DON'T WAIT UNTIL IT'S TOO LATE
TO SAVE ON NEXT YEAR'S TAXES!

Every year, millions of Americans wait until April 15 to figure out how they can cut their taxes. Although there are steps you can take to cut your taxes after the tax year ends, acting before December 31 allows you far greater tax-saving options. If you want significant tax savings, you've got to take action while there's still time.

J.K. Lasser's Year-Round Tax Strategies 1998, from the publishers of America's all-time best-selling tax guide, lets you in on the little-known secrets available to save money. You'll find

- ➤ Year-end reminders that highlight steps you can take NOW to save on THIS YEAR's taxes
- ➤ Tax planning ideas that will show you how to save on taxes year-round
- ➤ Filing pointers that will show you how to save taxes at preparation time
- ➤ Cautions of potential tax penalty traps, IRS trouble spots, and possible new laws
- ➤ Controversies where the IRS position may not be correct

With J.K. Lasser's exclusive investment allocation advice to help you make the most of your tax savings, you won't find a better pocket tax planner anywhere!

J.K. LASSER'S YEAR-ROUND TAX STRATEGIES 1998—
THE KEY TO TAX PLANNING FOR TAX SAVINGS!

ABOUT THE AUTHORS

David S. De Jong is an attorney and certified public accountant. A principal of the Rockville, Maryland, law firm of Stein, Sperling, Bennett, De Jong, Driscoll, Greenfeig & Metro, P.C., located outside Washington, D.C., he received his law degree from Washington & Lee University and his Master of Laws in Taxation degree from Georgetown University Law Center. Mr. De Jong has taught at four Washington, D.C., area universities and for many years has been an adjunct professor at American University. He is listed in *Who's Who in American Law.*

Ann Gray Jakabcin is a principal of Stein, Sperling, Bennett, De Jong, Driscoll, Greenfeig & Metro, P.C. She received her law degree from Temple University and her Master of Laws in Taxation degree from Georgetown University Law Center.

Both Mr. De Jong and Ms. Jakabcin are frequent speakers on various tax and estate planning topics. Each has been listed in *Washingtonian* magazine as among the top financial professionals in the Washington, D.C., area.

For over 50 years, the J.K. Lasser Tax Institute has specialized in writing tax and business publications for both nonprofessionals and professionals. The Institute is an editorial organization composed of tax attorneys, accountants, financial analysts, and writers—all experienced in presenting complicated tax, investment, and business material to the public and to professionals in related fields. J.K. Lasser's best-selling annual guide *Your Income Tax* has helped over 25 million taxpayers reduce their taxes and make informed financial decisions.

J.K. Lasser's™

Year-Round Tax Strategies 1998

David S. De Jong, Esq., C.P.A.
and
Ann Gray Jakabcin, Esq.

MACMILLAN • USA

J.K. Lasser Editorial and Production
Hilary Adler, Member of the New York Bar,
    Editor
Maryam Banikarim, Publishing Brand Manager
Claire Smith, Marketing
Nick Petro, Manufacturing

Design and layout: Michael Woyton
    for Kramer Communications

Publisher's Note: *Year-Round Tax Strategies* is published in recognition of the great need for useful information regarding the income tax laws, for the millions of men and women who must make out returns. We believe the research and interpretation by the J.K. Lasser Institute™ of the nation's tax laws to be authoritative and of help to taxpayers. Reasonable care has been taken in the preparation of the text. Taxpayers are cautioned, however, that this book is sold with the understanding that neither the publisher nor the author are engaged in rendering legal, accounting or other professional service. Taxpayers with specific tax problems are urged to seek the professional advice of a tax accountant, lawyer or preparer.

Macmillan General Reference
A Simon & Schuster Macmillan Company
1633 Broadway
New York, NY 10019

J.K. Lasser and the J.K. Lasser Institute are
registered trademarks of Simon & Schuster, Inc.
MACMILLAN is a registered trademark of Macmillan, Inc.

ISBN 0-02-861998-6

Manufactured in the United States of America

10 9 8 7 6 5 4 3 2 1

ACKNOWLEDGMENTS

The authors would like to thank Susan E. Anderson, CPA, for her continuing major substantive contributions and additionally wish to acknowledge the following individuals who contributed their time, ideas, and support:

Alan Bergamini, CPA
Edward A. Bortnick, CPA
Donald W. Burton, CDP
Karen Carolan, Esquire
Eugene C. Fisher, Esquire, CPA
Robert C. Hammond, CPA
Roland W. Johnson, EA
Robert J. Kopera, CPA
Philip Meade, Jr., CPA
Douglas A. Rausch, CPA
Isaac Reitberger, CPA
Jeffrey B. Rosenbloom, CPA
T. Theodore Schultz
Silvija A. Strikis, Esquire, CPA

Peter Wilhelm, CFP, EA
Alan Zipp, Esquire, CPA
Fred A. Balkin, Esquire
Millard S. Bennett, Esquire
David C. Driscoll, Jr., Esquire
Jack A. Garson, Esquire
Stuart S. Greenfeig, Esquire
A. Howard Metro, Esquire
Jeffrey M. Schwaber, Esquire
Donald N. Sperling, Esquire
Paul T. Stein, Esquire
Susan E. Webb
Tracy Barger De Jong, Esquire
George J. Jakabcin

CONTENTS

SUMMARY OF YEAR-END TAX STRATEGIES

Tax planning is a year-round concern. But it's a fact that most Americans neglect their tax planning until late in the year. As you will see, this can cost you in lost opportunities to save tax dollars. Still, there are certain moves that you can make during the last few months of the year to save money. In fact, there are steps you can take right up to December 31 (or even up to April 15) that may save you hundreds of dollars in taxes.

J.K. Lasser's *Year-Round Tax Strategies 1998* is intended to tell you about special tax strategies that you can use to cut your tax bill and increase your personal wealth. You may be facing a specific tax problem right now. The following table lists various year-end tax problems and possible steps you can take to cut your tax bil1l:

Problem	Possible Solution	Explained In
You support someone, but don't claim the person as a dependent	Provide additional support for possible dependent	Chapter 1
You face a penalty for not having paid enough taxes during the year	Increase your income tax withholding to avoid penalty	Chapter 1
You have homes in two states and want to pay as little in state taxes as possible	Watch time spent in the two states if you have more than one home and you seek to claim residence in the state with the lower tax rates	Chapter 1
You face payment of an alternative minimum tax	Preference items may be delayed to reduce tax	Chapter 1
You face a high tax bill; you want to defer taxes to a later year	Minimize December collections of income accounts	Chapter 1
	Purchase a CD maturing next year; sell assets on an installment basis	Chapter 2
	Use deferred compensation arrangement to postpone receipt of salary	Chapter 2
	Prepay next year's courses beginning before April 1 for an educational tax credit in the earlier year (not applicable 1997 year-end)	Chapter 4
	Use an escrow to delay closing until conditions satisfied	Chapter 5

Problem	Possible Solution	Explained In
You have passive losses, but can't use them because you don't have passive income against which to use them	Increase hours devoted to an activity to cause "material participation"	Chapter 2
You are in a higher than average tax bracket this year (or will be next year)	Consider timing of election of stock options	Chapter 2
	Determine whether stock, real estate, and other transactions should be closed in current year or next year	Chapter 4
Your income is low, and you may not be able to use the full Child Credit	Accelerate income to the extent needed and possible (not applicable 1997 year-end)	Chapter 3
You need to boost your itemized deductions	Accelerate the payment of medical bills	Chapter 4
	Make all planned cash charitable contributions	Chapter 4
	Donate used clothes and other property to a charity	Chapter 4
	Pay unescrowed property taxes	Chapter 4
	Pay educational expenses for the upcoming term if the courses will be deductible by you	Chapter 4
	Pay all anticipated state tax liability by December 31	Chapter 4
	Close on your new home to get deduction for points	Chapter 4
	Make next payment on mortgages and other obligations that bear interest	Chapter 4
	Pay professional and investment expenses if they will be deductible to you	Chapter 4

Problem	Possible Solution	Explained In
You own a vacation home	Increase or decrease use of vacation home for best tax results	Chapter 6
You have rental property income that you want to shelter	Pay all bills related to rental properties and consider needed repairs unless you will have unusable losses	Chapter 6
	Demonstrate "active participation" in rental property management and limit AGI	Chapter 6
You have capital gains you want to shelter	Sell securities at a loss (or at a gain if you would otherwise have unused capital losses)	Chapter 5
You wish to buy mutual fund shares but are concerned about capital gains	Avoid purchase of shares before a distribution, which is often in December	Chapter 5
You wish to sell securities but you want to delay taxes	Buy a "put" to protect your gain position	Chapter 5
You have securities which are "possibly" worthless	Sell the instrument for a small amount	Chapter 5
You're planning to get married	Accelerate marriage if it will reduce taxes	Chapter 8
You're planning to get divorced	Attempt to finalize divorce or legal separation if taxes will be lower filing as unmarried	Chapter 8
You're obligated to pay alimony to your ex-spouse	Make year-end alimony payment	Chapter 8
You need to shelter income	Set up qualified retirement plan or SEP for your business (the latter until extended due date of return in the following year)	Chapter 8
	Open up IRA (until April 15 of following year)	Chapter 9

Problem	Possible Solution	Explained In
	Make elective deferrals to your employer's 401(k) or Simple plan	Chapter 9
	Make elective deferrals to your employer's tax sheltered annuity plan	Chapter 11
You're considering purchasing equipment for your business	Make needed capital expenditures for your business assets	Chapter 10
You fear that a business activity may be deemed to be a "hobby"	Delay payment of bills to create a profit (if a cash basis taxpayer)	Chapter 10
You expect to sell your residence next year	Discontinue business or rental use of any portion of home	Chapter 10
You want to shift income to other relatives	Consider gifts of up to $10,000 to any family member	Chapter 12

HIGHLIGHTS OF THE TAXPAYER RELIEF ACT OF 1997

The Taxpayer Relief Act of 1997, signed into law by President Clinton on August 5, 1997 caused the most changes to the tax law since 1986. It created more opportunities for tax savings with new deductions and credits. However, it also created more complexity, particularly for middle income taxpayers with rising incomes who must contend with phaseouts of many benefits.

J. K. Lasser's Year-Round Tax Strategies 1998 is intended to inform you of the most recent tax developments and the newest strategies to cut your tax bill and increase your personal wealth. You may be able to use a particular strategy now. The following table lists the major provisions of the Taxpayer Relief Act, their effective dates, and where to look for the details and strategies.

Change	Effective Date	Explained in
Net operating loss carryback reduced generally to two years while carry-forward period increased to 20 years	Years beginning after 8-5-97	Chapter 1
Limited standard deduction for child claimed as dependent increased to greater of $650 indexed or earned income plus $250 indexed	1998	Chapter 1
Limited alternative minimum tax exemption for child claimed as dependent increased to earned income plus $5,000 indexed	1998	Chapter 1
Protective estimate "safe harbor" changed for higher income taxpayers	1998	Chapter 1
No penalty for estimated tax shortfall caused by Taxpayer Relief Act of 1997	1997	Chapter 1
Threshold for estimated tax payments increased to $1,000	1998	Chapter 1
Employer-provided education benefit plans extended retro-actively until 6-1-00	1997	Chapter 2
Prepaid tuition programs extended to include room and board	1997	Chapter 2

Change	Effective Date	Explained in
Education IRAs created with $500 contribution limit per beneficiary	1998	Chapter 2
Phase-in of deductible health insurance for self-employed and more than two percent S corporation shareholders accelerated	2000	Chapter 3
New deduction for student loan interest irrespective of itemizing	1998	Chapter 3
New child credit of $500 ($400 in 1998) for each dependent under age 17	1998	Chapter 3
New definition of modified adjusted gross income for phase-out of earned income credit	1998	Chapter 3
IRS can bar future use of earned income credit in event of abuse	1997	Chapter 3
HOPE scholarship credit created for first and second year under-graduate or vocational costs	1998	Chapter 3
Lifetime learning credit created for additional degree or career-related costs	7-1-98	Chapter 3
Charitable mileage rate increased to 14 cents per mile	1998	Chapter 4
Long-term capital gain rate lowered to 20 percent (ten percent to lowest bracketed individuals)	5-7-97	Chapter 5
Holding period for long-term capital gain changed to sales after 18 months	7-29-97	Chapter 5
Short sale must close by January 30 for gain to be taxed in prior year; identical securities must be held 60 days	6-9-97	Chapter 5

Change	Effective Date	Explained in
Exclusion of $250,000 ($500,000 for married couples filing jointly) once every two years on sale of principal residence	5-7-97	Chapter 6
Gain on sale of "small business stock" may be rolled over	8-6-97	Chapter 7
D.C. Homebuyer Tax Credit for "first-time" buyers of a principal residence in D.C.	8-6-97	Chapter 7
Phase-out income levels for deductible IRAs increased	1998	Chapter 9
Nondeductible Roth IRAs created for back-ended tax-free treatment	1998	Chapter 9
Penalty-free IRA withdrawals permitted up to $10,000 for "first-time" buyers of a principal residence and for certain educational costs	1998	Chapter 9
Excess withdrawal and excess accumulation penalties from retirement plans repealed	1997	Chapter 9
Office-in-home deduction expanded to cover administrative work at home if no other location for paperwork	1999	Chapter 10
Income-averaging over three years permitted on farm income	1998	Chapter 11
Income earned abroad exclusion increased	1998	Chapter 11
Insurance overrides to retired agents exempt from self-employment tax if statutory criteria satisfied	1998	Chapter 11

Change	Effective Date	Explained in
Compensation for purpose of 25 percent limit on contributions to tax-deferred annuities computed before elective deferrals	1998	Chapter 11
Unified credit increased in stages to $1 million	1998	Chapter 12
Estate exclusion for closely held business interests creates effective exemption equivalent of $1.3 million for qualified estates	1998	Chapter 12
Gifts of tuition certificates considered as transfers of present interests eligible for "five-year averaging"	8-6-97	Chapter 12
$10,000 gift exclusion to be indexed for cost of living	1999	Chapter 12
Clarification that direct gifts from revocable trusts treated as if made by creator	8-6-97	Chapter 12
$1 million generation skipping tax exemption to be indexed for inflation	1999	Chapter 12
Modification to levy rules	8-6-97	Chapter 13
IRS may accept credit cards under regulations to be drafted	5-5-98	Chapter 13

1

Introduction to Personal Tax Planning

PAYING TAX MAY BE INEVITABLE—PAYING TOO MUCH IS NOT

The word *tax* is derived from the Latin *tangere*; it means "to touch." Taxes touch us all as one of the absolute certainties in life. Over the last ten years, per capita taxes have increased 20 percent to an average of almost $22,000 per family and have outpaced housing, food, and all other necessary living costs. A family with two children making $25,000 annually loses 32 percent of earnings to federal, state, and local taxes. At $75,000 of income annually, the family loses 40 percent of earnings to taxes. If the family makes $200,000 annually, it pays a whopping 44.5 percent of earnings in taxes.

Studies indicate that you, as the typical American, work until May 9 to pay your taxes for the year and then you work for yourself. The average New York and Connecticut residents feel the greatest tax burden.

Despite the universal tax burden, numerous tax strategies remain for satisfying your tax obligation before April Fools' Day.

CHANGES TO THE TAX LAW ARE ALSO INEVITABLE

Louis XIV's finance minister once stated that "the art of taxation consists in so plucking the goose as to obtain the largest amount of feathers with the least amount of hissing." In the last four decades, the way in which the goose is plucked has changed almost annually. Hardly a year or two has passed since 1954 without tax law changes for one or more of the following purported reasons:

Tax reduction	Budget reconciliation	Equity or fairness
Revenue enhancement	Tax simplification	Economic recovery or growth

The year 1996 was particularly busy with four significant laws enacted only days apart, each with significant tax changes. Even before the ink had dried on these changes, The Taxpayer Relief Act of 1997 caused the largest overhaul of the Internal Revenue Code since 1986. With new deductions and credits generally phased out as income rises, the law has become more complicated. The Internal Revenue Code has grown from just over 400,000

1

words in 1954 to over 1.3 million words today. Regulations, which express the Internal Revenue Service's position on how the Code should be interpreted, run about 6 million words.

Individual tax compliance alone requires an estimated 3 billion hours per year. In dollars, total compliance costs number in the tens of billions of dollars annually. Then the IRS requires about 110,000 employees to be sure that everyone has filed and has reported accurately.

The public is ready for more change. In two recent surveys, clear majorities of Americans expressed support for either major changes to the tax law or complete replacement of the current system. Congress is in the early stages of studying both a "flat" individual income tax and a *value added tax* (sort of a national sales tax) as alternatives to the present structure.

THE BASIC TAX STRUCTURE FOR INDIVIDUALS— FROM GROSS INCOME TO TAX LIABILITY

Computation of your tax liability begins with an accounting of your *gross income,* which essentially constitutes your earnings and your gains. (Income and benefits constituting earnings are discussed in Chapter 2; gains are discussed in Chapter 5.)

From your gross income, certain expenses are deductible if you are eligible irrespective of whether you itemize. These expenses include, most importantly:

> Alimony paid (discussed in Chapter 8)
>
> Contributions to an Individual Retirement Account (IRA), Simplified Employee Pension Plan (SEP), Keogh Plan, or Simple Plan (discussed in Chapter 9)
>
> A portion of health insurance costs paid by a sole proprietor, partner, limited liability company member, or more than two percent S corporation shareholder not eligible to participate in a health insurance plan (discussed in Chapter 3)
>
> Contributions to a Medical Savings Account (MSA) (discussed in Chapter 3)
>
> Effective in 1998, certain student loan interest (discussed in Chapter 3)
>
> Limited types of moving expenses (discussed in Chapter 3)
>
> One-half of the self-employment tax paid by a sole proprietor or partner
>
> Penalties imposed by financial institutions on early withdrawals of savings

When these deductions are subtracted from gross income, the difference is your *adjusted gross income (AGI).* (Many tax deductions in reaching adjusted gross income are lost under the law if your adjusted gross income is too high. This would seemingly necessitate knowing your AGI to determine your AGI. However, in order to avoid the need for a degree in higher mathematics to solve this circular problem, the phaseout of deductions is actually based on *modified adjusted gross income*—which is AGI before computing certain of the deductions dependent on AGI and, in some contexts, after adding back the exclusion for income earned abroad (see Chapter 12). Consequently, modified adjusted gross income has a slightly different definition in each context.)

From adjusted gross income, you subtract itemized deductions (discussed in Chapter 4) or the standard deduction as well as personal exemptions to determine *taxable income*. *Marginal tax rates* of 15, 28, 31, 36, and 39.6 percent are then applied to levels of taxable income to determine your federal tax liability.

Credits reduce your tax liability dollar for dollar, including most importantly:

> Effective in 1998, the Child Credit for each dependency exemption (discussed in Chapter 3)
>
> The Adoption Expense Credit (discussed in Chapter 3)
>
> The Dependent Care Credit (discussed in Chapter 3)
>
> The Earned Income Credit (discussed in Chapter 3)
>
> Effective in 1998, the Hope Scholarship Credit and (after June 30) the Lifetime Learning Credit (discussed in Chapter 3)
>
> The Foreign Tax Credit (discussed in Chapter 11)
>
> The Credit for the Elderly or Disabled (discussed in Chapters 3 and 11)

ITEMIZED DEDUCTIONS VS. THE STANDARD DEDUCTION

Adjusted gross income is reduced by *itemized deductions* (claimed by about 29 percent of individual filers) or the *standard deduction*. Itemized deductions are write-offs for certain medical expenses, taxes, interest, charitable contributions, casualty and theft losses, as well as job expenses and other miscellaneous itemized deductions. In lieu of claiming itemized deductions, an individual generally has the option of using the standard deduction, which is a set dollar amount and varies with filing status. However, a nonresident alien, as well as a married individual filing separately whose spouse itemizes, cannot use the standard deduction and must itemize.

For 1997, prior to indexing in 1998 for cost of living, the standard deduction amounts are:

Filing Status	Standard Deduction
Married Filing Jointly	$6,900
Married Filing Separately	$3,450
Single	$4,150
Head Of Household	$6,050

If you are single or file as head of household, the standard deduction is increased by $1,000 if you are 65 years old or blind ($2,000 if you are both age 65 and blind). If you are married, the standard deduction is increased in multiples of $800 to a maximum standard deduction of $10,100, reflecting additional allowances for either or both spouses being over age 65, blind, or both. These increases are subject to indexing in 1998 and later years.

See the discussion later in this chapter on the "Kiddie" Tax for a special limited standard deduction in the case of an individual who can be claimed as a dependent on another's return.

CAUTION!   Individuals with adjusted gross income in excess of $121,200 ($60,600 for married individuals filing separately) must reduce the total of their itemized deductions except for medical expenses, casualty, theft, and gambling (see the restrictions in Chapter 11) losses, and investment interest. The reduction in otherwise allowable itemized deductions is an amount equal to three percent of adjusted gross income in excess of the threshold amount. However, the itemized deductions subject to the adjustment cannot be reduced by more than 80 percent. The threshold amounts will be indexed for inflation in 1998 and succeeding years. During the phase-out levels, the reduction in itemized deductions will generally increase the true marginal tax bracket of affected individuals by between .93 and 1.19 percent depending on tax bracket.

FILING POINTER   To receive the extra standard deduction, an individual need not be totally blind. For tax purposes, a taxpayer is blind if vision in the better eye does not exceed 20/200 with glasses or if the diameter of the visual field "subtends an angle no greater than 20 degrees."

FILING POINTER   If your itemized deductions barely exceed the amount of the standard deduction, you need to consider the effect on state taxes before itemizing. In some states you must itemize on the state return if you itemized on your federal return. Because state income taxes are not deductible on most state returns, you can have state itemized deductions far less than the state standard deduction when state income taxes constitute your largest federal itemized deduction. The result could be that itemizing on your federal return causes you to pay more to the state than you save with the IRS.

QUESTION: I feel deprived. Each year I fall short of being able to itemize deductions by a few hundred dollars. What can I do to save taxes?

ANSWER: Attempt to bunch deductions into alternating years. To the extent you can, time your payments of such deductible expenditures as charitable contributions, property taxes, and state income taxes (if you pay estimates) to double up every other calendar year. Then you'll be able to itemize once every two years and claim the standard deduction in the other years.

MAXIMIZING YOUR PERSONAL EXEMPTIONS

The final computation needed to reach taxable income is the subtraction for your *personal exemptions*. The amount of the deduction for each personal exemption, $2,650 in 1997 except for high-income individuals, will be adjusted annually for increases in the cost of living. You are entitled to claim a deduction for your own personal exemption unless you are claimed as a dependent on another's tax return. Consequently, a child cannot claim a deduction for a personal exemption on his or her own return when being claimed as a *dependent* on the tax return of either parent.

In addition to your own personal exemption, you are entitled to claim a personal exemption deduction for your spouse if a joint return is filed. If you are married but file a separate return, you will be able to claim a personal exemption for your spouse only if the spouse has no gross income and is not claimed as a *dependent* on someone else's return.

Additional exemptions are also available for certain dependents. To qualify for the dependency deduction, the following requirements must be met:

1. The dependent must have one of the following relationships to the taxpayer: child or stepchild; grandchild; parent or stepparent; grandparent; sibling or stepsibling; mother/father-in-law; brother/sister-in-law; son/daughter-in-law; or uncle, aunt, nephew, or niece related by blood. In addition, any other individual who is a member of the taxpayer's household for the entire year will qualify unless the living arrangement is in violation of local law.

2. The dependent must have less than the exemption deduction amount of $2,650 (increased in 1998 for cost of living) of gross income or be the taxpayer's child who has not attained the age of 19 or be the taxpayer's child who is a full-time student under age 24.

3. The dependent must receive more than one-half of his or her support from the taxpayer.

4. The dependent must be a U.S. citizen or resident or a resident of Canada or Mexico.

5. If the dependent is married, the dependent may not file a joint return with his or her spouse except for the purpose for getting a tax refund.

If a dependent was born during the year, or died during the year, or if a child was born alive but died shortly thereafter, the dependency deduction is available.

For purposes of satisfying the gross income test, only income that is taxable by the federal government is taken into account. Consequently, nontaxable Social Security benefits and tax exempt interest, for example, are not considered in determining whether the dependent exceeds the $2,650 gross income ceiling.

The most difficult issue usually associated with dependency deductions is whether a taxpayer provided over one-half of the support of the proposed dependent. It is necessary to consider the means of support for the potential dependent both from his or her own sources as well as from those of other parties. In other words, who *spent* what for the support of this individual?

Most sources of support, including items that are exempt from tax (if actually used for support), are counted in determining whether the support test has been met. Consequently, even though nontaxable Social Security benefits and tax exempt interest do not count toward the gross income test, they will be counted in determining whether the support test has been met.

Children can be claimed as dependents regardless of their gross income if they are under the age of 19, or are full-time students under the age of 24, and receive more than half of their support from the parents. In calculating the support provided to a child, nontaxable scholarships are not taken into account.

"Support" is interpreted broadly and includes such expenditures as food, clothing, lodging, education, and medical care. Lodging is based on the property's fair rental value. If a dependent lives in his or her own home, and the taxpayer seeking the exemption doesn't live with the dependent, the rental value of the home is deemed contributed by the dependent for his or her own support. If the taxpayer pays part of the expenses of the home (such as mortgage interest, taxes, fire insurance premiums, or repairs), the fair rental value is reduced by the taxpayer's payments in determining the dependent's contribution.

ILLUSTRATION

You provide $3,000 in cash for your father's support during the year. He lives in his own house which has a fair rental value of $3,600 a year. He uses $800 of the money you give him to pay real estate taxes. Your father's contribution for his own lodging is $2,800 ($3,600—$800 for taxes). Thus, if the lodging and the $3,000 in cash were the only support items involved for that tax year, you would be able to claim your father as a dependent as long as he satisfied the other dependency requirements such as the gross income test.

YEAR-END REMINDER   A few dollars wisely spent before the end of 1997 could result in a big tax saving. Suppose your child is a full-time student under age 24 with a part-time job earning, say, $6,000. You spend $5,500 a year for the child's support. Currently, you get no deduction because you provide less than half of your child's support.

Have your child bank $300 and increase your support by $300. Now you get an extra $2,650 exemption, because you provide more than half of your child's support—$5,800 compared to $5,700. Although your child loses his or her $2,650 personal exemption, that's only worth $398. If you're in a higher bracket, the extra exemption, if usable in full, is worth either $742 (28 percent bracket), $822 (31 percent bracket), or $954 (36 percent bracket). If your child is under age 17, the extra exemptions may be worth another $400 in 1998 and $500 in succeeding years as a result of the new child credit (discussed in Chapter 3).

CAUTION!   The benefit of each personal exemption is phased out based on levels of adjusted gross income. In 1997 the phase-out commences at $181,800 of adjusted gross income for married individuals filing jointly, $151,500 for heads of household, $121,200 for single individuals, and $90,900 for married individuals filing separately. Each exemption will be reduced by two percent (four percent in the case of married individuals filing separately) for each $2,500 or fraction by which adjusted gross income exceeds the threshold amount. Consequently, the benefit of all personal exemptions will be lost when adjusted gross income exceeds $304,300 in the case of married individuals filing jointly, $274,000 in the case of heads of household, $243,700 in the case of single individuals, and $152,150 in the case of married individuals filing separately. During this phase-out, the loss of exemptions will generally increase the marginal tax bracket of most affected individuals by between .55 and .78 percent (double for married individuals filing separately) for each exemption claimed. Thresholds will be indexed for inflation in 1998 and succeeding years. The phase-out of the new child credit is discussed in Chapter 3.

TAX PLANNING IDEA   As a result of the phase-out of personal exemptions, an exemption may be worth more to your child than you. In such case, help your child claim the exemption by decreasing your support or having the child spend more of his or her earnings.

FILING POINTER   When several family members collectively provide majority support of an individual by each contributing over ten percent of the support, but no one person contributes over one-half of the support, the contributors can enter into a *Multiple Support Agreement* in which all but one of the contributors waive the right to claim the individual in question as a dependent. The contributor who will be claiming the individual as a dependent should obtain signed IRS Forms 2120 from each of the other contributors of more than ten percent.

CAUTION!   When a majority of an individual's support is from public assistance, no one can claim the individual as a dependent (not even the person himself or herself).

CAUTION!   Social Security numbers of dependents must be shown on your tax return. The IRS uses this information to determine whether multiple individuals, such as both divorced parents, are claiming the same person as a dependent. Commencing with 1996 returns, the IRS has authority to disallow a dependent personal exemption by summary procedure—without a statutory notice of deficiency (discussed in Chapter 13) — where the proper Social Security number is not shown.

Prior to the requirement of listing Social Security numbers, the IRS believed that one in seven purported dependents was improperly claimed. In the first year of listed Social Security numbers, nine percent fewer individuals (7 million in number)—and probably 100 percent fewer household pets—were claimed as dependents. Nevertheless, the IRS still believes there are still millions of erroneous dependent claims each year.

QUESTION: I live in a large home with my girlfriend. We have a full-time housekeeper who has her own bedroom and bathroom. I provide all of the support for both my girlfriend and my housekeeper. Can I claim them as dependents?

ANSWER: For your girlfriend to be claimed as a dependent, she must have been a member of your household for the entire year and the relationship between the two of you must not violate state law. Some jurisdictions have criminal statutes prohibiting cohabitation between unmarried individuals and this would apparently prohibit claiming the dependency exemption, even though such laws may not be enforced. Live-in housekeepers will generally not qualify for the dependency exemption, even though they may have no other means of support, because the room and board furnished by the taxpayer are considered by the courts to have been furnished as compensation and not as items of support.

QUESTION: Last year my 17-year-old daughter had a child out of wedlock. They both live in my home and I provide all of the support of both of them. I guess that I can claim my daughter again this year. But can I claim my grandchild?

ANSWER: Sure. It makes no difference whether or not a child or grandchild is born out of wedlock.

QUESTION: My mother is a widow and, in order to help her make ends meet, I pay the rent on her apartment and all of her utility bills. Can I claim my mother as a dependent on my 1996 tax return? Her annual rent is $7,500 and her utilities are $1,200. My mother spends about $7,000 on food, clothing, and doctor bills and another $2,000 on incidentals. She receives about $5,000 per year in Social Security benefits, $1,000 in interest on her savings account, and $3,000 in interest on municipal bonds.

ANSWER: Your mother satisfies a crucial requirement to be claimed as a dependent— she will have less than $2,650 of gross income subject to tax. However, your mother will be deemed to have contributed $9,000 toward her total support, while you only have paid $8,700 of her total bills. If you simply increase the amount of your support by $151 and decrease the amount your mother provides herself by the same amount, you will be able to claim your mother as a dependent on your tax return and save between $742 (in a 28 percent bracket) and $954 (if the exemption is fully usable in a 36 percent bracket). Don't overlook other items of support you may pay—car insurance, repairs, new clothes, and the like.

QUESTION: My son attended "Chicken College" from January 20 until May 10, and as a result of this employee training course became an assistant manager in a fast-food restaurant. Aside from the months that he was away at "school," he lived at home. I definitely provided over one-half of his support for the year. He is 20 years old. Can I claim him as a dependent since he was only a full-time student for less than four months?

ANSWER: A student age 19 through 23 inclusive must be enrolled for some part of five calendar months at an educational institution on a full-time basis to be claimed as a dependent by a parent when the student earns over $2,650 (adjusted in 1998 and succeeding years for cost of living). Your son was in his training course for parts of five calendar months and would qualify. However, on-the-job training or other employee training programs are not considered as qualifying educational curricula. A regular vocational education program would have qualified, however.

QUESTION: I was more than eight months pregnant at the end of last year and gave birth to a baby boy on January 8 of this year. Can I claim my son as a dependent last year? I paid more than $2,000 out-of-pocket last year to my obstetrician.

ANSWER: The U.S. Court of Federal Claims in 1994 backed up the position of the IRS and ruled that taxpayers are not entitled to a dependency exemption for a child unborn at year-end.

MARGINAL TAX RATES—FROM 15 TO 39.6 PERCENT

After taxable income is determined, *marginal tax rates* are applied to determine regular tax liability before any available tax credits. Marginal tax rates reflect the percentage of the next dollar of taxable income which will be lost to taxes.

The 1997 marginal tax rates for various levels of taxable income are set forth below for the four filing status options from which an individual must choose—married filing jointly, married filing separately, single, or *head of household*. The levels of income to which these rates apply change as the cost of living increases.

For those who are married and file a joint return, their taxable income will be subject to the following marginal rates of tax:

Married Filing Jointly

If Taxable Income Is:	Marginal Tax Rate Is:
Up to $41,200	15%
$41,201–$99,600	28%
$99,601–$151,750	31%
$151,751–$271,050	36%
Over $271,050	39.6%

For those who are married but file separate returns, each spouse's taxable income will be taxed at the following rates:

Married Filing Separately

If Taxable Income Is:	Marginal Tax Rate Is:
Up to $20,600	15%
$20,601–$49,800	28%
$49,801–$75,875	31%
$75,876–$135,525	36%
Over $135,525	39.6%

For single individuals, taxable income will be taxed as follows:

Single

If Taxable Income Is:	Marginal Tax Rate Is:
Up to $24,650	15%
$24,651–$59,750	28%

$59,751–$124,650	31%
$124,651–$271,050	36%
Over $271,050	39.6%

For unmarried individuals who qualify as head of household, taxable income will be taxed as follows:

Head of Household

If Taxable Income Is:	Marginal Tax Rate Is:
Up to $33,050	15%
$33,051–85,350	28%
$83,351–$138,200	31%
$138,201–$271,050	36%
Over $271,050	39.6%

Taxpayers in a marginal tax bracket of 28 percent or more are now taxed at a maximum rate of 20 percent on long term capital gains; taxpayers in the 15 percent marginal tax bracket are now taxed at a maximum rate of ten percent on long term capital gains. See Chapter 5 on Gains—and Losses.

YEAR-END REMINDER To the extent that you have an ability to determine the timing of income, deferral of income to a succeeding year can take you out of a higher marginal bracket into a lower one where a decline in income from other sources is anticipated.

MARRIED—JOINT VS. SEPARATE RETURN

Individuals who are married on the last day of year (or whose spouse died during the year, provided the survivor did not remarry) have the option of filing a joint return, or each of them may file a separate return. By electing to file a joint return, the husband's and the wife's incomes and deductions are combined in computing the couple's taxable income. If a joint return is filed, the husband and wife are jointly and individually liable for the tax liability, regardless of whose income generated the tax liability.

Electing to file a joint return will usually produce a lower tax liability for a couple, particularly when there is substantial disparity between the levels of taxable income for each spouse.

ILLUSTRATION

Both John and Mary are wage earners and have some investment income. Both are eligible to contribute to their own Individual Retirement Accounts because neither participates in an employer sponsored retirement plan, and each has itemized deductions of $4,700 from qualified residence interest and taxes. If the couple elected to file a joint return for 1997, their federal tax liability would be $21,608. In contrast, if John and Mary chose to file separate returns, John's federal tax liability would be $4,504 while Mary would owe $17,891, for a combined total of $22,395, an increase of $787 over what would have been owed had they filed a joint return. Itemized deductions claimed do not equal total itemized deductions as a result of the overall reduction for individuals with AGI in excess of $121,200 ($60,000 for married individuals filing separately).

	John	Mary
Wages	$30,000	$75,000
Interest/Dividends	5,000	5,000
IRA	(2,000)	(2,000)
Adjusted Gross Income (AGI)	$33,000	$78,000
Itemized Deductions	(4,700)	(4,178)
Personal Exemptions	(2,650)	(2,650)
Taxable Income	$25,650	$71,172
Separate Return Tax	$4,504	$17,891
Joint AGI	$111,000	
Itemized Deductions	(9,400)	
Personal Exemptions	(5,300)	
Joint Taxable Income	$96,300	
Joint Return Tax	$21,608	
Savings Filing Jointly	$ 787	

About 97½ percent of married couples file a joint tax return for, in general, a joint return will produce a lower tax liability. However, there are exceptions. For example, suppose one spouse has substantial medical expenses or unreimbursed employee business expenses. Both types of expenses are permitted as itemized deductions only if the total of the expenses exceeds a percentage of adjusted gross income. Filing a separate return may produce a lower tax liability because of the ability of that spouse to claim a higher medical expense deduction or a higher deduction for the unreimbursed employee business expenses than would have been the case had the couple elected to file a joint return. The joint return election produces a higher AGI and as a result may eliminate or reduce the ability to claim the medical expenses or unreimbursed employee business expenses as itemized deductions.

ILLUSTRATION

Assume that in the prior illustration, in addition to the items of income and deduction shown, John had $2,000 of unreimbursed employee business expenses and $4,800 of unreimbursed medical expenses. If the couple opted to file a joint return, they would not be able to claim an itemized deduction for the $2,000 of employee business expenses because they are deductible (subject to the overall reduction by high income individuals) only to the extent that the total exceeds two percent of the couple's AGI ($111,000). Since $2,000 is less than two percent of the couple's AGI (2% × $111,000 = $2,220), the deduction for the $2,000 of unreimbursed employee business expenses is lost. Similarly, the couple loses the ability to deduct the $4,800 in medical expenses if they file a joint return. The medical expenses are deductible (subject again to the overall reduction by high income individuals) only to the extent that they exceed 7½ percent of AGI (7.5% × $111,000 = $8,325).

On the other hand, if John and Mary chose to file separate returns in 1997, John would have been entitled to an additional itemized deduction of $1,340, the amount by which his unreimbursed employee business expenses ($2,000) exceed two percent of John's AGI of $33,000 (2% × $33,000 = $660) and an additional itemized deduction of $2,325, the amount by which the medical expenses ($4,800) exceed 7½ percent of John's AGI (7.5% × $33,000 = $2,475). Consequently, John's itemized deductions have increased by $3,665 (the sum of $1,340 and $2,325) and John's federal tax liability on a separate return is $3,478. Mary's separate tax liability is not changed and remains at $17,891. Because John is able to claim the additional itemized deductions for his unreimbursed employee business expenses and for the medical expenses on his separate return, the couple's combined tax liability, if they were to file separate returns in 1997, is $21,369, as compared to a joint tax liability of $21,608, a savings of $239 as shown below:

	John	Mary
Wages	$30,000	$75,000
Interest/Dividends	5,000	5,000
IRA	(2,000)	(2,000)
Adjusted Gross Income (AGI)	$33,000	$78,000
Itemized Deductions	(8,365)	(4,178)
Personal Exemptions	(2,650)	(2,650)
Taxable Income	$21,985	$71,172
Separate Return Tax	$3,478	$17,891
Joint Taxable Income (from prior illustration)	$96,300	
Joint Return Tax (from prior illustration)	$21,608	
Savings Filing Separately	$239	

 CAUTION!   You may be legally married without ever having said "I do." And the IRS will say "you are."

About a quarter of the states plus the District of Columbia recognize *common-law marriages*. While each such jurisdiction has its own definition, a common-law marriage generally requires cohabitation coupled with public recognition as husband and wife (often for a set number of years). If you meet the criteria of your state of residence for a common-law marriage, the IRS will consider you as married even if you subsequently move to another state which does not recognize common-law marriages.

QUESTION: I said "I do" to my partner of the same sex in a formal ceremony. Can we file a joint return?

ANSWER: No single state currently recognizes the validity of a "marriage" between partners of the same sex whether through a formal ceremony or at common law. Irrespective, in 1996, President Clinton signed legislation to deny federal recognition of same sex marriages.

QUESTION: My son got married secretly last year to a girl who was under age at the time. When I found out about it a year later, I sent him to one of those islands where he could get a "quickie" divorce. When he got back, my lawyer told me that my state wouldn't recognize the divorce but that he could seek to get the marriage annulled. The annulment will be final this year, but my son has asked me if he can properly file as unmarried for last year.

ANSWER: Except for a "sham" divorce prior to year-end to save taxes with a planned remarriage in the following year, like a marriage, the IRS generally recognizes any divorce anywhere in the world unless set aside by a local court. Annulments are trickier. Although an annulment, foreign or domestic, should be recognized by the IRS unless set aside by a local court or unless a sham, applicable law determines whether your son's annulment relates back to the date of the marriage (in which case he files as unmarried for last year) or not (in which case he files as married for last year). In some states an annulment relates back as to rights and obligations of the couple as to themselves but does not relate back as to third parties such as the IRS (in which case your son also files as married for last year).

FILING POINTER   Very often a married couple will have to compute its tax liability under both options to determine which produces the lower tax cost. This is particularly true when either or both spouses have one or more deductions that are restricted based on adjusted gross income. Besides medical expenses and miscellaneous itemized deductions, other write-offs which may be more usable on a separate return include capital losses and casualty losses.

CAUTION!   A husband and wife who elect to file separate returns must allocate their itemized deductions between them. Only the spouse who paid the deductible expense is entitled to the write-off and then only if that spouse was legally obligated to make the payment. Thus, for example, when there is joint liability for real estate taxes, each spouse is entitled to claim a deduction on his or her separate return for the real estate tax which he or she actually paid. When there is joint liability for home mortgage interest, the spouse making the mortgage payment is entitled to the home interest expense deduction on his or her separate return. But if one spouse has no obligation for the mortgage debt, his or her payment of the mortgage interest will result in neither spouse being able to claim a deduction for that interest expense on the separate returns—the spouse who paid the interest is not liable for the debt and the spouse who is liable for the debt did not pay the interest.

CAUTION!   Separate tax returns in *community property* states must be prepared consistent with local law. In general, the spouses must equally divide all income from wages and self-employment as well as other community income net of allocable deductions. Itemized deductions are also divided equally except to the extent underlying expenses were paid from noncommunity funds. As a result, it is even more rare for residents of community property states, as opposed to other states, to save taxes by filing separately.

The community property states are Arizona, California, Idaho, Louisiana, Nevada, New Mexico, Texas, Washington, and Wisconsin.

TAX PLANNING IDEA   Married individuals who initially file separately may amend to file a joint tax return within a three-year period measured from the later of the original due date of the return or the date when the return was actually filed. Pursuant to the Taxpayer Bill of Rights-2 (see Chapter 13), effective with 1997 returns, any unpaid tax liability need not be paid with the amended return. Married individuals who file jointly may not amend to file separate tax returns with one narrow exception, when a surviving spouse has signed for a deceased individual prior to appointment of another as the decedent's *personal representative*.

CAUTION!   Despite the higher tax liability, separate filings are generally advisable when the tax liability from a joint return is attributable entirely or primarily to one spouse and can probably never be paid. As discussed in Chapter 13, separate filings place certain joint assets beyond the reach of the IRS, facilitate acceptance of an Offer in Compromise, and possibly save one spouse from a future filing for bankruptcy protection.

A married individual suspecting unstated income or overstated deductions on the spouse's part should hesitate to sign a joint return. See Chapter 8 concerning the advisability of separate returns by divorcing individuals.

UNMARRIED—FILING STATUS ALTERNATIVES

Unmarried individuals will generally file as single taxpayers. However, a widow or widower who has not remarried and who was eligible to file a joint tax return for the year of the spouse's death can use the tax rates (as well as the standard deduction) for married individuals filing jointly for the two years following the death of a spouse, provided he or she provides over one-half of the cost required to maintain a home for a dependent child as defined for head of household purpose.

If certain conditions are met, unmarried individuals can file as head of household. An individual who qualifies as head of household will have more of his or her income taxed at the 15, 28, and 31 percent rates than would be the case filing as a single taxpayer. If your 1997 taxable income is $80,000 and you file as a single taxpayer, you will owe $19,804; if you qualify for the head of household rate, you will only owe $18,104—a savings of $1,700.

You will qualify as head of household if you are a citizen or unmarried resident alien on the last day of the year and:

1. You pay more than one-half of the cost of maintaining your home which for more than one-half of the year is also the principal residence of your child or any other relative you are entitled to claim as a dependent on your tax return; or

2. You pay more than one-half of the cost of maintaining a parent's principal residence (which is not necessarily your home) and you are entitled to claim that parent as a dependent on your tax return.

For the purpose of determining who qualifies for the head of household rates, a married individual will be considered as unmarried for tax purposes if the taxpayer's spouse is a nonresident alien, or if the spouse does not live with the taxpayer during the last six months of the year and the taxpayer's household is the principal residence of a child for whom the taxpayer is entitled to claim the dependency deduction, or would have been entitled to claim the dependency deduction had it not been transferred to the noncustodial spouse (see Chapter 7).

Temporary absences from the home due to vacation or schooling, for example, will not prevent the home from qualifying as the principal residence for purpose of head of household status.

CONTROVERSY

Where the taxpayer seeking to claim head of household status maintains two households, the question may arise as to which home constitutes the principal residence of the child or other related dependent. To qualify for head of household status, the home maintained by the taxpayer must constitute the principal home of the child or other dependent. So long as the taxpayer spends a substantial amount of time at a residence, the Ninth Circuit Court of Appeals, with a Massachusetts federal district court in accord, would allow the head of household rates to apply. The IRS, the Fifth and Seventh Circuit Courts of Appeal, and the Tax Court take a more strict view, holding that a taxpayer cannot have two residences. However, no court will permit head of household status if an individual maintains one home for himself or herself and another where the child lives (at which location the individual is present only on an infrequent basis).

QUESTION: I'm a single parent. My ex-wife and I have joint custody of our only child. We alternate years claiming the child as a dependent. The child spends Monday through Wednesday at my house. On Thursday morning I take the child to school and after school he returns to his mother's home, where he spends Thursday and Friday nights. Saturday the child returns to my house. Sunday he goes back to his mother's. Can I use the head of household rates?

ANSWER: Yes. Your home is the child's principal residence (four out of seven days a week).

OPERATING AT A LOSS—CARRYBACK OR CARRYFORWARD

Although the ability to calculate tax liability in periods of rising income through the use of income averaging has been eliminated, individuals can still level out their tax liabilities over a number of years if they have *net operating losses*. A net operating loss is created whenever your deductions exceed your gross income. To the extent that this loss is attributable to trade or business deductions, you may elect to carry that loss back to offset up to two prior years of income and, if unused in the carryback years, carry the loss forward as many as 20 years to offset taxable income. Alternatively, you can elect to forgo the entire carryback period and simply carry the net operating loss forward. The election to forgo the carryback years must be made by the return due date, including extensions, for the year in which the net operating loss arises and, once made, the election is irrevocable.

If you had positive taxable income in previous years against which the net operating loss can be used, using a carryback will give you an immediate refund of previously paid taxes. On the other hand, forgoing the carryback period so that the net operating loss can be used against future income will delay the benefit to be derived from the net operating loss.

It is normally beneficial to use the net operating loss as a carryback when your marginal tax rate in the earlier years was higher than or equal to what is anticipated in the carry-forward years.

QUESTION: I expect a net operating loss of about $10,000 in 1998 arising from starting a new business. By 1999 I expect my sole proprietorship to be making at least $30,000 per year. I had small amounts of taxable income in 1996 and 1997 but not more than $6,000 in either year. Should I carry the loss back and then use the rest of the loss, if any, in 1999 and future years?

ANSWER: Although you can get an immediate refund by using the carryback, you will probably be better off to skip the carryback, file the election, and use the net operating loss to offset future income. Your marginal rate of tax in the carryback period was lower than your likely rate in the future.

CAUTION!   Prior to 1998, a net operating loss carryback offset up to three prior years of income. A net operating loss carry-forward could be used for only 15 years. The Taxpayer Relief Act of 1997 left a carryback period of three years only for individual casualty and theft losses and for farm and small business losses attributable to disaster areas declared by the President. See Chapter 4 for a discussion of these types of losses.

AVOIDING THE ALTERNATIVE MINIMUM TAX

In addition to the regular income tax, over 600,000 individuals each year are required to pay the *alternative minimum tax (AMT)* which is an additional tax equal to the *tentative minimum tax* (determined through a special computation) less the regular income tax liability.

The starting point in computing the alternative minimum tax is the determination of *alternative minimum taxable income.* In general terms, this is regular taxable income increased by many deductions used in computing the regular taxable income, but which are disallowed in the computation of alternative minimum taxable income, and further increased by certain *tax preference items* such as accelerated depreciation on real property acquired before 1987 (see Chapter 5), percentage depletion and intangible drilling costs (see Chapter 7), and the spread between the fair market value of incentive stock options that were exercised during the year and the option price (see Chapter 2). Additionally, a special net operating loss deduction for alternative minimum tax purposes is substituted for any regular net operating loss deduction.

After alternative minimum taxable income has been computed, married individuals who file a joint return are entitled to an exemption amount of $45,000 ($33,750 for single individuals and $22,500 for those who are married and file separate returns) but the exemption amount is phased out for those on a joint return with alternative minimum taxable income over $150,000 ($112,500 for single individuals and $75,000 for married taxpayers filing separately). The exemption amount is completely phased out when the alternative minimum taxable income on a joint return is $330,000 ($247,500 for single taxpayers and $165,000 for married taxpayers who file separately).

A tax rate of 26 percent is applied to the first $175,000 ($87,500 for married taxpayers who file separately) of alternative minimum taxable income less the applicable exemption, if any. A tax rate of 28 percent is applied to the excess. A special foreign tax credit is computed and subtracted if the taxpayer paid any foreign taxes. The result is a tentative minimum tax from which the regular tax liability before all credits except the foreign tax credit is subtracted. The difference is the additional tax arising from the alternative minimum tax.

The number of individuals paying the alternative minimum tax is expected to rise dramatically in coming years in that, unlike in the case of regular tax liability, the AMT exemption and rates are not indexed for cost of living. Additionally, new tax credits created by the Taxpayer Relief Act of 1997 (see Chapter 3) offset regular tax liability but not alternative minimum tax liability. However, the new low tax rates for capital gain (see Chapter 5) are also used in the computation of AMT.

YEAR-END REMINDER   Whenever tax benefits such as accelerated depreciation, incentive stock options, intangible drilling costs, percentage depletion, net operating losses, or passive activity losses are being considered, the impact of the transaction on both regular tax liability and on the alternative minimum tax must be considered. The refinancing of a principal home or a designated second home may cause or increase alternative minimum tax as discussed in Chapter 6. Certain preference items (such as the exercise of an incentive stock option) can often be timed in order to avoid alternative minimum tax.

NO KIDDING—YOU CAN MINIMIZE THE "KIDDIE" TAX

A child under the age of 14 will be taxed on unearned income (interest and dividends, for example) at his or her parents' top marginal tax rate (perhaps as high as 39.6 percent) rather than at his or her own marginal tax rate (perhaps as low as 15 percent). The first $650 of the child's unearned income is not taxed because it is offset by a special $650 standard deduction, and the next $650 of unearned income is taxed at the child's own tax rates. However, the child's unearned income in excess of $1,300 will be taxed at the parents' top marginal rate. The special $650 standard deduction and the $650 of unearned income taxed at the child's own rates will be indexed in 1998 and succeeding years. Use IRS Form 8615 to compute the *"Kiddie"* tax.

If a child's gross income is more than $650 but less than $6,500, the parents can elect on IRS Form 8814 to include the child's income in excess of $1,300 in their adjusted gross income and the child's tax on the first $1,300 of his or her income as part of their tax liability. If the election is made, the child will not be required to file a tax return. The election is available only if the child's income consists solely of interest and dividends and if no estimated tax payments or backup withholding payments have been made on behalf of the child. All dollar figures relating to IRS Form 8814 will be indexed in 1998 and succeeding years for cost of living.

CAUTION!   By making the election to include your child's income on your tax return, you avoid having to file a separate return for your child. However, including the child's income over $1,300 on your personal return will increase your adjusted gross income and may have an adverse impact on your ability to claim deductions for Individual Retirement Account contributions as well as itemized deductions for medical expenses, casualty losses, and miscellaneous itemized deductions. State tax liability may also increase. In addition, your withholding and estimated tax obligations will rise to cover the increased tax liability.

QUESTION: My son (12 years old) has a paper route this year for which he will probably earn $2,800. He'll also receive dividends and interest totaling about $1,950. The interest ($450) is earnings on his paper route savings and the dividends ($1,500) that he receives are from stock that his grandmother gave to him. My taxable income will be $46,000. How will the "Kiddie" tax affect us, if at all? Also, I didn't file a tax return for him last year, although he had the same income. Can he be penalized for my mistake?

ANSWER: The "Kiddie" tax will cost your son $85 in taxes because a portion of his income will be taxed at a 28 percent rate rather than at a 15 percent rate. Of the investment income, $650 will not be taxed because it is sheltered by $650 of your son's $3,050 standard deduction, which is normally $4,150 (prior to indexing in 1998) for unmarried taxpayers but is specifically limited to the greater of $650 or earned income plus $250 for those who can be claimed as a dependent on another's return. The next $650 is taxed at your son's 15 percent rate and the remaining $650 is taxed at your 28 percent rate. It doesn't make any difference that $450 of the investment income was earnings on your son's salary. His earned income ($2,800) is sheltered in part by the remaining $2,400 of his $3,050 standard deduction ($3,050 − $650 = $2,400) and the balance is taxed at a 15 percent rate:

$650 investment income × 15%	=	$ 98
$650 investment income × 28%	=	182
$400 net earned income × 15%	=	60
		$340

You are not eligible to use Form 8814 to include your son's income on your tax return because your son had some non-investment income.

As for the penalties, several years ago the Tax Court decided that actress Skye Bassett was liable for penalties when her parents failed to file for her when she was ages 11 through 14. Only if her parents' conduct as her guardians was reasonably justified might she have avoided the penalties. Bassett's father was a college graduate, and the Court determined that he ignored his responsibility. See a full discussion of penalties in Chapter 13.

CAUTION!   Prior to 1998 the standard deduction of an individual who could be claimed as a dependent by another was the lesser of the regular standard deduction or earned income ($650 as indexed if greater.)

CAUTION!   A child who is subject to the "Kiddie" tax may be subject to the alternative minimum tax if his or her parents have to pay AMT. The child's alternative minimum tax exemption is limited to his or her earned income plus $5,000 indexed in 1999 and succeeding years for cost of living rather than a full $33,750 which is normally available to single individuals. For 1997 the AMT exemption for a child subject to the "Kiddie" tax was the greater of his or her earned income plus the greater of $1,300 or the parents' unused exemption.

QUESTION: Which parent's tax rate is used if the parents aren't married? I am in a 15 percent bracket, but I'm certain my ex-husband is in a higher bracket. And does it make sense for either of us to transfer funds into an account in the name and Social Security number of our nine-year-old?

ANSWER: Use the rate of the parent who has custody. If you were married but filed separate returns, the "Kiddie" tax would have been imposed at the rate used by the parent with the higher income.

Parents often want to make gifts to their children of investment assets both from a financial planning point of view, meaning providing them with a nest egg to finance college education, business start-up costs, and the like, as well as with a view toward shifting the income tax burden of these investment assets to children who are generally in lower tax brackets. However, as a result of the "Kiddie" tax, to the extent that the investment income exceeds $1,300, no income tax savings can be accomplished. The key then is to limit the taxable investment income of the child who is under the age of 14 to $1,300.

TAX PLANNING IDEA   If a child's investment income might be expected to exceed $1,300, consider purchasing U.S. Series EE Bonds in the child's name. Series EE Bonds mature in ten years and no federal taxes need be paid on the interest until the bonds are cashed. If a bond is purchased for a child no earlier than age four, then the interest at maturity will be taxed at the child's rate rather than at the parent's marginal tax rate. Other investments that will produce a similar result are growth stocks (those that pay little or no current dividends but are expected to appreciate in value) and municipal bonds, the interest from which is exempt from federal tax. If the child is closer to age 14, consider purchasing certificates of deposit in the child's name that will mature after the child attains the age of 14. The interest on these certificates will be taxed at the child's rate after age 14.

CAUTION!   When shifting investment assets from your portfolio to a child's portfolio, keep in mind that no more than an aggregate of $10,000 in gifts ($20,000 for gifts from both parents) indexed in 1999 and succeeding years may be made in any single tax year to each recipient without causing potential adverse estate and gift tax consequences. (See Chapter 12 for a detailed discussion of the tax consequences of gifts.)

AVOID PENALTY BY PINPOINTING YOUR TAX PREPAYMENT AMOUNT

Wage earners are all required to prepay income tax liabilities by having amounts withheld from each paycheck. If there is non-wage income, such as investment income or income from sole proprietorships or partnerships, prepayments of income tax liabilities through quarterly payments of the estimated tax bill may be required. Correctly calculating both the amount of tax to be withheld from your paycheck as well as correctly calculating the quarterly estimated tax payments are important tasks in year-round tax planning.

CAUTION!   Failure to have the correct amount withheld from your paycheck or failure to make the appropriate deposits of estimated tax payments may lead to the imposition of a penalty, normally applicable when 90 percent of the liability has not been prepaid through withholding or estimates. However, the penalty can generally be avoided even when there is a substantial liability due on April 15 because too little has been withheld or too little has been paid in estimated tax payments, provided these prepayments total at least 100 percent of the previous year's tax bill. For example, if your 1996 federal tax obligation (line 51 of the 1996 Form 1040) was $10,000 and your withholding or estimated tax payments during 1997 total at least $10,000, then even though the actual 1997 tax bill turns out to be more, no penalty will normally be imposed for failure to properly prepay this obligation. Of course, the additional liability must still be paid on April 15, 1998.

CAUTION!   For 1997 estimates, individuals with prior year adjusted gross income in excess of $150,000 ($75,000 on a married filing separate return) were required to prepay 110 percent of the previous year's tax bill for a *protective estimate* based on prior liability. The Taxpayer Relief Act of 1997 suspended the 110 percent rule for 1998 estimates and adjusted it for 1999–2001 to 105 percent of the previous year's tax liability. However, the requirement climbs to 112 percent for 2002 before reverting in the following year to the current 110 percent.

FILING POINTER   No penalty for underpayment of withholding or estimates can properly be imposed on a 1997 tax return to the extent it arose out of law changes in the Taxpayer Relief Act of 1997.

FILING POINTER   You should prepay in estimated taxes and withholding only the minimum amount certain to keep you from being penalized so that you, rather than IRS, have the use of your money during the year for cash flow and for earning more money. If you prepay more than that which is needed to avoid penalty, you are, in essence, giving the IRS an interest-free loan. In 1997, two-thirds of individual filers received refunds with cumulative checks of approximately $100 billion—lost opportunities for taxpayers and found money for the IRS.

HELP WITH FORM 1040-ES

The IRS provides Form 1040-ES to assist taxpayers in computing the appropriate amount of estimated tax payments. This form should be completed each year if it is anticipated that the amount withheld from your paycheck will not be sufficient to pay at least 90 percent of the current year's expected tax bill (or, if less, 100 percent or, for higher income taxpayers, the applicable percentage of the preceding year's tax bill depending upon AGI). If it is determined that estimated tax payments are needed, they are due on April 15, June 15, September 15, and January 15 of the following year. No estimated payments are required if the estimated tax liability is less than $1,000.

Here is an example of the completed Form 1040-ES for 1997. Fred and Ethel are married and have one child. Fred is a wage earner and anticipated his 1997 annual salary to be $60,000. Ethel has her own business, from which she anticipated a profit of approximately $30,000. The couple will receive about $8,000 in investment income and each will contribute $2,000 to an Individual Retirement Account. Itemized deductions will be $11,000. To enable Fred and Ethel to continue their respective jobs, their child is taken to a day-care center, the cost of which is $5,000 per year.

Fred and Ethel completed the 1997 Form 1040-ES at the same time they did their 1996 income tax return, which showed a tax liability of $20,000. Based on the information available to them at that time, the couple decided that estimated tax payments for 1997 were in order. The minimum amount of quarterly payments needed to be made by the couple was $1,367. Assuming that their estimates of salary, self-employment income, investment income, and itemized deductions were accurate, Fred and Ethel's 1997 tax bill will be $18,823, including $4,239 of self-employment tax arising from Ethel's profitable sole proprietorship. If the amounts of tax to be withheld from Fred's salary checks were as predicted and the couple makes the four quarterly payments of $1,367, they will owe the Internal Revenue Service $1,883 on April 15, 1998.

The computation of Ethel's self-employment tax reflects a reduction in the tax base equal to 7.65 percent of the business profit. The computation of adjusted gross income reflects a deduction for one-half of the self-employment tax.

CAUTION!   Unless your expected tax liability for a year will decline significantly from the previous year, it is often best to ensure that you won't be penalized by prepaying for the current year based on 100 percent or, for higher income taxpayers, the applicable percentage of the previous year's liability (whichever is applicable). This guarantees

Fred and Ethel's 1997 Form 1040-ES, page 4

1997 Estimated Tax Worksheet (keep for your records)

1	Enter amount of adjusted gross income you expect in 1997 (see instructions)	1	91,880
2	• If you plan to itemize deductions, enter the estimated total of your itemized deductions. **Caution:** If line 1 above is over $121,200 ($60,600 if married filing separately), your deduction may be reduced. See Pub. 505 for details. ⎫ • If you do not plan to itemize deductions, see **Standard Deduction for 1997** on page 2, and enter your standard deduction here. ⎭	2	11,000
3	Subtract line 2 from line 1	3	80,880
4	Exemptions. Multiply $2,650 by the number of personal exemptions. If you can be claimed as a dependent on another person's 1997 return, your personal exemption is not allowed. **Caution:** If line 1 above is over $181,800 ($151,500 if head of household; $121,200 if single; $90,900 if married filing separately), see Pub. 505 to figure the amount to enter	4	7,950
5	Subtract line 4 from line 3	5	72,930
6	**Tax.** Figure your tax on the amount on line 5 by using the 1997 Tax Rate Schedules on page 2. DO NOT use the Tax Table or the Tax Rate Schedules in the 1996 Form 1040 or Form 1040A instructions. **Caution:** If you have a net capital gain and line 5 is over $99,600 ($85,350 if head of household; $59,750 if single; $49,800 if married filing separately), see Pub. 505 to figure the tax	6	15,064
7	Additional taxes (see instructions)	7	0
8	Add lines 6 and 7	8	15,064
9	Credits (see instructions). Do not include any income tax withholding on this line	9	480
10	Subtract line 9 from line 8. Enter the result, but not less than zero	10	14,584
11	Self-employment tax (see instructions). Estimate of 1997 net earnings from self-employment $................. ; if **$65,400 or less,** multiply the amount by 15.3%; if **more than $65,400,** multiply the amount by 2.9%, add $8,109.60 to the result, and enter the total. **Caution:** If you also have wages subject to social security tax, see Pub. 505 to figure the amount to enter	11	4,239
12	Other taxes (see instructions)	12	0
13a	Add lines 10 through 12	13a	18,823
b	Earned income credit and credit from **Form 4136**	13b	0
c	Subtract line 13b from line 13a. Enter the result, but not less than zero. **THIS IS YOUR TOTAL 1997 ESTIMATED TAX** ▶	13c	18,823

14a	Multiply line 13c by 90% (66⅔% for farmers and fishermen)	14a	16,941	
b	Enter the tax shown on your 1996 tax return (110% of that amount if you are not a farmer or a fisherman and the adjusted gross income shown on that return is more than $150,000 or, if married filing separately for 1997, more than $75,000)	14b	20,000	
c	Enter the **smaller** of line 14a or 14b. **THIS IS YOUR REQUIRED ANNUAL PAYMENT TO AVOID A PENALTY** ▶	14c		16,941

Caution: Generally, if you do not prepay (through income tax withholding and estimated tax payments) at least the amount on line 14c, you may owe a penalty for not paying enough estimated tax. To avoid a penalty, make sure your estimate on line 13c is as accurate as possible. Even if you pay the required annual payment, you may still owe tax when you file your return. If you prefer, you may pay the amount shown on line 13c. For more details, see Pub. 505.

15	Income tax withheld and estimated to be withheld during 1997 (including income tax withholding on pensions, annuities, certain deferred income, etc.)	15	11,472
16	Subtract line 15 from line 14c. **(Note:** *If zero or less, or line 13c minus line 15 is less than $500, stop here. You are not required to make estimated tax payments.*)	16	5,469
17	If the first payment you are required to make is due April 15, 1997, enter ¼ of line 16 (minus any 1996 overpayment that you are applying to this installment) here and on your payment voucher(s)	17	1,367

that you won't be penalized if you miscalculate 90 percent of the current year's liability. In our example above, Fred and Ethel would protect against a miscalculation of 1997 liability by increasing estimated payments by $3,060 ($765 per quarter). Their total prepayment would then be the $20,000, equalling the previous year's liability. Of course, Fred must still monitor his withholding so that it is not less than projected.

 CAUTION!   For 1997 estimated tax payments were required if the estimated tax liability was at least $500.

HELP WITH FORM W-4

IRS Form W-4 is the paper that every employee fills out in order to determine how much of each paycheck will be withheld and paid over to IRS by the employer. Proper completion of Form W-4 will help pinpoint the proper prepayment of taxes through withholdings.

Here is an example of the completed Form W-4. Assume the same facts about Fred and Ethel as previously described except that Ethel gave up her own business on December 31, 1996 and now has a salaried position which will pay her $30,000 in 1997. Based on these assumptions, Fred and Ethel want to compute their withholding allowances on one Form W-4 worksheet. Once the withholding allowances for the couple have been calculated, they can divide the withholding allowances between them and file their own separate Forms W-4 with their respective employers. The employers then determine the appropriate amount of withholding from tables prepared by IRS.

If the form is properly completed by the couple and then each properly files his or her own W-4 with the respective employers, Fred and Ethel will each claim "0" allowances and Fred will have $478 withheld from each of his semimonthly paychecks (including an additional $62 over the amount determined from the IRS tables) for a total of $11,472 withheld for the year. Ethel will have $147 withheld from each of her semimonthly paychecks for a total withholding of $3,528. The couple's combined withholding for 1997 will be $15,000. Assuming that the estimates of the couple's income were exact, their 1997 federal income tax liability will be $15,178. Thus, the couple will have an additional payment of $178 due on April 15, 1998. However, they will not be penalized for underwithholding in that they will have prepaid 90 percent of the tax liability for 1997.

 CAUTION!   Even careful completion of Form W-4 may cause overwithholding in certain instances. Wage earners should monitor their expected tax liability versus withholding throughout the year and make adjustments as needed.

CHANGING YOUR TAX PREPAYMENT AMOUNT

What do you do if circumstances change during the year after you have completed the Form 1040-ES or Form W-4? For example, let's assume that on October 1, 1997, Fred and Ethel

Fred's Form W–4.

Form W-4 (1997)

Want More Money In Your Paycheck?
If you expect to be able to take the earned income credit for 1997 and a child lives with you, you may be able to have part of the credit added to your take-home pay. For details, get Form W-5 from your employer.

Purpose. Complete Form W-4 so that your employer can withhold the correct amount of Federal income tax from your pay. Form W-4 may be completed electronically, if your employer has an electronic system. Because your tax situation may change, you may want to refigure your withholding each year.

Exemption From Withholding. Read line 7 of the certificate below to see if you can claim exempt status. If exempt, only complete lines 1, 2, 3, 4, 7, and sign the form to validate it. No Federal income tax will be withheld from your pay. Your exemption expires February 17, 1998.

Note: You cannot claim exemption from withholding if (1) your income exceeds $650 and includes unearned income (e.g., interest and dividends) and (2) another person can claim you as a dependent on their tax return.

Basic Instructions. If you are not exempt, complete the Personal Allowances Worksheet. Additional worksheets are on page 2 so you can adjust your withholding allowances based on itemized deductions, adjustments to income, or two-earner/two-job situations. Complete all worksheets that apply to your situation. The worksheets will help you figure the number of withholding allowances you are entitled to claim. However, you may claim fewer allowances than this.

Head of Household. Generally, you may claim head of household filing status on your tax return only if you are unmarried and pay more than 50% of the costs of keeping up a home for yourself and your dependent(s) or other qualifying individuals.

Nonwage Income. If you have a large amount of nonwage income, such as interest or dividends, you should consider making

estimated tax payments using Form 1040-ES. Otherwise, you may find that you owe additional tax at the end of the year.

Two Earners/Two Jobs. If you have a working spouse or more than one job, figure the total number of allowances you are entitled to claim on all jobs using worksheets from only one W-4. This total should be divided among all jobs. Your withholding will usually be most accurate when all allowances are claimed on the W-4 filed for the highest paying job and zero allowances are claimed for the others.

Check Your Withholding. After your W-4 takes effect, use **Pub. 919,** Is My Withholding Correct for 1997?, to see how the dollar amount you are having withheld compares to your estimated total annual tax. Get Pub. 919 especially if you used the Two-Earner/Two-Job Worksheet and your earnings exceed $150,000 (Single) or $200,000 (Married). To order Pub. 919, call 1-800-829-3676. Check your telephone directory for the IRS assistance number for further help.

Sign This Form. Form W-4 is not considered valid unless you sign it.

Personal Allowances Worksheet

A	Enter "1" for **yourself** if no one else can claim you as a dependent	**A** __1__
B	Enter "1" if: { • You are single and have only one job; or • You are married, have only one job, and your spouse does not work; or • Your wages from a second job or your spouse's wages (or the total of both) are $1,000 or less. }	**B** _____
C	Enter "1"for your **spouse.** But, you may choose to enter -0- if you are married and have either a working spouse or more than one job (this may help you avoid having too little tax withheld)	**C** __1__
D	Enter number of **dependents** (other than your spouse or yourself) you will claim on your tax return	**D** __1__
E	Enter "1" if you will file as **head of household** on your tax return (see conditions under **Head of Household** above) .	**E** _____
F	Enter "1" if you have at least $1,500 of **child or dependent care expenses** for which you plan to claim a credit . .	**F** __1__
G	Add lines A through F and enter total here. Note: This amount may be different from the number of exemptions you claim on your return ▶	**G** __4__

For accuracy, complete all worksheets that apply.	• If you plan to **itemize or claim adjustments to income** and want to reduce your withholding, see the Deductions and Adjustments Worksheet on page 2. • If you are **single** and have **more than one job** and your combined earnings from all jobs exceed $32,000 OR if you are **married** and have a **working spouse or more than one job,** and the combined earnings from all jobs exceed $55,000, see the Two-Earner/Two-Job Worksheet on page 2 if you want to avoid having too little tax withheld. • If **neither** of the above situations applies, **stop here** and enter the number from line G on line 5 of Form W-4 below.

---------------------- **Cut here and give the certificate to your employer. Keep the top portion for your records.** ----------------------

Form **W-4** Department of the Treasury Internal Revenue Service	**Employee's Withholding Allowance Certificate** ▶ **For Privacy Act and Paperwork Reduction Act Notice, see reverse.**	OMB No. 1545-0010 **1997**

1 Type or print your first name and middle initial	Last name	**2** Your social security number
Fred Mertz		000 : 00 : 0000

Home address (number and street or rural route) 518 Crestview Drive	**3** ☐ Single ☒ Married ☐ Married, but withhold at higher Single rate. **Note:** If married, but legally separated, or spouse is a nonresident alien, check the Single box.
City or town, state, and ZIP code Mayfield, Ohio 99999	**4** If your last name differs from that on your social security card, check here and call 1-800-772-1213 for a new card . . . . . . ▶ ☐

5	Total number of allowances you are claiming (from line G above or from the worksheets on page 2 if they apply) .	**5**	0
6	Additional amount, if any, you want withheld from each paycheck	**6** $	62
7	I claim exemption from withholding for 1997, and I certify that I meet **BOTH** of the following conditions for exemption: • Last year I had a right to a refund of **ALL** Federal income tax withheld because I had **NO** tax liability; **AND** • This year I expect a refund of **ALL** Federal income tax withheld because I expect to have **NO** tax liability. If you meet both conditions, enter "EXEMPT" here . . . . ▶	**7**	

Under penalties of perjury, I certify that I am entitled to the number of withholding allowances claimed on this certificate or entitled to claim exempt status.

Employee's signature ▶   Date ▶   , 19

8 Employer's name and address (Employer: Complete 8 and 10 only if sending to the IRS)	**9** Office code (optional)	**10** Employer identification number

Cat. No. 10220Q

Fred's 1997 W–4 worksheet.

Form W-4 (1997)   Page **2**

Deductions and Adjustments Worksheet

Note: *Use this worksheet only if you plan to itemize deductions or claim adjustments to income on your 1997 tax return.*

1	Enter an estimate of your 1997 itemized deductions. These include qualifying home mortgage interest, charitable contributions, state and local taxes (but not sales taxes), medical expenses in excess of 7.5% of your income, and miscellaneous deductions. (For 1997, you may have to reduce your itemized deductions if your income is over $121,200 ($60,600 if married filing separately). Get Pub. 919 for details.)	1	$ 11,000
2	Enter: { $6,900 if married filing jointly or qualifying widow(er) / $6,050 if head of household / $4,150 if single / $3,450 if married filing separately }	2	$ 6,900
3	**Subtract** line 2 from line 1. If line 2 is greater than line 1, enter -0-	3	$ 4,100
4	Enter an estimate of your 1997 adjustments to income. These include alimony paid and deductible IRA contributions	4	$ 4,000
5	**Add** lines 3 and 4 and enter the total	5	$ 8,100
6	Enter an estimate of your 1997 nonwage income (such as dividends or interest)	6	$ 8,000
7	**Subtract** line 6 from line 5. Enter the result, but not less than -0-	7	$ 100
8	**Divide** the amount on line 7 by $2,500 and enter the result here. Drop any fraction	8	0
9	Enter the number from Personal Allowances Worksheet, line G, on page 1	9	4
10	**Add** lines 8 and 9 and enter the total here. If you plan to use the Two-Earner/Two-Job Worksheet, also enter this total on line 1 below. Otherwise, **stop here** and enter this total on Form W-4, line 5, on page 1	10	4

Two-Earner/Two-Job Worksheet

Note: *Use this worksheet only if the instructions for line G on page 1 direct you here.*

1	Enter the number from line G on page 1 (or from line 10 above if you used the Deductions and Adjustments Worksheet)	1	4
2	Find the number in **Table 1** below that applies to the **LOWEST** paying job and enter it here	2	6
3	If line 1 is **GREATER THAN OR EQUAL TO** line 2, subtract line 2 from line 1. Enter the result here (if zero, enter -0-) and on Form W-4, line 5, on page 1. **DO NOT** use the rest of this worksheet	3	

Note: *If line 1 is LESS THAN line 2, enter -0- on Form W-4, line 5, on page 1. Complete lines 4–9 to calculate the additional withholding amount necessary to avoid a year end tax bill.*

4	Enter the number from line 2 of this worksheet	4	6
5	Enter the number from line 1 of this worksheet	5	4
6	**Subtract** line 5 from line 4	6	2
7	Find the amount in **Table 2** below that applies to the **HIGHEST** paying job and enter it here	7	$ 740
8	**Multiply** line 7 by line 6 and enter the result here. This is the additional annual withholding amount needed	8	$ 1,480
9	Divide line 8 by the number of pay periods remaining in 1997. (For example, divide by 26 if you are paid every other week and you complete this form in December 1996.) Enter the result here and on Form W-4, line 6, page 1. This is the additional amount to be withheld from each paycheck	9	$ 62

Table 1: Two-Earner/Two-Job Worksheet

Married Filing Jointly				All Others			
If wages from **LOWEST** paying job are–	Enter on line 2 above	If wages from **LOWEST** paying job are–	Enter on line 2 above	If wages from **LOWEST** paying job are–	Enter on line 2 above	If wages from **LOWEST** paying job are–	Enter on line 2 above
0 - $4,000	0	35,001 - 40,000	8	0 - $5,000	0	75,001 - 90,000	8
4,001 - 7,000	1	40,001 - 50,000	9	5,001 - 11,000	1	90,001 - 110,000	9
7,001 - 12,000	2	50,001 - 60,000	10	11,001 - 15,000	2	110,001 and over	10
12,001 - 17,000	3	60,001 - 70,000	11	15,001 - 20,000	3		
17,001 - 22,000	4	70,001 - 80,000	12	20,001 - 24,000	4		
22,001 - 28,000	5	80,001 - 100,000	13	24,001 - 45,000	5		
28,001 - 32,000	6	100,001 - 110,000	14	45,001 - 60,000	6		
32,001 - 35,000	7	110,001 and over	15	60,001 - 75,000	7		

Table 2: Two-Earner/Two-Job Worksheet

Married Filing Jointly		All Others	
If wages from **HIGHEST** paying job are–	Enter on line 7 above	If wages from **HIGHEST** paying job are–	Enter on line 7 above
0 - $50,000	$400	0 - $30,000	$400
50,001 - 100,000	740	30,001 - 60,000	740
100,001 - 130,000	820	60,001 - 120,000	820
130,001 - 240,000	950	120,001 - 250,000	950
240,001 and over	1,050	250,001 and over	1,050

unexpectedly sell some stock which generates a long-term capital gain of $20,000. Obviously, their tax liability will be substantially increased.

The couple has several available options. They can make a fourth quarter estimated tax payment due January 15, 1998, or they can have additional amounts withheld from either or both their remaining 1997 wages to cover the increased liability. Alternatively, no additional amount of withholding or estimated taxes need be paid under these facts despite the unexpected increase in taxable income in 1997 if the current rate of withholding and/or estimated tax payments will at least equal their 1996 tax liability. In our example, we had assumed that the couple's 1996 tax liability was $20,000 so this alternative will be unavailable to Fred and Ethel.

Consequently, Fred and Ethel should calculate what the additional $20,000 of capital gain will cost them in taxes. Given the 20 percent maximum applicable tax rate (see Chapter 5), the capital gain will increase their tax liability by $4,000. To cover this additional liability, Fred and Ethel can either have an additional amount withheld from their remaining 12 paychecks (six each) or pay the $4,000 by January 15, 1998 as an estimated tax payment.

YEAR-END REMINDER   Estimated payments must be made *pro rata* for the four calendar quarters unless changed circumstances cause a modification. Taxpayers are credited with prepayment when estimated taxes are paid. In contrast, withholding is presumed to be divided equally among the four calendar quarters unless the taxpayer demonstrates to the contrary. Consequently, increasing your withholding at the end of the year can help you avoid the penalty for being underwithheld. Suppose that, in November, you realize that you have been drastically underwithheld during the year and that you will not only owe tax to Uncle Sam, but will also be liable for the penalty. Here's a way out.

File a new W-4 and increase your withholding to a level that will bring your total within 90 percent of this year's or, depending on AGI, 100 percent or the applicable higher percentage of last year's tax liability. You don't even have to have a job to use this loophole; you can have your spouse hike his or her withholding. Many people don't realize that they may have as much withheld from their pay as they want, up to the full amount of their salary. It may mean tightening the belt through the Christmas season, but this beats paying an underpayment penalty come filing time the next Easter. This loophole also works for taxpayers who have fallen behind in their estimated tax payments. The only catch is that you or your spouse must earn enough money from employment to be able to have enough money withheld to avoid the penalty.

TAX PLANNING IDEA   Effective tax planning and the prepayment of one's federal tax liability will involve careful computations of withholding allowances and estimated tax obligations. These computations will have to be reviewed whenever there is a change in marital status, a change in the number of dependents, or an increase or decrease in the amount of estimated non-wage income or in deductible expenses. Household employers should see Chapter 11 concerning additional prepayments needed to cover employee payroll taxes.

YOUR HOME STATE AND ITS IMPACT
ON YOUR INCOME TAX LIABILITY

Regardless of your home state, the federal tax laws will apply to you in the same manner as they apply to your friend who lives across the state line. However, the two of you will likely be subject to two different state tax structures. There are a few jurisdictions (the largest being Texas and Florida) which do not impose any income taxes on individuals. Other jurisdictions, such as California and New York, impose heavy tax burdens.

In many situations, there is no choice in selecting a home or place of employment. However, retirees in particular may have flexibility, and locating in a state without an income tax can save thousands of dollars.

YEAR-END REMINDER   Many retirees enjoy spending part of the year in Florida. For individuals who divide time between two homes, one of which is in a state such as Florida which does not have an individual income tax, it is important to become familiar with the law of the taxing state and possibly to limit time there as year-end approaches. By restricting time in the taxing state, usually just under one-half of the year, you typically avoid being considered as a *resident* of that state. You must also typically avoid being treated as a *domicile* of the taxing state. This test is subjective and is based on what you consider as your home state as shown by voting records, automobile registration, driver's license, and other indicia.

2

TAXABLE AND TAX-FREE INCOME AND BENEFITS

INCOME CLASSIFICATIONS: PORTFOLIO, ACTIVE, AND PASSIVE

Depending upon its source, income will fall into one of three categories which are not always easily distinguishable: portfolio (also known as investment) income, active income, and passive income. Your ability to claim certain types of deductions will hinge on the existence of a particular type of income.

Portfolio income or *investment income* is income generated by an activity which is not considered a trade or business. Portfolio income consists primarily of interest (even interest paid by the IRS, according to an IRS private letter ruling) and dividends, though self-charged interest income related to an individual and a pass-through entity (partnership or S corporation) in which he or she owns at least ten percent as a passive investment may be recharacterized as passive in order to prevent inequity. (See Chapters 6 and 10 for discussions of the various types of business entities including limited liability companies taxed as partnerships in the contexts of real estate and operating businesses.)

The amount of portfolio income is significant in that individuals can claim a deduction for investment interest expense only to the extent of net investment income (investment income less expenses) for the year.

Active income is income from salary, income derived from a sole proprietorship business in which the individual *materially participates,* and income from partnerships and S corporations in which the partner or shareholder materially participates in the entity's business operations.

Passive income is income generated by a business operation in which the taxpayer does not materially participate, whether that business activity is conducted in the form of a sole proprietorship, a partnership, or a corporation. Except for non-recurring casualties or thefts, losses from passive business enterprises can be used only to offset passive income. Any losses that are not deductible as a result of the passive loss rule can be carried forward indefinitely and deducted against passive income generated in a subsequent year or any income upon disposition of the passive activity.

The distinction between active income and passive income turns on the extent of the individual's participation in the business operations. If the participation is on a regular and continuous basis, it will be deemed to be material. In that case, any income or loss generated by that business enterprise will be active in nature with any loss fully deductible.

Unless the individual's participation in the business enterprise meets the standards for material participation, any income or loss generated by the business will generally be considered passive in nature. But see Chapter 7 concerning how income otherwise passive in nature will be recharacterized as non-passive where material participation standards are not met but the lesser standards for significant participation are satisfied.

Except for certain individuals in real estate–related businesses (see Chapter 11), real estate rentals are automatically passive activities. Short-term rentals (those of seven days or less, or 30 days or less if services are provided) are not automatically passive according to a Temporary Regulation but, in fact, are passive absent material participation.

Gains and losses on dispositions of income-producing assets are generally classified in an identical manner as the income produced (i.e., investment, active, or passive).

Temporary Regulations define material participation in terms of the number of hours devoted to the activity. If you work more than 500 hours a year, or work more than 100 hours during the year and no one else works more than 100 hours, you will meet the definition of material participation and any loss generated will be deductible. Other tests are available for meeting the material participation standard. They include situations when:

1. The individual's work constitutes substantially all of the work in the activity;

2. In the last ten years, the individual satisfied a material participation standard in at least five years, but only the 500-hour test can be used for pre-1987 years; and

3. With respect to personal service activities such as medicine, law, accounting, engineering, architecture, or performing arts, the individual satisfied a material participation standard in at least three years, but only the 500-hour test can be used for pre-1987 years.

To determine your degree of participation in an activity, you are permitted to include your spouse's participation in the activity.

CAUTION!   The rules on utilization of suspended passive losses on disposition of an investment are complex. When you sell the passive investment, the losses that have been carried forward will be used to offset income in the following order:

1. Current year income or gain from the passive activity, including any gain recognized on the sale;

2. Net income or gain from all other passive activities; and

3. Any other nonpassive income or gain, including wages and investment income.

If the gain on the sale of the passive investment is reported on the installment method (see Chapter 5), then the losses can only be used as your buyer makes payments.

If you sell your passive investment to certain related parties, for example, your family or your closely held corporation, the losses that have been carried forward cannot be used. Rather, you continue to carry forward the losses against other passive income until the related party sells the passive investment to an unrelated party. Then you can claim any losses from the particular investment which you never used.

To be eligible to use the suspended passive losses, your disposition of the passive activity must generally be a taxable transaction. If you make a gift of the passive investment, you are not entitled to use the losses. Instead, the recipient of your gift adds your losses to his or her basis in the investment.

You get a limited right to use any suspended losses that may remain at the time of your death. On your final tax return, remaining passive losses may be used only to the extent that they are greater than the difference between the value of the investment and your basis in the investment just prior to your death. For example, if you have $18,000 of suspended losses and your passive investment is worth $15,000 against a basis of $7,000, $10,000 of the suspended losses are usable to offset both passive and nonpassive income. The remaining $8,000 of losses is wasted. If the amount of the suspended losses had been $8,000 or less, nothing would have been deductible on your final tax return.

 CAUTION!   Congress has periodically considered legislation to allow individuals with minimal passive losses in any year to use those losses without carryover.

QUESTION: I am receiving payments under a covenant not to compete with the person to whom I sold my business. Are these payments passive in nature since I get paid for doing nothing?

ANSWER: Although your payments appear to be the exact opposite of active income, the Tax Court in 1995 upheld a Regulation which makes payments under a covenant not to compete as active income. The Court observed that restraint from work has traditionally been considered as akin to work itself.

QUESTION: I own an arts and crafts business. I operate only during the summer weekends. I have no employees. Do I materially participate in my business?

ANSWER: Yes. Even if you don't work 100 hours a year, you will be treated as materially participating in the business when no one else is helping out and you are doing all of the work. This meets the definition of material participation even when the total hours of work are less than 100.

QUESTION: I have been a general partner in a retail clothing firm since 1975. I retired on New Year's Eve of 1993, but I continue to be a partner. Is my share of the profit active or passive income?

ANSWER: Through 1998 you will be treated as materially participating in this business under the five out of ten year rule. However, any profit that you receive in 1999 and subsequent years will be passive income.

YEAR END REMINDER As year end approaches, watch the number of hours which you have devoted to an activity if losses are expected. Increase the number of hours that you work in order to cause material participation.

TAX PLANNING IDEA Your recordkeeping with respect to the type of work done and the amount of time spent is critical. When you wish to show material participation in an activity, you must maintain time records, appointment books, or other written documentation detailing the amount of time devoted to an activity.

CAUTION! According to a 1993 Tax Court decision, activities in an individual's capacity as an investor do not count toward satisfying the requisite number of hours for material participation. The Court threw out most of the 341 hours claimed by the taxpayer as not part of the day-to-day operations and management.

REPORTING INCOME PROPERLY AGAINST THE IRS MATCH

The IRS has a sophisticated program by which it can match, by using the Social Security number or other taxpayer identification number, data on information returns against that reported on the tax return. Any discrepancy will usually trigger IRS correspondence. When income-producing property is owned by two or more persons, the income derived from the property must be reported in accordance with the type of co-ownership involved. On the federal return, if the only co-owners are husband and wife and they file a joint income tax return, it makes no difference whose income it is or whether the property is jointly owned or owned in individual names. However, when the co-owners are other than husband and wife, each co-owner should report his or her share of the income generated. That share is generally determined under state law. This usually requires the reporting of income proportionate to ownership interests, but in some cases each co-owner will include on his or her return the same proportion of income as contributed to the acquisition of the asset.

The payor of income to these co-owners, such as a bank or brokerage firm, will normally issue only one IRS Form 1099 to the party whose taxpayer identification number it was given. Even though a bank account or brokerage account may have been opened in joint name, only one taxpayer identification number will be accepted by the institution. The co-owners are entitled to split the income in accordance with their entitlement to the property under state law but, because only one of the co-owners will receive the information return, he or she will have to report all of that income and then issue the other co-owner(s) their own 1099s. The co-owner who received the 1099 from the institution will then reduce his or her income by the portion of the income for which he or she is a *nominee*.

ILLUSTRATION

If two sisters, Cathy and Chris, have a joint bank account to which they made equal contributions, each should report one-half of the interest earned on that account annually. If Cathy's Social Security number was given to the bank at the time the account was opened, Cathy will receive a 1099 for all of the interest. If the account generated $1,000 of income in 1997, Cathy will receive a 1099 for $1,000. Cathy must report the $1,000 on her Schedule B for 1997. Since her sister, Chris, is the true owner of one-half of the account, Cathy should issue her sister a Form 1099 in the amount of $500. On Cathy's 1997 income tax return, she reports the entire interest on Schedule B and then subtracts the *nominee distribution* of $500 from her other interest income. Chris, having received the 1099 from her sister, will include the $500 reported on that information return on her Form 1040, Schedule B.

FILING POINTER When tax preparation time rolls around, you should check data reported on information returns (Form 1099, 1099B, W-2, W-2P, etc.) against the records received during the year from the payor of the income, whether it's your employer, bank, credit union, or brokerage firm. If the records do not confirm the information received on the 1099 or similar form, you should obtain clarification from the payor. If the original information return is incorrect, you must request a corrected tax form.

TAX PLANNING IDEA In an effort to tax income at the lowest possible marginal rate, income splitting may be undertaken. Family members can title bank accounts, securities, or other property in joint names in an effort to divide the total tax burden among the family members. However, as a result of the creation of the "Kiddie" tax, this technique has been substantially limited where a co-owner is a child under the age of 14. This approach is still available between parents and older children or between siblings.

CAUTION! Where one of the co-owners is a child who has attained 14 years of age, income splitting will work effectively but caution must be exercised so as to prevent the loss of the dependency exemption for that child. Otherwise, the tax savings generated by the shifting of income will be reduced.

ILLUSTRATION

Assume you own stock worth $11,000. It has been paying you an annual dividend of $800. You are in the 36 percent tax bracket. You will lose $288 (36% × $800) of the dividend income in federal taxes.

If you give the stock to your two children, they will be subject to tax on $400 each. If this is their only income, there will be no tax—a savings of $288.

Don't lose a dependency exemption through income shifting; in 1997 it could cost you as much as $908 (36% × $2,650) and save only $288—a net loss of $620! After 1997, in the case of a child under 17, the loss of the child credit (see Chapter 3) would involve greater cost.

CAUTION! Be careful of potential issues in the estate tax area discussed in Chapter 12 if the value of your gift to any beneficiary is more than $10,000 in any single year; the threshold is indexed in 1999 and succeeding years for cost of living.

USING THE TAX BENEFIT RULE TO AVOID INCOME

If you claimed a deduction in an earlier year (such as for state and local taxes) and you receive a refund or reimbursement of the deducted amount in a later year, you generally have taxable income in that later year. However, under the "Tax Benefit Rule," you only have taxable income to the extent of your *tax benefit* in the prior year.

For example, suppose your itemized deductions in the earlier year, excluding the state tax deduction, exceeded your adjusted gross income. Under these circumstances, claiming an additional deduction for state taxes provided you with no tax benefit because your other itemized deductions more than offset your adjusted gross income resulting in no tax liability. A refund of state taxes in the subsequent year will therefore be excludable from your income.

ILLUSTRATION

In 1997, Kevin's adjusted gross income will be $15,000 and his itemized deductions will total $18,000, including $2,000 of state income taxes withheld from his paycheck. In 1998, after filing his state income tax return, Kevin will receive a refund of $1,200 in state taxes paid during 1997. The $1,200 refund will not be taxable in 1998 because Kevin received no tax benefit when he filed his 1997 return and claimed a deduction for the withholding from his paycheck.

See the discussion of Damage Awards and Settlements later in this chapter for an illustration of the tax benefit rule.

FILING POINTER Individuals who claimed the standard deduction in the prior year are *never* required to report any attributable state tax refund as income in the subsequent year.

QUESTION: Last year I lost out on $2,500 of $22,500 of itemized deductions shown on my return, because high adjusted gross income got me caught in the phase-out. My deduction for state income taxes would have been $7,200. The remaining $15,300 was from mortgage interest and property taxes. This year I received a $3,000 refund from the IRS. Do I have to report the entire refund as income even if I couldn't use one-ninth of the deduction? Or can I report eight-ninths of the refund as income?

ANSWER: The IRS position is that an individual caught in the phase-out of itemized deductions must recompute what prior-year itemized deductions would have totaled after the phase-out if the taxes paid had been netted with the subsequent-year refund. If, as in most situations, the recomputation would have caused a reduction in allowable deductions equal to the tax refund, the IRS says that the individual received a benefit from the entire deduction of state taxes and must consequently report the entire tax refund as income.

To illustrate, in your case, if your prior year allowable itemized deductions after the phase-out would be recomputed at $17,000, the IRS says you must report the full $3,000 state tax refund as income. Your reduction in itemized deductions on the recomputation is equal to the amount of the tax refund.

CAUTION! Upon recomputation, some individuals will find their deductions reduced by less than the amount of their tax refunds. These individuals may limit their income from the refund to the amount by which their deductions are reduced. They include taxpayers whose reductions would have caused them to claim the standard deduction and those affected by the maximum 80 percent phase-out of itemized deductions.

LOWER-YIELD TAX-EXEMPT BONDS MAY GIVE YOU A HIGH YIELD

One significant way to reduce your taxable investment income is to invest in state and local bonds. The interest paid on most state and local bonds will be exempt from federal income tax and, if the bonds that you purchase are issued by your state of residence or a locality within that state, they will generally be exempt from state taxes as well.

The yields on state and local bonds will generally be lower than the yields on corporate bonds and other investments, but you will want to compare the after-tax yield of the investments. For example, if you are in a 36 percent marginal federal tax bracket and in a state marginal tax bracket of seven percent, and you invest $1,000 in a corporate bond yielding eight percent, you will earn $80 of interest annually. However, you will lose $34.40 in federal and state taxes (ignoring the state tax benefit on the federal return, $28.80 to the federal government, and $5.60 to your state of residence). Thus, from that $80 of interest income, you will net only $46.60. If you invested $1,000 in a tax-exempt municipal bond of your state yielding six percent, the same $1,000 investment produces only $60 of income per year but will cost you nothing in taxes.

Although most state and local bond interest is exempt from federal taxes, the exemption will be lost if the bond was issued after August 15, 1986, in an unregistered form; that is, if the bond is a bearer bond. Also, there is no tax exemption for state and local bonds when the proceeds are used for private business purposes rather than for governmental business purposes unless the proceeds are used for particular kinds of private activities sanctioned by the Internal Revenue Code such as to build residential rental projects, sewage facilities, airports, or hazardous waste disposal facilities; to finance student loans; or to invest in empowerment zones (see Chapter 7).

CAUTION! Before investing in any state or local bond, it is important to have your investment adviser check into the tax-exempt status of the bond as well as the financial stability of the issuing jurisdiction. The bond will be rated based on that financial stability. If there is a greater risk of default by the jurisdiction issuing the bond, then the bond may have a lower rating but a higher yield to attract investors. The two primary rating services are Standard and Poor's and Moody's. Standard and Poor's top rated bonds receive an AAA rating, while a bond in default receives a D rating. If you wish a higher rate of return and are willing to take a greater degree of risk, look into state and local bonds that receive less than the AAA rating. If you are a conservative investor, look only for the highest rated bonds for your investments.

CAUTION!   The value of a tax-exempt bond, particularly one with a lengthy maturity, could fall dramatically in the event of enactment of a low-rate flat federal income tax.

FEDERAL OBLIGATIONS MAY GIVE YOU AN EVEN HIGHER YIELD

Lending money to the federal government by purchasing Treasury bills, Treasury notes, or Treasury bonds will yield interest income that is exempt from state and local taxes but is taxed by the federal government. Treasury bills have a short maturity date of three, six or 12 months. Treasury notes mature within two years to ten years, while Treasury bonds are long-term investments of ten to 30 years.

CAUTION!   Although Treasury bills, Treasury notes, and Treasury bonds are exempt from state and local tax, other types of federal obligations may not be exempt from tax at the state or local level. Each jurisdiction must be consulted to determine whether or not another particular federal government investment is exempt.

TAX PLANNING IDEA   The purchase of certain federal government obligations can result in a deferment of taxes. The interest from Treasury bills with a maturity of one year or less is taxed only at maturity. Thus, if in December 1997, you purchase a three-month Treasury bill, the interest will not be taxed until April 15, 1999, when you pay your 1998 federal tax bill.

Additionally, the interest on the Series EE bonds is not taxable until the bond is cashed unless you elect to report the interest currently. Since the Series EE bonds do not pay interest until the bond is cashed, it is rare that anyone chooses to currently report income as it accrues. If the bond is disposed of prior to maturity, for example, by gift, then the donor must include the accrued interest prior to the date of the gift in income.

TAX PLANNING IDEA   Individuals over age 24 who purchase series EE bonds may use IRS Form 8815 to exclude some or all of the series EE bond interest from their income if, in the same year that the bond is redeemed, the bond owner pays tuition and other fees so that the bond owner, spouse, or dependent is able to attend college. If the bond redemption proceeds exceed the total tuition and fees paid during the year, only the ratio of expenses to redemption proceeds multiplied by the bond interest received is exempt.

Furthermore, the amount that can be excluded from income in 1997 is phased out if the bond owner's modified adjusted gross income exceeds the threshold amount of $50,850

($76,250 in the case of a joint return) and is completely phased out at AGI of $65,850 ($106,250 in the case of a joint return). Married individuals must file a joint return to be eligible for the exclusion. The ranges of income at which the exclusion is phased out are adjusted annually for changes in the cost of living.

This limited exclusion was intended to encourage savings for education; however, the purchase of savings bonds has barely increased since its enactment.

CAUTION!   Tax legislation in 1996 changed the base year for inflation adjustments retroactive to 1993, effectively raised the income levels at which the exclusion is phased out in order to correct a technical error in the law. Affected individuals may file amended tax returns within the limitations period (see Chapter 13).

SOCIAL SECURITY—NETTING THE BENEFIT

If your adjusted gross income, determined without Social Security benefits but increased by tax-exempt interest plus one-half of the Social Security benefits ("modified AGI"), exceeds a base amount, then up to 85 percent of the benefits is taxable. The net effect to an individual in the highest marginal tax bracket of 39.6 percent is a loss of more than one-third of the gross Social Security check. To an individual in a more modest 31 percent bracket, the loss to taxes is still more than one-fourth of the check.

If you are single and your modified AGI is more than $25,000 but no more than $34,000, the computation will be relatively easy. One-half of your benefits (or, if less, one-half of the modified AGI over the $25,000 base) will be taxed.

ILLUSTRATION

John, a widower, is retired and receives Social Security benefits of $10,000. His other income consists of a pension ($18,000), bank interest ($2,000), and tax-exempt interest ($3,000).

$18,000	Pension
2,000	Bank Interest
3,000	Tax-Exempt Interest
5,000	½ Social Security Benefits
$28,000	Modified AGI
(25,000)	Base Amount, Single
$ 3,000	Excess

John must include in his income an amount equal to one-half of the excess of modified AGI over the base or one-half of the Social Security benefits, whichever is less. In this case, John includes $1,500 of his Social Security benefits in income (½ of $3,000 is less than ½ of $10,000).

Different thresholds apply if you are married. If your modified AGI as a couple filing jointly is more than $32,000 but no more than $44,000, the computation will also be relatively easy. One-half of your benefits (or, if less, one-half of the modified AGI over the $32,000 base) will be taxed.

If you are single and your modified AGI is more than $34,000, or if you are married and your modified AGI is more than $44,000, the computation will be much more complex and, depending on the extent that your modified AGI exceeds this higher base, can result in a full 85 percent of benefits being taxed.

ILLUSTRATION

Mildred and Pete file jointly. Together they receive a total of $8,000 in Social Security benefits. Their other income consists of Pete's military pension ($35,000), dividends ($4,500), and tax-exempt interest ($6,500).

$35,000	Pension
4,500	Dividends
6,500	Tax-Exempt Interest
4,000	½ Social Security Benefits
$50,000	Modified AGI
(44,000)	Base Amount, Married Filing Joint
$ 6,000	Excess

Mildred and Pete must include in their income an amount equal to 85 percent of their Social Security benefits or, if less, the sum of (1) 85 percent of the excess of modified AGI over the base amount of $44,000; plus (2) one-half of the Social Security benefits (or, if less, $6,000). In this case, Mildred and Pete include $6,800 of their Social Security benefits in income (85% of $8,000 is less than the sum of 85% of $6,000 plus $4,000).

The following tables illustrate the taxable portion of $10,000 in Social Security benefits at various levels of modified AGI:

Single Individual with $10,000 of Social Security Benefits

Taxable and Tax-free Income	Modified AGI	Taxable Social Security
≤$20,000	≤$25,000	$ 0
21,000	26,000	500
22,000	27,000	1,000
23,000	28,000	1,500
24,000	29,000	2,000
25,000	30,000	2,500
26,000	31,000	3,000
27,000	32,000	3,500
28,000	33,000	4,000
29,000	34,000	4,500
30,000	35,000	5,350
31,000	36,000	6,200
32,000	37,000	7,050
33,000	38,000	7,900
≥33,706	≥38,706	8,500

Married Individuals Filing Jointly with $10,000 of Social Security Benefits

Taxable and Tax-free Income	Modified AGI	Taxable Social Security
≤$27,000	≤$32,000	$ 0
28,000	33,000	500
29,000	34,000	1,000
30,000	35,000	1,500
31,000	36,000	2,000
32,000	37,000	2,500
33,000	38,000	3,000
34,000	39,000	3,500
35,000	40,000	4,000
36,000	41,000	4,500
37,000	42,000	5,000
38,000	43,000	5,000
39,000	44,000	5,000
40,000	45,000	5,850
41,000	46,000	6,700
42,000	47,000	7,550
43,000	48,000	8,400
43,118	48,118	8,500

The lump sum Social Security death benefit is not subject to tax.

CAUTION!   Thresholds for single individuals also apply to married individuals who live apart for the entire year and who file separately. Married individuals who live together for at least part of the year and who file separately are generally taxed on 85 percent of benefits.

QUESTION: In 1998 I will receive a lump sum payment of back Social Security monthly benefits covering periods back to 1996. The lump sum payment, when combined with my other income, will cause this check to be taxable. If I had received monthly payments all along, my income under the formula each year would have been less than $25,000. This doesn't seem fair.

ANSWER: It isn't fair. Consequently, you may elect to compute the portion of the lump sum payment which would have been taxed in each year, if any, using the applicable threshold for each year, and add these amounts together. The sum of the excess amounts is taxed in the year that you received the lump sum payment.

YEAR END REMINDER   When Social Security recipients make investments, they must keep in mind the potential that income generated by the investments will cause the otherwise nontaxable Social Security benefits to be taxable. This is particularly true when acquiring investments that throw off tax-exempt income. Even though the income generated by these investments is itself exempt from federal tax, it may be sufficient to cause the Social Security recipient to be taxed on a portion of Social Security benefits. If your AGI, as modified above, is approaching the applicable base amount, try to minimize your income for the remainder of the year. Buy CDs that mature next year or consider the use of installment reporting to defer recognition of gain on sales of assets. Also, if you are comfortable in taking this step, give income producing assets to your children. However, as discussed in Chapter 12, avoid gifts of highly appreciated assets and, in most cases, limit any gift each year to $10,000 per recipient ($20,000 if you are married) or as increased for cost of living beginning in 1999.

HEALTH COVERAGE—INSURANCE AND REIMBURSEMENTS

Employers may offer health insurance coverage in a select manner to employees as long as there is a "rational basis" for any discrimination. Subject to that subjective standard, an employer's payment of the cost of health (including dental) insurance coverage for employees, their spouses, and their dependents is not taxable. Payments made by the insurance carrier to employees or for their benefit (for example, to physicians providing medical care for the family) are also not taxable, except to the extent that you benefited from a deduction for the medical expenses in a prior year and received the reimbursement in a subsequent year.

If the carrier makes payments for the permanent loss of a part of your body or permanent disfigurement, such payments are not includable in income unless the amount of the payment is computed by reference to the period of absence from work. For example, assume an employer financed insurance policy pays an employee $125 per week up to 52 weeks for absence from work as the result of the loss of an arm. The $125 weekly payment would be taxable since it is computed by reference to the employee's absence from work. But, if the payment from the health insurance plan were determined by the nature of the injury, rather than on the basis of service, the benefit payments would be excludable from income.

Tougher nondiscrimination rules apply to *self-insured* medical reimbursement plans. An employer's payment of medical and dental expenses of employees and their families pursuant to a *written nondiscriminatory* plan is not taxable to any employee. However, if the self-insured medical reimbursement plan fails to comply with the statutory nondiscrimination requirements mandating coverage generally for full-time workers over age 25 with three years of service, *highly compensated employees,* as defined under the law, will be taxed on the discriminatory portion of the medical reimbursements.

A medical reimbursement plan may be set up quite broadly to cover any medical expense which would be deductible by the employee as an itemized deduction were it not for the AGI floor (discussed in Chapter 3) or may be set up narrowly to cover only certain types of unreimbursed expenses including possibly only the *deductible* amount which the employee has to pay before the insurance carrier's coverage commences.

Under a new law effective in 1997, contributions by an employer averaging no more than 50 employees during the two preceding years to Medical Savings Accounts of employees with high deductible health insurance coverage are excludable from income. The maximum contribution is 65 percent of the individual deductible or 75 percent of the family deductible. Employer contributions may not discriminate among employees with extended health insurance coverage. See Chapter 3 for a discussion of Medical Savings Accounts.

TAX PLANNING IDEA   In the case of a small corporation where the only employees are owners, group health insurance and a medical reimbursement plan are excellent fringe benefits and there is no concern with the nondiscrimination rules. Few individuals, even among those who itemize deductions, are able to enjoy the benefit of itemizing medical and dental expenses due to the 7½ percent of adjusted gross income floor. A health insurance or medical reimbursement plan permits the payment of these expenses with before-tax dollars. For example, a single individual with $70,000 of adjusted gross income in a 31 percent marginal tax bracket will save $1,395 in taxes under a medical reimbursement plan if he or she has $4,500 in medical expenses not covered by insurance.

The pre-tax payment of 100 percent of the cost of participation in a group health plan or in a medical reimbursement plan is not available to shareholders of more than a two percent interest in an S corporation. Sole proprietors and partners (who cannot be employees of their own unincorporated businesses), but not S corporation shareholders with more than two percent, can achieve pre-tax payment of all health costs in the event that their spouses can be placed on the payroll as bona fide employees. (See Chapter 10 for a discussion of various types of business entities.)

CAUTION!   Owners of C corporations with medical reimbursement plans who must cover non-family members should consider a ceiling on benefits to protect against the possibility of catastrophic costs.

CAUTION!   See Chapter 3 concerning the special deduction of a portion of health insurance costs which is available to sole proprietors, general partners, and more than two percent S corporation shareholders.

CAUTION!   See Chapter 4 concerning a new law effective in 1997 expanding the definition of health insurance to include coverage for long-term care up to a maximum premium cost. Unless provided by a cafeteria plan (see the discussion later in this chapter), such employer-paid insurance will be tax-free (except for the same limitations for sole proprietors, partners, and shareholders of more than a two-percent interest in an S corporation). However, tax-free benefits will be limited to the greater of $175 per day adjusted for changes in the cost of living or actual expenses.

QUESTION: My employer offers free family health coverage which extends to domestic partners of the same or opposite sex. My live-in girlfriend, who has a job but is not covered by health insurance, is afraid that she must pay taxes on this benefit. Is she right?

ANSWER: No, according to the IRS in a 1997 letter ruling, but *you* must pay taxes on the benefit, since it is provided by *your* employer and your girlfriend is not family (neither spouse nor dependent).

QUESTION: Five years ago I organized a corporation. I now have six employees, four of whom work full-time (two salary and two hourly), and two of whom are part-time hourly and work only about four hours a day. Can the corporation pay for the four full-time employees' health insurance without paying for the two individuals who work only part-time?

ANSWER: It is clear that you have a "rational basis" for the distinction under which you would be providing health insurance for only the full-time workers. You should be able to provide this fringe benefit for all of them on a tax-free basis. Avoid coverage of *only* salaried or owner employees.

EXCLUDING DISABILITY BENEFITS

Payments by an employer for employee disability insurance coverage are nontaxable to the employee. However, if the premium cost is excluded from the employee's income, subsequent disability benefits would be taxable to the employee. In contrast, disability insurance paid by the employee (or paid by the employer as additional compensation to the employee and reported as income by the employee) will allow payments made by the carrier, in the event of disability, to be nontaxable.

CAUTION!   In a closely owned corporation, or in a larger business when the employer offers disability insurance coverage to the employee, the initial reaction is to attempt to provide disability insurance on a tax-free basis. However, most disability insurance policies limit benefits to about two-thirds of an employee's usual income. A disabled employee who receives two-thirds of his or her usual pay, and is taxed on the benefit, may incur a cash shortage. On the other hand, a nontaxable disability benefit of two-thirds of usual compensation may be comparable in after-tax dollars to the pre-disability situation.

QUESTION: My employer pays my disability insurance premium. I have no reason to believe that I'm ever going to draw benefits under the policy. Suppose I exclude the premium cost from income now. In the unlikely event that I become disabled, I'll have my employer report that year's premium cost on my W-2.

ANSWER: Good luck with the IRS. Under scrutiny, your idea would undoubtedly be considered a "sham" and your disability income determined to be taxable.

EXCLUDING WORKER'S COMPENSATION BENEFITS

If a worker is injured on the job, he or she may be eligible to receive worker's compensation benefits. These benefits, to the extent that they are paid under a state or federal worker's compensation statute or under an equivalent law, are not taxable. No exclusion is available if the payments are for nonwork-connected disabilities or if the amount of the payment is based on age or service.

QUESTION: My husband was a firefighter with the County for 25 years. Six months ago he had a heart attack and was given a disability pension. The County determined that the heart attack was probably work related, inasmuch as it occurred two days after he had fought a major fire for 36 hours straight. Under worker's compensation he was awarded disability pay of 50 percent of his compensation at the time that he had the heart attack plus an additional one percent for each year of service. Do we have to pay taxes on the payments?

ANSWER: If it was determined for other purposes that a disability was work connected, it should be accepted by IRS. The base portion of the pension equal to 50 percent of pay will be nontaxable. The IRS would consider the balance as taxable income linked to years of service. However, the Tax Court would probably find the balance tax-free as well if the service add-on was a distinction between work-related injuries and others.

CAUTION!   While a worker's compensation award is excludable from income, the Tax Court determined several years ago that interest on a back award is taxable. However, see the discussion on Damage Awards and Settlements later in this chapter, which provides authority for a pro-taxpayer result if a state's worker's compensation law makes such interest part of the compensation itself.

ACQUIRING LIFE INSURANCE CHEAPLY

Employers commonly offer an employee group life insurance coverage, usually the amount of the insurance coverage being determined by reference to the employee's salary. To the extent that the insurance coverage provided is term insurance and the amount of the insurance coverage does not exceed $50,000, this benefit is nontaxable to the employee. If the amount of the insurance coverage exceeds $50,000, the employee is taxed on the *deemed* cost of this excess insurance. Following is the table for the current *PS-58* cost of excess insurance coverage.

Age	Monthly Cost per $1,000
Under 30	8 cents
30–34	9 cents
35–39	11 cents
40–44	17 cents
45–49	29 cents
50–54	48 cents

55–59	75 cents
60–64	$1.17
65–69	$2.10
Over 69	$3.76

Even though this excess insurance coverage is taxable to the employee, the employee will often still derive a benefit in that the tax cost of the excess insurance coverage should be less than the actual premium paid by the employer or what the employee would have to pay for the excess coverage if purchased individually.

ILLUSTRATION

Sally's employer offers her group term insurance coverage on her life in an amount equal to twice her salary. Sally earns $60,000 a year. She is 37 years old and in a 28 percent tax bracket.

$120,000	Total Insurance Coverage
(50,000)	Exempt Insurance Coverage
$ 70,000	Taxable Insurance Coverage
$ .11	Monthly Cost per $1,000
$ 1.32	Annual Cost per $1,000
$ 92.40	Taxable Amount ($1.32 × 70)
$ 25.87	Added Taxes ($92.40 × .28)

If the employer provides group term life insurance protection on a discriminatory basis, *key employees*, as defined under the law, are charged with income based upon the value of the discriminatory excess coverage. Sole proprietors, partners, and greater than two percent S corporation shareholders may not enjoy coverage with pre-tax dollars in any event.

Other employer paid insurance premiums will be includable in the employee's income if the beneficiary of the insurance proceeds is the employee's personal beneficiary rather than the employer. Where the employer is the beneficiary (for example, in a *key person* policy), the employee is not taxed on the insurance coverage since he or she receives no policy benefit.

Life insurance proceeds received by the insured's beneficiary are generally tax-exempt even when the employer has paid the cost of the insurance protection.

CAUTION!   Employer-paid group term life insurance providing a benefit on the death of a spouse or dependent of no more than $2,000 is automatically exempt from tax as a *de minimis* fringe benefit. Coverage in excess of $2,000 may also be exempt as *de minimis*. Treasury Regulations which have been indefinitely delayed, if implemented, would require employees to include the cost of all spouse or dependent coverage in income.

Split-dollar life insurance is a means of providing additional insurance above group coverage to select employees. Under a typical *split-dollar* policy, the employer pays for the policy and is the policy beneficiary to the extent of the premiums it paid while the employee's personal beneficiary receives the difference.

Since the mid-1960s it has been clear that the employee is required to include in his or her income each year the one year term cost of the insurance protection (determined under the PS-58 table issued by the IRS or, if lower, the rate charged by the insurer) less the amount the employee may have contributed to the premium.

In 1996 the IRS issued a Technical Advice Memorandum which, although binding only on the taxpayer for whom it was prepared, has shaken the insurance industry and compensation planners. In the ruling the IRS held that the employee was not only taxed annually on the term cost of insurance protection but also on the excess of the cash surrender value of the policy over the premiums paid by the employer. The tax on the excess cash surrender value was based on the position that, since the employer would only receive a repayment of the premiums it had paid and the excess would be kept by the employee or his or her beneficiaries, the excess was an additional economic benefit for the employee which is properly taxed each year.

TAX PLANNING IDEA   Under a new law effective in 1997, except in a business context, policy owners may receive tax-free *accelerated death benefits* from both insurance carriers and certain third parties. The law benefits both *terminally ill* (expected to die within 24 months) and *chronically ill* (substantial loss of physical or mental functions) individuals. Tax-free benefits to chronically ill individuals are limited to the greater of $175 per day adjusted for changes in the cost of living or actual expenses when considered in conjunction with benefits paid out under long-term care insurance policies (see Chapter 4). Expenses do not include amounts paid to related individuals who are not health care professionals.

EMPLOYER PROVIDED DEPENDENT CARE PLANS— A BENEFIT FOR YOU AND YOUR EMPLOYER

A very valuable fringe benefit that an increasing number of employers are offering to their employees is the opportunity to participate in a dependent care plan. Through such a plan, an employer can provide the employee with the ability to exclude from income the value of the dependent care services up to the lesser of $5,000 per year ($2,500 in the case of a married couple filing a separate return) or the employee's earned income.

Under a dependent care assistance program, the employer can pay the child care costs for the employees on a tax-free basis. The dependent care assistance must be offered to both rank and file as well as to owners and other highly paid employees in order to qualify. No more than 25 percent of the amounts paid under the dependent care plan can be provided for more than five-percent owners of the employer, their spouses or dependents, and the rank and file must receive benefits under the plan which are at least 55 percent of those paid to owners, officers, and certain other highly compensated workers.

(A related benefit for employees is a new exclusion effective in 1997 for employer-paid adoption expenses pursuant to a nondiscriminatory plan under which no more than five percent of the amounts paid can be provided to more than five-percent owners or their family members. The exclusion, which expires after 2001, generally parallels the tax credit for employee-paid adoption expenses discussed in Chapter 3).

QUESTION: I am a single parent earning $40,000 a year, and I am due to receive a $5,000 raise. My only child, Cathy, lives with me. I have to pay a babysitter $5,000 per year to care for

Cathy while I go to work. If I expect taxable income for the year of $35,000, how can I benefit from a dependent care plan?

ANSWER: If you don't participate in a dependent care plan, using 1997 rates, you will owe $5,024 in federal taxes on taxable income of $35,000, computed by using the head of household rates and taking into account a $480 child care credit. If you participate in a dependent care plan, you will owe $4,500 in federal taxes on taxable income of $30,000, computed by using the head of household rates. By participating in the plan, you have $35,500 left ($40,000 – $4,500 taxes) of your $40,000 salary as opposed to $34,976 left of your $45,000 salary ($45,000 – $5,000 child care costs – $5,024 taxes). You save $524! Additionally, you and your employer save another $383 each because the $5,000 child care reimbursement is not subject to Social Security taxes.

"CAFETERIA" PLANS—A FULL "MENU"

In a *cafeteria plan* an employer provides employees with a "menu" of various nontaxable fringe benefits such as health insurance, medical reimbursement, life insurance, and dependent care coverage. Each employee can then choose the benefits which best suit his or her particular needs. Such a plan provides employees with a great deal of flexibility. For example, an employee may not wish to participate in any health insurance coverage offered by an employer if the employee is covered by the spouse's employer provided insurance program. The employee may then choose the dependent care fringe benefit and the life insurance coverage instead of health insurance coverage with the cafeteria plan dollars. If the plan so provides, the employee can choose to receive unspent plan dollars in cash or have the unspent dollars contributed to a 401(k) profit sharing plan.

A cafeteria plan must be nondiscriminatory in order to qualify for favorable tax treatment, and key employees, as defined, may not received more than 25 percent of benefits.

QUESTION: My employer has just instituted a cafeteria plan which allows me to choose coverage in a major medical plan, dental plan, group term life insurance plan, or a dependent care assistance plan. How often can I change my selection of benefits from the cafeteria plan menu?

ANSWER: Except in limited instances, generally involving a change in family circumstances such as your marriage or divorce, the death of your spouse, or the birth or death of a dependent, your selection of benefits under the cafeteria plan must be irrevocable for each plan year. Should there be a change in family circumstances, you will be permitted to make a new selection of benefits necessitated by this change in circumstances.

⚠ CAUTION! Employees who select reimbursement under a cafeteria plan for uninsured medical expenses should be careful to limit this choice so that there is no unused portion at year-end. You may not make a new selection simply because you have not incurred uninsured medical expenses in excess of the amount of medical reimbursement coverage which you have elected. You will forfeit the unused portion which could otherwise have been used by another benefit under the plan.

TAX-FREE MEALS AND LODGING

When an employer provides an employee with free food and lodging, the employee normally pays a tax on the value of the benefit. However, employees are not taxed on certain employer-provided meals and housing.

QUESTION: My wife and I own our own family farm. It is incorporated and not an S corporation. Running the farm requires that we be available for duty 24 hours a day, seven days a week, in case of occurrences such as storms, stampedes, etc. Therefore, the corporation pays for the house on the farm and meals for my wife and me. Do I have to pay tax on this?

ANSWER: In order to qualify for the tax-free treatment, the meal or lodging must be provided to the employee by the employer to further a business purpose of the employer (compensating the employee doesn't qualify) and it must be furnished on the employer's business premises. An additional condition exists to qualify the value of lodging (but not meals) for the exclusion—the employee must accept the lodging in order to properly fulfill job responsibilities.

Here are some typical situations in which the employee would not be taxed on the value of employer provided meals or housing:

1. Lunch served to a waiter or waitress who works the lunch shift;
2. Room and board provided to a live-in babysitter; or
3. Meals and lodging provided by an employer at a remote job site where no other facilities other than those provided by the employer exist.

If the value of a meal is taxable because one or more of the above conditions is not satisfied, the amount that is taxed is the cost of the meal to the employer, even though it may have cost the employee much more to have gone to a restaurant to eat.

The nontaxability of meals and lodging applies only to situations where the meals or lodging are provided *in-kind* and not to cash allowances. If the employer provides supper money to employees who work late, the supper money will not be exempt from tax under the meals and lodging rule, although it may be exempt from tax as a *de minimis* fringe benefit.

The meals and lodging rule applies irrespective of whether the employer is a closely held corporation and the employee is a stockholder in that corporation, so long as the statutory requirements are met. However, the IRS will not allow the value of meals or lodging furnished by an S corporation to a more than two percent shareholder, by a partnership to a partner, or by a sole proprietorship to its owner to qualify for the exclusion.

In your case, all three conditions for exclusion are met because:

1. The furnished lodging is on the business premises of the employer (the corporation);

2. The lodging is furnished for the convenience of the employer; and

3. You are required to accept this lodging as a condition of your employment, because the nature of your jobs requires that you both "be available for duty at all times."

Therefore, you won't have to pay tax on the value of the meals and lodging.

TAX PLANNING IDEA   Let's say you and an investor own and operate a motel in a resort area. You have converted three motel rooms into your home. You have to be at the motel 24 hours a day. If you run the business as a partnership, the value of the three rooms will be taxed to you. However, if you incorporate the business and work as an employee, the value of your home isn't taxed.

CAUTION!   The placing of real property in a corporation can potentially cause double taxation in the event of sale, first at the corporate level and then again when remaining proceeds are distributed to the shareholders. Consequently, real property should only be placed in a corporation after extensive consideration of both the advantages and disadvantages.

THE COMPANY CAR AND OTHER EMPLOYER-PROVIDED TRANSPORTATION BENEFITS

Often, an employer will provide an employee with an automobile as part of the employment package. More often than not, the vehicle provided will be used both for business purposes and for personal purposes. Any personal use of the company car, including commuting use, is taxable to the employee, while use of the vehicle for business purposes is not taxable. The value of personal use of the car is determined by the employer under various guidelines provided by the IRS, including *annual lease value* multiplied by the percentage of personal use or, for some cars costing less than $15,700 when placed in service during 1997, a standard mileage rate of 26 cents per mile. Both the dollar maximum for use of the standard mileage rate and the rate itself are indexed for inflation in 1998 and succeeding years. Under either method, if an employer provides gas and oil for the vehicle, the employee will normally report an additional 5½ cents per personal mile as income.

The employer can choose to include 100 percent of the lease value of a car in the employee's income. The employee then deducts the business use portion as a miscellaneous itemized deduction subject to the two percent floor.

Even when the employee must include 100 percent of the lease value in income, he or she will be better off taking the company car than receiving reimbursement for business use of a personal car. The employee has to buy a car with after-tax dollars and must earn $23,438 to buy a $15,000 car if he or she is in the 36 percent bracket. If the employer buys the car and allows the employee to use it for personal as well as business purposes, the employee's income is increased by only $4,350 per year and the tax liability by $1,566. This $1,566 in extra taxes will be reduced as a result of the costs associated with the business use of the car if the employee itemizes deductions and the costs coupled with other miscellaneous itemized deductions exceed two percent of adjusted gross income.

If an employer requires employees to commute to and from the workplace in the company car and has a written policy banning other personal use of the automobile, the employer has the option (usually favorable to the employee) of valuing the personal commuting use at $3 per round trip commute. This method of valuing personal use is not available if the employee is an officer, director, or a one percent or more shareholder. Stock owned by your spouse, children, parents, and grandparents is considered to be owned by you for purposes of determining stock ownership here.

CAUTION!   Careful substantiation records must be maintained when an employee uses a company car in order to establish business versus personal use. This is a high audit area.

TAX PLANNING IDEA   Employees who drive to work can enjoy employer-paid parking privileges or cash reimbursements on a tax-free basis up to $170 per month indexed for inflation in 1998 and succeeding years. This exclusion from income is not available to sole proprietors, partners, and greater than two percent shareholders in an S corporation. (See Chapter 10 for a discussion of alternative types of business entities.)

Employees who would otherwise walk or use public transportation to commute to or from their job site can receive an employer-paid taxi ride to or from work and need only include $1.50 per one way trip in income as the *deemed* value of the fringe benefit. This special valuation rule is only available if the taxi ride is furnished because of unsafe conditions, such as a high crime area, and the employer has a written policy to that effect. Only employees paid on an hourly basis are eligible for this special tax break. Other employees who receive a taxi ride home from their employer must include the *actual* value of the taxi service in income.

Public transit passes, fare cards, or tokens provided by employers to employees for their use in commuting as well as van pooling (six or more workers plus driver) costs paid by employer are not taxable to the extent of a benefit of up to $65 per month indexed for inflation in 1997 and succeeding years. This exclusion too is not available to sole proprietors, partners, and greater than two percent S corporation shareholders.

FILING POINTER   Employee parking benefits are valued based on the regular commercial rate at the same or similar location. The IRS has acknowledged the lack of value in suburban and rural lots where free parking is offered, thus the law is directed at employees who work in urban areas where parking is costly.

STOCK OR PROPERTY FOR SERVICES—AN IMPORTANT ELECTION

Particularly in the case of start-up companies, many employers provide their employees with the opportunity to acquire stock (or other equity interest) in the company at a discount or for no consideration. If there are no restrictions on the ability to sell or otherwise transfer the stock or there is a minimal chance that the stock will have to be forfeited, then the difference between the value of the stock and any amount which is paid for stock is taxable upon receipt of the stock. However, if the employer places restrictions on the transferability of the stock and imposes restrictions on the employee's ability to retain the stock in certain circumstances (for example, if the employee would be required to forfeit the stock upon termination of employment), then the employee has no income tax consequences until such time as the stock becomes fully transferable or there is no longer a substantial risk of having to forfeit the stock.

Stock will be considered freely transferable when the employee can sell, assign, or pledge the stock without having the transferee subject to any conditions as an owner of the stock.

The IRS considers the following to be *substantial risks of forfeiture*:

1. The stock is subject to a requirement that it be returned if the employer's earnings do not increase above a specified level; or

2. The stock must be returned to the employer if the employee terminates employment.

However, the following are not considered to be substantial risks of forfeiture:

1. Return of the stock is required if the employee is terminated for cause; or

2. The employer is required to pay the employee the fair market value for the stock upon its return.

The existence of these conditions upon receipt of the stock would not prevent the employee from having to include the value of the stock less any amount paid for it in income in the year of receipt.

When such stock first becomes transferable or is not subject to a substantial risk of forfeiture, then the value of the stock at that time over any amount paid for the stock is additional compensation. However, the employee has the option to include the value of this restricted stock in income in the year that it is received rather than in a later year when the stock becomes transferable or the substantial risk of forfeiture is eliminated. This *Section 83(b) election* permits the employee to be taxed prior to any rise in value of the stock, thereby reducing the compensatory element of the presumably appreciating property and ensuring that future appreciation will not be taxed until disposition of the property and that it will be taxed at capital gain rates.

The Section 83(b) election must be made within 30 days from the date that the employer transfers the property to the employee. The election is made by filing a written statement with the IRS Service Center where the employee expects to file his or her individual income tax return. A copy of that statement is attached to the tax return for the year in which the property is received. The Section 83(b) election must contain certain prescribed information.

Once the Section 83(b) election is made, it is generally irrevocable. Consequently, even if the value of the stock declined rather than appreciated in value, the employee who has made the Section 83(b) election cannot change his or her mind.

QUESTION: As part of my employment package, my employer, Mainco, Inc., will sell me ten shares of Mainco stock for $10 per share. Mainco stock is currently worth $100 per share. If I terminate my employment within the next two years, I am obligated to sell the stock back to Mainco for $10 per share. In addition, I am prohibited from transferring the Mainco stock to any other person for two years. As I understand it, these conditions will be stamped on the face of the stock certificate. Mainco is doing very well and there is every indication that in two years the stock will double in value. What are the tax consequences to me, if any, if I buy the ten shares?

ANSWER: Because the Mainco stock is nontransferable and subject to a substantial risk of forfeiture, there will be no tax consequences to you when you buy the stock. However, on the second anniversary, you will be taxed on the difference between the stock's value at that time and your $10 per share cost. If your estimate of value is correct, you would have to include $1,900 in income ($200 per share value—$10 per share cost × 10 shares). Alternatively, you should consider making the Section 83(b) election. By making the election, you would be taxed on your receipt of the Mainco stock. The amount that you would be taxed on is the difference between today's value of the stock and your cost, $900 ($100 per share value—$10 per share cost × 10 shares).

    CAUTION!   The Section 83(b) election must be made even when there is no compensation element in the transfer (that is, the property is purchased by an employee at its fair market value) or else the rise in value will be taxed as ordinary income when the property becomes transferable or there no longer exists a substantial risk of forfeiture. For example, an employee who receives restricted shares of a second class of stock with no rights in existing equity and sharing only in future growth should probably make a Section 83(b) election and avoid any immediate tax or any tax, in fact, prior to disposition of the shares.

TAX PLANNING IDEA   A partnership interest granted for services is taxed similarly. Several years ago the IRS announced that it was relenting from a prior position and agreeing that such partnership interests sharing only in future income (as opposed to interests in existing capital) are *generally* not taxed upon grant. Exceptions include interests in publicly traded partnerships (see Chapter 7), interests sold within two years of receipt, and interests in partnerships with a predictable income stream.

TAX PLANNING IDEA   While the IRS is silent on the issue, receipt of a corporate interest sharing only in future income should also be tax-free, whether a formal equity interest in a second class of stock (C corporations only) or a quasi-equity interest under a contract giving the employee a percentage of future net income and gain.

CAUTION!   The transfer of almost any property by an employer to an employee for services rendered is treated in the same manner as stock. If an employer gives an employee a house in exchange for services, the value of the house is taxable to the employee if the employee is able to transfer title to the house, or if his or her rights to fully enjoy the property are not conditioned upon performance of future services or other substantial restriction. However, see the exception in Chapter 11 for members of the clergy.

TAX PLANNING IDEA   Although the general rule is that property provided to employees for free or at a discount is taxable, some such fringe benefits can be provided on a tax-free basis. Employees who receive employer services costing the business little or nothing are not taxed on the value received. For example, as a *no additional cost service,* airline employees may be given the opportunity to travel for free or at a discount. Employee discounts on the purchase of merchandise are tax-free if the discount does not exceed the gross profit percentage or, in the case of services paid by the employer, 20 percent of the price of the service to customers. Employers must offer these fringe benefits on a nondiscriminatory basis.

De minimis fringe benefits—those of little value to justify the record keeping—are not taxed to employees. Examples include occasional personal use of business telephones, copiers, and postage meters. A 1994 IRS letter ruling distinguishes a *de minimis* fringe benefit from one of value. The IRS determined in its ruling that employer-paid tax return preparation is not a *de minimis* benefit but use of the employer's computer equipment for electronic filing is a *de minimis* benefit.

STOCK OPTIONS—A PREMIER FRINGE BENEFIT

The ability to acquire stock in an employer corporation—an option to buy stock—remains one of the premier fringe benefits available to employees. There are currently two general categories of stock options, *nonqualified stock options* and *incentive stock options.* The tax consequences of the two types of options are significantly different.

The grant of a nonqualified stock option will not be taxable to the recipient unless the option is capable of being valued. This is normally not the case unless the option is traded on an established market. Thus, the mere grant of a nonqualified stock option will generally have no tax consequences to the employee. However, when the employee exercises the option to buy the stock, the difference between the value of the stock at that time and the amount paid for the stock (the bargain element) is additional compensation. Any future appreciation in the stock received upon the exercise of the nonqualified stock option would not be recognized as income until the stock is sold. At that time, the appreciation would be considered a capital gain rather than ordinary income.

If the stock that is acquired upon the exercise of a non-qualified option is *restricted,* as previously discussed, then the taxation of the bargain element of the transaction is delayed until the stock becomes transferable or is not subject to a substantial risk of forfeiture. The Section 83(b) election, however, is available as a hedge against future appreciation of the stock.

If an employer establishes an Incentive Stock Option (ISO) Plan in accordance with the Internal Revenue Code, there are no tax consequences to the employee upon the grant of an incentive stock option. Nor is there any regular income tax as a result of the exercise of the incentive stock option, even though the value of the stock at the time of the exercise exceeds the option price. Upon exercise of an incentive stock option, however, the spread between the value of the stock at the time of the exercise and the purchase price is a tax preference item and may result in the imposition of the alternative minimum tax. With this exception, tax liability is delayed until disposition of the stock when it is taxed at capital gain rates.

To qualify as an incentive stock option:

1. An option must be issued pursuant to a plan approved by the shareholders within 12 months of Board of Directors' approval;

2. The option must be granted within ten years from the earlier of Directors' or shareholders' approval;

3. The option must only be exercisable within ten years from the date of grant;

4. The price for which the option can be exercised must at least equal the value of the stock on the date the option is granted;

5. No more than $100,000 worth of stock (valued at the time the option is granted) may become exercisable for the first time in any one year;

6. The option must be nontransferable during the employee's lifetime; and

7. The employee to whom the option is granted cannot own more than ten percent of the stock of the company unless the option is no less than 110 percent of the stock's value on the date of grant and the life of the option is limited to five years.

The $100,000 limitation still permits your employer to grant you incentive stock options to purchase $1 million worth of stock (as valued at the time of the grant) so long as the terms of the option provide that only $100,000 worth of the stock can be purchased in 1998, for example, a second $100,000 in 1999, and so forth. However, these rights to acquire stock are cumulative such that, if in 1998 you decide to exercise your option with respect to only $20,000 worth of the stock, in 1999 you would be able to buy not only the $100,000 worth of stock that first became exercisable in 1999 but also the $80,000 worth of stock that you chose not to purchase in 1998.

If you sell the stock received upon the exercise of the incentive stock option, any gain realized will be a long-term capital gain, as long as you hold on to the stock for two years from the time the option was granted to you and one year from the time you exercised the option. If the stock is disposed of prematurely, the gain will instead be taxed as ordinary income.

QUESTION: I have heard a lot about stock options as part of a compensation package. Should I insist that my employer comply with the incentive stock option rules or is it okay if my employer issues me an option to buy stock which does not comply with the incentive stock option rules?

ANSWER: From your point of view, the incentive stock options certainly present an advantage. You will have no tax consequences on the receipt of the option or on its exercise; however, on the exercise of the option, the spread between the value of the stock and the exercise price is a tax preference item which may expose you to the alternative minimum tax.

The disadvantage for you in being given an option to buy your company's stock under an incentive stock option plan is that the option price may be higher than what your employer is willing to sell you the stock for under a nonqualified plan. The employer must make the option price under the ISO plan equal to or greater than the value of the stock on the date the option is granted whereas the nonqualified option price need not be related to the stock's value.

Your employer may insist on the nonqualified option as opposed to the ISO. The ISO has more restrictions than does the nonqualified option, and your employer gets no tax deduction when an ISO is exercised but does get a deduction when a nonqualified option is exercised.

If your employer will not structure the option as an ISO, you might negotiate for your employer to pay you additional compensation equal to the extra tax that you are going to pay in the year that you exercise the option.

YEAR END REMINDER Employees with stock options exercisable over a period of multiple years should not let December pass without considering the tax consequence of exercise versus nonexercise before year end. Don't forget to consider the alternative minimum tax (discussed in Chapter 1).

DEFERRED COMPENSATION ARRANGEMENTS

For any number of reasons, you may want to defer the receipt of your salary until a subsequent year. For example, you may wish to defer income to a year in which you believe you will be in a lower tax bracket or you may want to provide for financial security following retirement. In order to effectively defer the tax consequences of the compensation income to the time when you actually receive the salary, there must be a binding agreement between you and your employer entered into prior to the time that the compensation was earned, that is, before you render the services to which the compensation relates.

Unfortunately, you cannot turn your back on your employer's paycheck and avoid including it in income. If the paycheck is available on the last day of the year, even if you do not pick up the check until the following year, that salary check is includable in your income in the earlier year.

A deferred compensation arrangement is simply an employer's unfunded promise to pay the employee at a later date. For example, on December 31, 1997, you and your employee may enter into an agreement whereby $10,000 of your 1998 salary (plus perhaps a factor reflecting the time value of money) will be paid to you upon your termination of employment rather than in 1998.

QUESTION: My financial situation is such that I can afford to defer a portion of my salary ($5,000) until I retire. The company that I work for has agreed to pay me my $5,000 plus a time value factor upon retirement. However, the company is fairly small and I am concerned that, if I enter into a deferred compensation agreement, the company won't be around when I retire or will have spent "my" money for general operations. Isn't there something that I can do to protect what I am owed yet not have to pay tax on it currently?

ANSWER: Your concerns are well justified. It does you no good whatsoever to defer compensation and then lose it completely. However, if your employer sets the funds aside or otherwise secures its obligation to you, then you are exposing yourself to current income tax even though you do not actually receive the money until retirement.

If you wish to defer income, take two precautions. First, negotiate a trust arrangement (often known as a "Rabbi Trust") whereby your employer will place the amount of deferred compensation in a special trust fund. The trust will then pay over the accumulated funds to you when you retire. The income generated by the trust will be taxed to your employer and the trust fund will be within reach of the general creditors of the company. However, at least you know that the company has set the funds aside to cover its future obligation to you. Second, obtain personal guarantees of the owner and the owner's spouse. These unsecured personal guarantees should not accelerate taxation of your deferred compensation.

YEAR END REMINDER   Examine your income level as year end approaches and determine if it is advisable to defer future compensation. Note, however, that the IRS will closely scrutinize deferred compensation agreements and will disregard any agreement that doesn't impose substantial limits on your right to receive the salary. One factor the IRS will consider in its examination of the limits on your right to receive the deferred amount is the length of the deferral period. Where the deferral period is for just a few weeks, say from mid-December to mid-January, the IRS will likely rule that you must pay taxes on the deferred salary in the year you would have received the salary if there had been no agreement.

CAUTION!   While income tax liability is delayed on deferred compensation, Social Security and Medicare taxes are generally computed on the value of deferred compensation when earned. Payroll tax liability may consequently be lowered when compensation in that year (both paid and deferred) exceeds the Social Security base. If payroll taxes were not computed on deferred compensation when earned, the base would need to be met in each year of payment before only the Medicare portion would apply to the year's payments.

LOSING YOUR JOB—A TAXING TIME

Unemployment compensation is fully taxable. Consequently, if you are receiving unemployment benefits, make sure that your withholdings from your job or your estimated tax payments are adequate to cover your obligation to prepay your current year's income tax liability, including the tax on the unemployment benefits.

QUESTION: The division of the company that I work for was closed down. I received six months' severance pay and job placement assistance. I assume my severance pay is taxable. What about the job placement services?

ANSWER: Your assumption is correct; the severance pay is taxable. The value of the job placement assistance, however, is excludable from your income so long as you did not have the option of taking the job placement counseling in lieu of additional severance pay. The mere ability to choose between the counseling and the money would force you to include the value of the job placement counseling in your income.

EMPLOYER-PAID EDUCATIONAL BENEFITS

When an employer pays for an employee's education, the employee normally pays a tax on the value of the benefit. However, employees are not taxed on employer-provided educational assistance (tuition, fees, books, and supplies) pursuant to an educational benefit plan even when the courses are primarily for the employee's benefit. However, graduate level courses do not qualify and payment must be pursuant to a nondiscriminatory plan under which no more than five percent of the amounts paid can be provided for more than five-percent owners of the employer or their family members. (See Chapter 3 concerning tax credits for employee-paid educational expenses and Chapter 4 concerning a deduction for such expenses.)

 FILING POINTER   The exclusion for employer-provided educational benefits originally expired after 1994 but was extended retroactively by 1996 legislation. This retroactive extension also covered graduate level courses commencing before July 1, 1996. Individuals who failed to claim a proper exclusion should file amended returns before the expiration of the statute of limitations (see Chapter 13). The exclusion again expired on June 30, 1997 but was quickly extended retroactively for courses commencing before June 1, 2000.

TAX PLANNING IDEA   Employer-provided educational assistance for the primary benefit of the employer is excludable from an employee's income.

FAMILY-PAID EDUCATIONAL BENEFITS

Effective in 1997, states may create tax-exempt programs under which individuals purchase tuition certificates to pay future educational expenses including room and board pursuant to a retroactive change in the Taxpayer Relief Act of 1997. The beneficiary, generally a child or grandchild, who is usually in a low tax bracket, pays tax on the earnings only on receipt of the educational expenses. Contributions may be returned to the transferor, but earnings which are returned are subject to a substantial penalty.

Effective January 1, 1998 individuals may contribute to nondeductible Education IRAs of up to $500 per beneficiary under age 18 at the date of the contribution. The ability to make contributions is phased out at modified gross income between $150,000 and $160,000 for married couples filing jointly and between $95,000 and $110,000 for others. Earnings from an Education IRA are excludable from income unless distributions in a year exceed qualified undergraduate, graduate, or post-high school vocational education expenses (including room and board of at least a half-time student), in which case a pro rata portion of the contributions is recovered tax-free and the balance is taxable.

 CAUTION! An individual beneficiary may not receive *both* a prepaid tuition certificate *and* a contribution to an Education IRA in the same year.

FILING POINTER Contributions of the maximum $2,000 to a traditional IRA or new Roth IRA (discussed in Chapter 9) will not preclude or limit a contribution to an Education IRA.

CAUTION! Unlike a traditional IRA or a new Roth IRA to which contributions for a year may be made until April 15 of the following year, contributions to an Education IRA must be made by December 31 of the year for which they are to apply.

CAUTION! Prior to the Taxpayer Relief Act of 1997, the purchase of a tuition certificate in the name of another was not considered a gift. Rather, the gift arose on receipt of the educational benefits. Effective August 6, 1997 the purchase of a tuition certificate in the name of another is considered to be a gift at the time of the purchase, but the gift is considered to be that of a present interest eligible for the annual exclusion on gifts. The same rule applies to Education IRAs. (See Chapter 12 for a discussion of the annual exclusion as well as a special five-year averaging upon the purchase of a tuition certificate gift in order to enjoy a larger exclusion.)

TAX PLANNING IDEA If a potential beneficiary's parents are barred from an Education IRA contribution by high modificated adjusted gross income, the $500 per beneficiary contribution may alternatively originate from grandparents with lower income or from the child's own money.

TAX PLANNING IDEA Even though the contribution is not deductible, the value of an Education IRA is in the tax-free growth over the years. Unlike traditional IRAs for retirement where the tax liability is only deferred, the liability can be *totally avoided* in an Education IRA.

CAUTION! No exclusion is available in a year for which either of two new educational credits, the HOPE scholarship credit or the lifetime earning credit is claimed for expenses of the same individual. Both credits are discussed in Chapter 3. Because the HOPE scholarship credit may be claimed only for the first two years of undergraduate study, distributions from Education IRAs should normally be deferred to cover courses in years thereafter.

CAUTION! The taxable portion of a distribution from an Education IRA, meaning the portion not used to pay qualifying expenses, is subject to a ten percent penalty unless the withdrawal is on account of death or disability or to the extent of a scholarship received by the account holder. An Education IRA account must be distributed before the account holder is age 30, thus the penalty is likely to apply unless education is completed by that time.

QUESTION: What can my daughter do to avoid the penalty; she may not go back to school. In the meanwhile, what can be done to increase the yield on the account? It's earning five percent in the bank.

ANSWER: Before your daughter turns age 30, she can transfer her account balance without penalty to a younger family member (and without gift tax considerations to a same generation beneficiary) by direct transfer or rollover with possession for up to 60 days under rules similar to those which have applied for many years to traditional Individual Retirement Accounts (see Chapter 9). Prior to any such transfer, she may change investments in a similar manner by direct transfer or rollover.

CAUTION! In the rush to enact the Taxpayer Relief Act of 1997, the age 30 limit was omitted. Inasmuch as the legislative history is clear, a technical correction can be expected.

DAMAGE AWARDS AND SETTLEMENTS—NO MORE CONTROVERSY

The 1996 tax law changes and a 1997 decision of the U.S. Supreme Court clarified the taxability of damage awards and settlements. Amounts received as a result of litigation or settlement of litigation involving *physical* injury are exempt from tax if the payments are *compensatory* in nature, even if the payments represent back pay. With narrow exceptions, other damages including *punitive* damages are taxable as of August 21, 1996.

FILING POINTER In a situation involving physical injury when compensatory damages are tax-free and punitive damages are taxable, a settlement should allocate substantially to the compensatory damages. However, the Fifth Circuit Court of Appeals has determined that the IRS is not bound to a settlement allocation of the parties and may seek to redetermine the taxable portion. The Eighth Circuit Court of Appeals agreed in an August 6, 1997 decision.

FILING POINTER Recipients of large tax-free settlements will often benefit taxwise from *structured settlements* under which payments are received over a number of years. The additional amounts paid, although constituting the equivalent of interest, are also tax-free when the underlying damages are tax-free. If the recipient of the settlement were to take a lump sum payment instead, interest received on the invested proceeds would be subject to tax. Of course, recipients of structured settlements must investigate the financial solvency of the insurance carriers or others who are legally liable for the deferred payments.

CAUTION!   Post-judgment interest on damages received in litigation and pre-judgment interest, arising when state law provides for interest from the date of contract breach or injury until judgment, are both taxable.

FILING POINTER   If you receive a judgment in your favor and are entitled to pre-judgment and/or post-judgment interest of a type nondeductible to the other party (see Chapter 4), everyone may come out ahead by entering into a consent judgment for a higher principal amount without the interest. However, the IRS might challenge such an arrangement.

FILING POINTER   Here's how a corporate owner received tax-free compensation for injury on the job as the result of a Tax Court case several years ago. The corporate owner sued the corporation for medical expenses plus additional damages resulting from the injury, and the corporation made a quick cash settlement. The corporation deducted the amount of the settlement as a business expense, and the owner excluded the payment as settlement for physical injuries. The result was conversion of otherwise taxable compensation into a tax-free payment.

CAUTION!   Notwithstanding all other rules, damage awards from settlements with foreign sources may be governed by treaty with the foreign country. For example, compensation paid to Americans by Germany for property confiscated by the Nazi government is tax free.

CAUTION!   The only remaining uncertainty concerning the taxability of damage awards and settlements involves the taxability of compensatory damages received prior to August 21, 1996 for employment discrimination based on race, sex, or handicap under the Americans with Disabilities Act; however, excludability of such damages is unlikely as a result of a 1995 U.S. Supreme Court decision taxing compensatory damages for age discrimination.

GAMBLING AND LOTTERY WINNINGS

Taxable income includes any winnings from gambling or lottery drawings. If you itemize your deductions, losses can be deducted as miscellaneous itemized deductions to the extent of winnings (the gross amount of which is reported as "other income").

If you are a professional gambler involved in gambling activities on a regular basis, your gambling losses are still deductible only to the extent of your gambling winnings (which include complimentary enticements by a casino, according to a 1996 Tax Court decision involving a gambler who lost more than $1.6 million in excess of $2.5 million in "comps" over a three-year period). However, income and expenses are reported on a Schedule C and, if the winnings exceed the losses, the profit is subject to self-employment tax.

TAX PLANNING IDEA   It makes sense to hold on to losing lottery tickets, losing horse track tickets, and the like so that, should you later get lucky, your losses can offset your winnings. The IRS looks with suspicion at losing tickets to see if they were picked up off the ground or perhaps even "borrowed." In 1996, a New Hampshire man and his accountant were indicted for "renting" 200,000 losing tickets to reduce the tax impact of a $2.7 million lottery payoff.

PRIZES—WHEEL OF "MISFORTUNE"

With the principal exception that employees can exclude certain length of service and safety awards from their income, amounts received as prizes and awards will be fully taxable to the recipient.

QUESTION: I appeared on a television quiz show and won a new car and a round trip to Antarctica. I was given a Form 1099 that placed a value on the car at $4,000 more than my local dealer says would have been the price that he would have charged me for the car. I had no interest in going to Antarctica and I sold this round trip to a crazy friend of mine for one-third of the retail value. How do I report all of this on my tax return? And how do I handle my $1,800 of travel expenses to appear on the show?

ANSWER: The IRS takes the position that the value of the prizes must be measured by the fair market value at the time that you won them. However, the Tax Court has been liberal in determining what constitutes the value of a prize. As regards the car, it would be advisable to obtain an affidavit from your dealer and hold onto it for use in the likely event that you are audited. Report the value of the car at what you could have reasonably acquired it for. In the case of the trip, as long as you made a reasonable effort to sell this prize, report the resale price. You may wish to include a statement with your tax return explaining the difference between the amounts shown on the Form 1099 and the amounts reported on your tax return.

The Tax Court in 1995 determined that prizes from a television quiz show are not gambling winnings and, consequently, the expenses incurred in winning the prizes are not gambling losses fully deductible as miscellaneous itemized deductions to the extent of winnings. The expenses should be deductible as miscellaneous itemized deductions for expenses incurred in the production of income. However, as such, they would be subject both to the two percent floor on most miscellaneous itemized deductions (see Chapter 4) and the overall phase-out levels of itemized deductions (see Chapter 1).

FREQUENT FLIER MILES—WILL THEY BE GROUNDED BY THE IRS?

More than four out of five business travelers admit to redeeming business miles for personal use. However, the IRS left frequent flier miles alone for years, electing not to commence any nationwide enforcement program to scrutinize the millions of annual awards. The first volley in what could be a war was fired in Orlando during 1993. The IRS adjusted personal tax returns of several employees of a corporation under an apparent theory that business miles redeemed for personal purpose are an employer-derived benefit.

The second volley was fired in Washington during 1995 when the IRS issued a letter ruling which stated that an employee had income on business frequent flier miles retained without accountability for personal use. One day later the IRS announced it was reconsidering its ruling.

Among the many issues affecting the possible taxation of frequent flier awards unaddressed in the letter ruling are:

1. Does the taxable event, if any, occur on earning the miles, redeeming the miles, or using the miles?

2. How do you separate awards in which both business and personal miles are redeemed?

3. Is the value of an award computed on a "cents-per-mile" basis, or is the value dependent on the underlying use of an award (i.e., midweek travel or travel over a Saturday night)?

What is the future of taxing frequent flier miles? Callers seeking tax information from the IRS are typically told that employer-based frequent flier awards are taxable. However, the IRS denies that a major "compliance" program directed at frequent fliers is imminent.

CAUTION!   An individual who sells a frequent flier award would appear subject to tax on the proceeds by virtue of a sale of a zero basis asset at a gain. However, to the extent that the award arose from personal miles, such a sale could arguably be considered tax-free as a reduction in the cost of travel. In a 1996 decision, the Ninth Circuit Court of Appeals agreed with the Tax Court that a businessman had taxable income when he billed customers for first-class air travel, paid for coach, used upgrades to move to first class, and pocketed the savings for future personal travel.

WHEN IS A LOAN REALLY A TAX-FREE LOAN— AND WHEN IS A GIFT REALLY A TAX-FREE GIFT?

Money or property received as a loan is not includable in the recipient's income. However, a loan taken without any intention of repayment may be considered as income in the year of the borrowing. Likewise, an unauthorized loan is treated like a theft and will constitute income in the year of the "borrowing" despite an intention of repaying the loan.

Money or property received as a gift is not includable in the recipient's income. However, it is often difficult to distinguish between a gift and a transfer of money or property in exchange for services or other valuable consideration. (See the discussions of clergy and tip-earning employees in Chapter 11.) A scholarship "grant," normally excludable from income by a degree candidate to the extent of tuition and related expenses, is not a gift to the extent that the recipient must perform services such as teaching or research as a *quid pro quo*.

CAUTION! Under scrutiny by the IRS, a shareholder in a closely owned corporation who takes loans instead of compensation from the corporation may be charged with personal income in the year of the borrowing unless a promissory note and/or repayment pattern exists.

TAX PLANNING IDEA While true scholarships covering tuition, books, supplies, and equipment are tax-free, grants for room, board, and travel are taxable. Students receiving lump sum scholarship grants should keep records of qualifying expenses to minimize or eliminate the taxable portion of a grant.

QUESTION: I received a scholarship grant for tuition from my college on condition that I engage in public service or nonprofit work after graduation for a period of at least five years. I don't have to pay taxes on the scholarship, do I?

ANSWER: No, the IRS determined in a 1995 letter ruling that there is no *quid pro quo* in such a situation. In other words, the source of the grant is receiving no benefit from your services.

FILING POINTER Pursuant to a 1994 decision of the Tax Court, certain fellowships or taxable portions of scholarship grants are not subject to self-employment tax under which individuals in business for themselves contribute to their future Social Security and Medicare benefits. The Tax Court ruled that an individual receiving such grant who is not required to perform services is not in a trade or business even though he or she derives taxable income as a non-degree candidate or as a degree candidate receiving free room, board, or travel.

QUESTION: I have been living with a man for the past six months in an exclusive condominium which he bought me. My companion is a very generous man and has given me furs, jewelry, and two automobiles over the period of time that we have been together. Are the condominium, furs, jewelry, and automobiles taxable to me?

ANSWER: The tax treatment of property and money made in this context turns on the intention of the donor. If these items were given to you by your companion out of a "disinterested generosity" on his part rather than in exchange for any *consideration* from you, then none of these items, irrespective of their values, would be taxable to you. However, the courts have ruled that individuals are taxable on the value of similar "gifts" received from their companions where IRS successfully argued that the property was received in exchange for sexual services. In a case several years ago, an appeals court reversed the conviction of twin sisters sentenced to jail for failing to report more than $1 million "given" to them by an elderly Milwaukee man.

QUESTION: I work for a corporation which has a plan of "leave sharing" under which employees can donate their paid vacation time to other employees who need extra time off to take care of family emergencies but who have no remaining leave. If I donate my leave to the plan in order to help a friend with a sick child, will I be taxed on this transfer of unpaid vacation time?

ANSWER: According to the IRS, the employee who uses another employee's paid vacation time in a leave sharing program will be taxed on the vacation pay received from the vacation bank. The employee who surrenders the paid vacation time to the leave sharing program will not be taxed.

QUESTION: I went out on strike and received union welfare benefits as gifts. I never worked for the union. All of us received $100 per workday, no questions asked. The union only asked us to walk a picket line two days a week. I also received another $200 per week in unemployment. These are tax-free gifts or welfare benefits, aren't they?

ANSWER: No, by law, unemployment benefits are taxable. While public welfare benefits are tax-free, your union benefits will be taxable pursuant to a 1995 decision of the Tax Court. They aren't welfare because everyone got them irrespective of need, and they aren't gifts because there is no disinterested generosity on the part of the union.

QUESTION: I have a rare type of blood, and I am paid each time that I make a donation. The IRS is trying to tell me that this money is taxable. Is the IRS right?

ANSWER: The IRS does not consider the "giving" of blood to be a donation for tax purposes. Donors throughout the country are being taxed on the money they earn for donating their blood. Regular donors are also being subjected to the 15.3 percent self-employment tax.

EASY TO FORGIVE?—NOT WITH THE IRS

The general rule is that taxable income includes the amount by which your liabilities have decreased as a result of a creditor's forgiveness of your obligation to that creditor. The additional income is the result of an increase in your net worth by the freeing of your assets that would otherwise have been required to be used to pay the debt. Thus, if you settle a personal or business obligation for less than the amount owed, the difference is generally taxable to you.

There are limited exceptions to the debt cancellation rule. When a disputed debt is compromised, the portion that is written off is not considered income. If a debt is forgiven in a gift context (for example, parents forgiving a loan that they made to their child), then there would be no debt forgiveness income. In addition, if a debtor is insolvent or has filed for bankruptcy, or on discharge of certain real estate debt, the forgiveness of debt does not result in income; however, such a debtor is required to reduce favorable tax attributes such as net operating loss carryovers, credit carryovers, and capital loss carryovers and may be required to reduce the tax basis of remaining assets.

CAUTION! Even without formal forgiveness of a debt, the IRS may take the position that relief from the indebtedness constitutes taxable income upon expiration of the statute of limitations on collection—in other words, at the time when you can raise a valid defense under state law that the creditor took too long to collect on the debt.

QUESTION: When I bought my house in 1970, I was able to obtain a 6½ percent 30-year mortgage. The bank contacted me and has offered to consider my mortgage paid off if I pay $3,000 of the outstanding $6,000 principal. It would otherwise be paid off in 2000. Does it sound like a good deal?

ANSWER: Your bank is trying to clean out its loan portfolio by ridding itself of low-interest loans so additional funds will be available to the bank to lend at a higher rate of return. While it still would appear to make sense to accept the bank's offer, the $3,000 savings will be taxable to you as debt forgiveness income which could mean more than $1,000 in additional taxes if you are in a 36 or 39.6 percent tax bracket.

CONTROVERSY

A forgiven student loan may or may not constitute taxable income depending on the program under which the loan is discharged. The lack of clarity is causing litigation and may force modification of the law.

QUESTION: I guaranteed a debt of my wholly owned corporation which went bankrupt with no assets for creditors. I settled my guarantee for 15 cents on the dollar. Do I have debt cancellation income?

ANSWER: Not according to the Tax Court in a 1996 decision. It reasoned that forgiveness of debt income can arise only on an increase in net worth, which happens on an obligor's but not a guarantor's debt cancellation.

3

DEDUCTIONS AND CREDITS— FOR ITEMIZERS AND NON-ITEMIZERS

DEDUCTIBLE HEALTH INSURANCE

While employees may enjoy employer-provided health insurance and medical reimbursements on a tax-free basis, self-employed individuals must generally claim their medical expenses as itemized deductions (see Chapter 4)—where most often they are lost due to the 7½ percent of adjusted gross income floor.

FILING POINTER Certain sole proprietors, general partners, and more than two percent shareholders of S corporations, unable generally to enjoy the tax benefit of deducting costs of participation in a group health plan or medical reimbursement plan on a tax-free basis, as discussed in Chapter 2, are able to deduct 45 percent of the cost of health insurance coverage for themselves and their families irrespective of the 7½ percent floor applicable to itemized medical deductions. This special deduction, limited to earned income from the business (wages in the case of an S corporation shareholder), is available even if you don't itemize to those self-employeds and more than two percent S corporation shareholders who are not eligible to participate in another health plan by virtue of their employment or their spouse's employment. This test is applied on a monthly basis. Insurance costs in excess of 45 percent are combined with other itemized medical expenses and are subject to the 7½ percent floor.

CAUTION! For 1997 the deduction was 40 percent of health insurance costs; Pursuant to the Taxpayer Relief Act of 1997, the deduction rises from 45 to 50 percent in 2000 and will gradually climb until it reaches 100 percent by 2007.

DEDUCTIBLE MEDICAL SAVINGS ACCOUNTS

Effective in 1997, without itemizing, an individual who participates in a health insurance plan of an employer which averaged no more than 50 employees during the two preceding years or is self-employed may create a deductible *Medical Savings Account (MSA)* (or may receive excludable employer contributions as discussed in Chapter 2) if his or her health insurance coverage has a deductible of between $1,500 and $2,250 with a maximum $3,000 out-of-pocket for individual coverage or between $3,000 and $4,500 with a maximum $5,500 out-of-pocket for family coverage.

Under this experimental program, the maximum deductible amount is 65 percent of the individual deductible or 75 percent of the family deductible. Contributions can be made until April 15 for the preceding year; this date is not changed by placing a tax return on extension. Excess contributions are subject to a six percent penalty.

Distributions from an MSA are only includable in income if not used for medical expenses in which case they are also subject to a 15 percent penalty unless paid out following age 65, death, or disability. An MSA account may only retain its character following death if it passes to a surviving spouse. Otherwise, the beneficiary is taxed on the date of death value.

CAUTION! No new MSA accounts may be set up except by a participating employer after 750,000 accounts have been opened (treating married couples as a single account and excluding certain previously uninsured individuals), or after December 31, 2000 in any event. Rush because of the tax savings but not because of the maximum number of accounts. In the first six months of the program, only 17,000 MSAs counting toward the limitation were created.

DEDUCTIBLE MOVING EXPENSES

Certain moving expenses are deductible to qualifying individuals irrespective of whether they itemize or not. However, the deductibility of moving expenses is limited. To qualify for the deduction, your new place of employment must be at least 50 miles further from your old residence than your former job was from your old residence. If you moved in order to start work at your very first job, then the job site must be at least 50 miles from your former residence. In addition, during the 12 months immediately following the move, you must be employed on a full-time basis for at least 39 weeks or, alternatively, during the two-year period after the move, you must be a full-time employee or self-employed on a full-time basis for at least 78 weeks, half of which occurred during the first 12-month period.

You may claim the moving expenses even if you are not able to satisfy the 39-week/78-week requirement, if your failure to do so was a result of death or disability, if your employment was involuntarily terminated (other than for willful misconduct), or if your employer transferred you to another job location.

Moving expenses which qualify for the deduction are limited to the cost of moving your household goods and furnishings and the cost of moving your family. If you drive, you can either claim your actual expenses of operating the car (gas and oil) or, alternatively, claim an amount equal to ten cents for each mile traveled. Any parking fees and tolls while en route to the new residence may also be claimed.

If your new or continuing employer pays your qualifying moving expenses, this payment will not constitute additional income unless you claimed a deduction in a prior year.

See the special rule in Chapter 11 for members of the military.

QUESTION: I moved across the country in November. How can I file my tax return not knowing if I meet the time requirements for deducting moving expenses?

ANSWER: You are entitled to claim the moving expense deduction even though the time test is not satisfied by the date your tax return is filed for the year in which the moving expenses were incurred. However, if after filing the return and claiming the deduction for the moving expenses, you fail to satisfy the time test (other than for reason of death, disability, involuntary termination, or transfer), then you must include the deducted amount as *other income* in the year you failed to satisfy the time test.

DEDUCTIBLE STUDENT LOAN INTEREST

While personal interest has generally been nondeductible for many years, interest paid on loans for educational expenses (tuition, fees, room and board) is partially deductible for undergraduate, graduate or vocational study effective for interest payments due and paid after 1997.

The maximum deduction is $1,000 in 1998, $1,500 in 1999, $2,000 in 2000, and $2,500 in 2001 and subsequent years. The deduction is phased out at modified adjusted income between $60,000 and $75,000 for married couples filing jointly and between $40,000 and $55,000 for single individuals, in each case indexed for cost of living beginning in 2003. The deduction may not be claimed by a married individual filing separately or by an individual claimed as a dependent on a return of another.

The deduction is only available for interest paid during the first five years of repayment of original or refinanced debt incurred to pay for at least half-time education of the individual or anyone else who was the individual's dependent at the time of the loan.

   CAUTION!   Don't refinance by borrowing from a relative to pay off existing student loans. Payments to the relative are nondeductible.

THE NEW CHILD CREDIT

Your children give you credit—a new tax credit. In 1998 you receive a $400 reduction in your tax bill for *each* dependency exemption (see Chapter 1) for a child, grandchild, stepchild, or foster child under age 17 at year-end. After 1998 the credit jumps to $500 for each year.

The *child credit* is phased out in $50 increments for each $1,000 or fraction of modified adjusted gross income in excess of $110,000 (one-half of that amount on a separate return) for married couples and $75,000 for single individuals.

CAUTION!   The child must be a U.S. citizen or resident to be eligible for this credit. Additionally, a Social Security number must be obtained for the dependent in order to be eligible.

TAX PLANNING IDEA   A dependency allowance is more valuable in 1998 than it has ever been for individuals who can utilize the child credit. The exemption for a dependent, expected to be $2,700 in 1998 after adjustment for cost of living, is worth $756 to a taxpayer in a 28 percent bracket. Tack on the child credit and the dependency allowance is worth $1,156—right off your bottom line. Care should be given to avoid inadvertent loss of the ability to claim a dependent by failure to meet all of the conditions. Divorcing individuals see Chapter 8 for a discussion of how to keep the dependency allowance away from your ex-spouse.

YEAR-END REMINDER   Except for an individual with three or more eligible dependents who can get a refund of the credit (to the extent that the individual's Social Security contribution, including one-half of the self-employment tax, exceeds the earned income credit discussed later in this chapter), the child credit is nonrefundable. Take income to the extent possible before year-end in order not to waste the credit. Before computation of the earned income credit, you need tax liability of $400 per dependent ($500 after 1998) in order not to waste the credit.

ADOPTION EXPENSE CREDIT

A new nonrefundable tax credit took effect in 1997 for the first $5,000 of unreimbursed qualified adoption expenses per child, shared in the case of two unmarried adopting individuals. The limit is $6,000 in the case of a citizen or resident child determined by a state as hard to place due to background, age, or handicap. The *adoption expense credit* is phased out at modified adjusted income levels of between $75,000 and $115,000. Unused credits carry forward for five years.

The definition of qualified adoption expenses is broad but excludes adoptions of stepchildren, surrogate parenting, and illegal adoptions. Expenses of unsuccessful adoptions of a citizen or resident child count. Except for the $6,000 credit for hard to place children, the credit expires for expenses after 2001.

CAUTION!   The adoption expense credit is claimed in the year of the final adoption. However, expenses for adopting a citizen or resident child are claimed in the year *after* they are incurred even if the adoption is not completed by year-end.

DEPENDENT CARE CREDIT

If you incur expenses to care for your child so that you or, if married, you and your spouse are able to go to work, you may be eligible for a *dependent care credit* equal to at least 20 percent of your expenses (up to $2,400 of expenses for one child or $4,800 of expenses for more than one child).

To be eligible for the credit:

1. You must provide over one-half of the cost of maintaining your household which is also the principal residence of the child;
2. The child must be your dependent (except in the case of divorced parents when only the custodial parent can claim the credit);
3. The child must be under 13 years old or must be physically or mentally unable to care for himself or herself; and
4. If you file as married, you must file a joint return.

In addition to being able to claim a credit for the cost of caring for your child, the credit is available with respect to expenses incurred for the care of your spouse, any other dependent who is under 13 years old, or any dependent (including an individual who would be a dependent but who earned over the income limitation which is $2,650 in 1997 and indexed in succeeding years for cost of living) who is physically or mentally unable to care for himself or herself.

The amount of the credit is 30 percent of the lesser of your earned income (or, if married, your spouse's earned income if that is less) or the expenditures incurred for the dependent's care (up to $2,400 of expenses, $4,800 if there is more than one dependent). The credit percentage is reduced, but not below 20 percent, by one percent for each $2,000 (or fraction thereof) by which adjusted gross income exceeds $10,000. Earned income means income from working such as salary, tips, and self-employment income.

For the purpose of determining the deemed earned income of a spouse who is a full-time student or is not capable of self-care, the spouse is considered to be employed and to have $200 of earned income ($400 if there are two or more dependents for whom expenses are incurred) for each month that he or she is a full-time student or is not capable of self-care. Without this special rule, no credit would typically be available where one of the spouses was a student or was disabled because the spouse would often have no earned income.

The kinds of expenses that qualify for the credit include babysitting costs, day care fees, and payments to a housekeeper (so long as the housekeeper's duties include care of the child or other individual) as well as nursery and kindergarten tuition. Tuition for first and higher grades do not count. Overnight camps do not qualify.

CAUTION!   To be eligible for the credit, your tax return must include the name, address, and taxpayer identification number of the person or organization providing the dependent care services unless you can establish that you made diligent efforts to obtain the information and were unable to do so. See Chapter 11 concerning withholding requirements on certain household workers. Additionally, if you fail to provide the Social Security number of the person cared for, the IRS may disallow the credit by summary procedure—without a statutory notice of deficiency (discussed in Chapter 13).

QUESTION: My mother-in-law cares for our two infants while my wife and I go to work. We pay her $150 a week. Do we qualify for the dependent care credit?

ANSWER: Yes, you get the credit so long as you cannot claim your mother-in-law as a dependent. No credit is available for payments made to a dependent or for payments to your child who is under 19 years of age. If your mother-in-law comes to your house to care for the children, you are required to pay Social Security and unemployment taxes based on her salary as well as to withhold and pay over Social Security taxes from her wages. If you take your children to your mother-in-law's home, you will not have these payroll responsibilities but she will still be subject to income and self-employment tax on the earnings.

QUESTION: My husband and I both work full time outside of the home, and we pay over $11,000 annually for child care for our two children. I participate in my employer's dependent care assistance program, and as a result, I am reimbursed for $5,000 of these expenses. Are we still eligible to claim the dependent care credit with respect to the $6,000 of unreimbursed child care expenses?

ANSWER: Unfortunately, you will be unable to claim the dependent care credit with respect to your unreimbursed expenses. The dollar limitations on the dependent care expenses ($2,400 for one dependent and $4,800 for two or more dependents) are reduced dollar for dollar for each reimbursement dollar that you receive from your employer's dependent care assistance program. Consequently, your maximum $4,800 ceiling is reduced to $0 as a result of the $5,000 reimbursement from your employer.

FILING POINTER   Once children enter the first grade, educational expenses paid on their behalf cannot qualify as expenses for the care of qualifying individuals. However, the expenses of before- or after-school care may qualify.

EARNED INCOME CREDIT

The *earned income credit,* traditionally of benefit to low-income workers with one or more children at home, now also benefits certain low-income workers not supporting a child at home. This credit is particularly valuable to 19 million eligible individuals in that it is *refundable.* This means that, if your tax liability is less than the amount of the credit, the excess credit is refunded to you.

Certain low-income workers caring for a child at home are entitled to a tax credit based on their earned income in 1997 of 34 percent (40 percent if the worker has two or more children living at home for more than one-half of the year) of the first $6,500 of earned income ($9,140 for a worker with two or more children living at home). The credit amount is reduced when the modified adjusted gross income (or, if greater, earned income) exceeds $11,930 and no credit is available when modified adjusted gross income (or, if greater, earned income) exceeds $25,760 ($29,290 for a worker with two more children living at home). "Modified adjusted gross income" in this context is AGI increased by certain losses, tax-exempt interest, and nontaxable distributions from pensions and annuities which are not rolled over (see Chapter 9).

To be eligible for the earned income credit, if you have one or more children at home, you must:

1. File a joint return if you are married;
2. Have less than the applicable annual thresholds of adjusted gross income and earned income;
3. Not have taxable and tax-exempt interest, dividends, net rents and royalties, net capital gain, and other net passive income (see Chapter 2) of more than $2,250 prior to increase for cost of living in 1998;
4. Not be a qualifying child of another individual;
5. Not be an illegal alien; and
6. Have a child who is under 19 years old, is a student under age 24, or is permanently disabled live with you more than one-half of the year.

Individuals at least 25 years old but less than 65 years old who satisfy the first three criteria above, do not have an eligible child living with them, and cannot be claimed as a dependent on another's tax return qualify for the earned income credit on a reduced basis. These individuals are entitled to the credit at the rate of 7.65 percent of the first $4,340 of earned income. The credit for these individuals will begin to phase out when modified AGI (or, if greater, earned income) exceeds $5,430 and no credit is available when modified AGI (or, if greater, earned income) exceeds $9,770.

The dollar amounts on which the earned income credit is based will change in 1998 and succeeding years to reflect increases in the cost of living.

 FILING POINTER   You may receive an advance payment of the credit from your employer by filing a Form W-5 with your employer. A portion of the credit will be paid to you with each paycheck. Many individuals who are entitled to the earned income credit are unaware that they can receive advance payment during the year instead of waiting until they file their tax return. Notify your employer if you are eligible.

CAUTION!   For 1997 "modified adjusted gross income" did not include tax-exempt interest and nontaxable pension and annuity distributions.

CAUTION!   The IRS may disallow the credit by summary procedure—without a statutory notice of deficiency (discussed in Chapter 13)—upon failure to provide the qualifying child's Social Security number.

CAUTION!   The earned income credit has been abused by taxpayers and their income tax preparers. Effective with 1997 returns, an individual who claims the earned income credit erroneously and due to reckless or intentional disregard of rules is barred from claiming the credit for two years (ten years in the event of fraud). Additionally, the individual must be "recertified" by the IRS in order to claim the credit again.

HOPE SCHOLARSHIP AND LIFETIME LEARNING CREDITS

The Taxpayer Relief Act of 1997 created two new education tax credits designed to help ease the cost of higher education.

First, the *HOPE scholarship credit*, effective for costs paid after 1997 for courses beginning after 1997, is designed to cover 100 percent of the first $1,000 and 50 percent of the next $1,000 of qualified out-of-pocket first and second year tuition and fees (not books or room and board) in a program leading to an undergraduate degree or post-high school vocational certificate.

Second, the *lifetime learning credit*, effective for costs paid after June 30, 1998 for courses beginning after that date, covers 20 percent of the first $5,000 ($10,000 after 2002) of qualified out-of-pocket tuition and fees in a program leading to *any* degree or vocational certificate.

Both the HOPE scholarship and lifetime learning credits may be claimed by a parent of a dependent student or by a student who is not the dependent of another individual. The student must attend school on at least a half-time basis. Both credits are phased out at modified adjusted gross income between $80,000 and $100,000 for married couples and between $40,000 and $50,000 for single individuals. The credits are not available to married individuals filing separately. Indexing for cost of living begins in 2002 on the credit amounts and on the income levels of the phaseout.

CAUTION!   As in the case of the child credit discussed earlier in this chapter, the education credits are only available to a parent who can claim his or her child as a dependent. A parent wishing to claim the credit must be careful to ensure that he or she is entitled to the dependency allowance and not the child (see Chapter 1) or, in the case of divorced parents, not the other parent.

FILING POINTER   A parent of a dependent child claiming the credit is entitled to tack on any expenses paid by the dependent child prior to computing the credit. The converse, however, does not apply.

YEAR-END REMINDER   Except for 1997, inasmuch as the credits are not effective until 1998, a year-end payment of tuition and fees for courses starting in January will get you a tax credit for the year ending in the previous December.

CAUTION! No credit is available for a prepayment for courses not commencing within three months of the start of the following year.

CAUTION! The HOPE scholarship credit but not the lifetime learning credit is denied to a parent or child if the student has been convicted of a felony involving distribution or possession of drugs. Hope parents don't learn anything they don't know from the IRS!

FILING POINTER The HOPE scholarship credit may only be claimed, whether by the parent or by the child, as to a particular student in two calendar years and may not be claimed for any year in which the student has third year status as of January 1. If the first two years of higher education will be spread over three or more calendar years, the HOPE scholarship credit should be claimed in the two years of greatest benefit.

CAUTION! For expenses of a particular student, only one of three benefits (the HOPE scholarship credit, the lifetime learning credit, or the Education IRA exclusion discussed in Chapter 2) may be claimed in any year. A choice will need to be made each year, recognizing that the exclusion expires when the student reaches age 30. Even though the student may claim only one of these benefits, added costs may be deductible as an itemized deduction (see Chapter 4).

CREDIT FOR THE ELDERLY

Individuals who are 65 or older may be entitled to a *credit for the elderly* equal to 15 percent of a base amount. The base amount is $5,000 for single individuals and for married individuals where only one spouse is 65 or older. The base amount is $7,500 for married individuals where both spouses are 65 or older. Married individuals who file separate returns do not qualify for the credit, unless the couple did not live together for the entire year. If such a married person has attained age 65, the base amount is $3,750.

Before calculating the credit, the base amount is reduced by nontaxable Social Security, veterans, Railroad Retirement, and disability pensions. The base amount is further reduced by one-half of the AGI in excess of $7,500 ($10,000 for married individuals who file jointly and $5,000 for married individuals who file separately).

ILLUSTRATION

Harry and Mabel are married. They are both 70 years old. During the year they have received $4,000 in Social Security benefits, $8,500 in taxable dividends and interest, a $3,000 capital gain, and $5,000 in municipal bond interest.

$ 7,500	Base Amount
$(4,000)	Nontaxable Social Security Benefits
(750)	½ excess AGI ($11,500) over $10,000

| $ 2,750 | Credit Base |
| $412.50 | Credit (15% × $2,750 Credit Base) |

This credit is calculated in conjunction with the credit for disabled individuals discussed in Chapter 11.

4

DEDUCTIONS — FOR ITEMIZERS ONLY

REPORTING DEDUCTIONS PROPERLY ON CO-OWNED PROPERTY

Just as sources of income are the subject of sophisticated IRS matching programs (see Chapter 2), certain deductions are also subject to the IRS match program. For example, mortgage interest paid to financial institutions is required to be reported to the IRS by financial institutions. If there is a discrepancy between the taxpayer's reporting of the interest expense and that shown on the IRS records, an IRS inquiry will likely result.

When real property is owned by two or more persons, the deductions associated with the property must be reported in accordance with the type of co-ownership involved. Where a husband and wife own the property as co-owners and they file a joint return, it makes no difference whose deduction it is. However, when the co-owners are other than husband and wife, tracking the deductions becomes critical.

Under most states' laws there are two types of co-ownerships for unmarried individuals— *joint ownership with rights of survivorship* and a *tenancy in common*. Each type of co-ownership has particular attributes under applicable state law. Generally, however, joint ownership with rights of survivorship means that the surviving owners will own the property upon the death of a co-owner whereas, in a tenancy in common, each co-owner has a separate and distinct interest which passes pursuant to a deceased owner's Will.

For tax purposes, each co-owner is entitled to deduct expenses associated with the real property only to the extent of his or her interest in the property, as determined under state law.

QUESTION: My brother and I own a condominium as tenants in common. From the time my brother was laid off from his job a year ago, he has been unable to contribute his share of the mortgage and taxes and I have covered for him. Am I entitled to claim a deduction for the interest and taxes?

ANSWER: The answer depends on the law of the state in which the property is located. Very often, state law will provide that you would only be entitled to claim one-half of the deductions (and report only one-half of the income) associated with the property because you were under no legal obligation to pay the expenses or you were entitled to be reimbursed by your brother for his share of the expenses. Other states' laws would hold that you are jointly liable for the expenses. If state law makes you jointly liable for the expense or if your payment of the expense was required to protect your beneficial interest in the building, you may claim 100 percent of the expenses generated by the property.

DEDUCTIBLE VS. NONDEDUCTIBLE INTEREST EXPENSE

Interest expense of an individual must be classified into the following categories:

1. Qualified residence interest;

2. Investment interest;

3. Passive activity interest;

4. Business interest; or

5. Personal interest.

Interest expense is allocated among the various categories based on the use to which the proceeds are put. Where the debt proceeds are commingled in a single account with unborrowed money, a complicated set of rules controls how to determine the use to which the proceeds were put.

Of the five classifications of interest, only *qualified residence interest* and *investment interest* are deductible as itemized deductions.

Business interest, meaning interest incurred in carrying on a trade or business in which you materially participate, is fully deductible without any limitations. This interest in the case of a sole proprietorship is typically deducted on Schedule C where business profit or loss is reported.

Passive activity interest, meaning interest incurred in a passive activity, is coupled with other expenses in passive activities and is compared with passive income. If the result is a loss, it is unusable except as a carry-forward to future years. Rental of real estate except on a short-term basis is a passive activity, and interest expense associated with rental properties is covered by these rules. However, see Chapter 6 concerning the deductibility by certain taxpayers of up to $25,000 in rental losses and the special treatment for certain individuals in a real property trade or business.

Personal interest, meaning interest falling outside of the other four categories, is nondeductible except after 1997 for certain student loan interest (see Chapter 3) deductible whether or not deductions are itemized. Personal interest includes credit card interest and interest incurred to purchase an automobile used solely for personal purposes.

Interest is only deductible in any event by an individual who is liable for the underlying debt. If you pay the interest on another person's obligation, no interest deduction is available. Where two or more individuals are jointly liable for a debt, each of the obligors is entitled to a deduction for the interest that he or she actually pays, subject to the statutory limitations, even if the obligor pays more than a proportionate share of the debt.

CAUTION!   Meticulous recordkeeping throughout the year will be very important in order to maximize your deduction for interest expenditures. Properly classifying each of the expenditures and maintaining the appropriate records to trace the use of the loan proceeds will be crucial to the interest deduction.

TAX PLANNING IDEA   To avoid getting into the recordkeeping and complications of the allocation rules, consider establishing separate bank accounts in which to deposit loan proceeds earmarked for different purposes. For example, you might deposit loan proceeds to be used for investments in one account and deposit proceeds intended for personal purposes in another.

CONTROVERSY

The IRS position is that all interest attributable to a federal or state income tax deficiency (see Chapter 13) is personal interest irrespective of whether the deficiency giving rise to the interest was allocable in whole or in part to a business, passive activity, or investment. The Eighth Circuit Court of Appeals agrees.

However, the Tax Court takes the position (except in Arkansas, Iowa, Minnesota, Missouri, Nebraska, North Dakota, and South Dakota where the Tax Court is bound by the Eighth Circuit decision) that interest on a tax deficiency *may* be deductible by an individual depending on the facts. In a 1995 case, the Tax Court denied a business interest deduction to a sole proprietor on late paid taxes arising from business income. However, that Court reached an opposite result in a 1996 decision, permitting a business interest deduction to another sole proprietor on a tax deficiency caused by accounting errors. The distinction in the latter case was that the interest payments there were "ordinary and necessary", a requirement for any business expense (see Chapter 10).

The issue will probably take several years to resolve, probably by the U.S. Supreme Court if one or more federal Courts of Appeal agree with the Tax Court.

QUALIFIED RESIDENCE INTEREST

Qualified residence interest of an individual, on a principal residence or on a combination of a principal home and a designated second home, is fully deductible subject to the overall reduction in most itemized deductions by high-income individuals (see Chapter 1). In order to constitute qualified residence interest of the taxpayer, the debt must be secured by a *qualified residence*, and the debt cannot exceed certain dollar limitations. Qualified residence interest is claimed by almost one-fourth of individual filers.

The definition of a qualified residence is quite liberal, so you can deduct interest on financing to purchase not only typical single family homes, but also condominiums, cooperatives, mobile homes, boats, recreational vehicles, and time-share units. Temporary Regulations indicate that so long as the facility has basic living accommodations such as sleeping space and toilet and cooking facilities, the boat, recreational vehicle, or similar "home" will fall within the definition of a qualified residence. The definition of purchase is also liberal, so as to include an acquisition from a spouse in a marital termination situation (see Chapter 8).

An individual can have two qualified residences, one *principal residence* and one *secondary residence*. Generally, determining an individual's principal residence will not be a problem except when he or she spends considerable time in a number of homes throughout the year. The determination of what is a principal residence will depend upon all the facts and circumstances, including where the individual votes, files a state income tax return, registers a vehicle, and spends more time.

In addition to an individual's principal residence, mortgage interest on a second residence may also qualify as qualified residence interest. The second residence may be a home used by an individual for personal purposes such as a weekend place. When the second residence is not rented out at all to any other party, then the mortgage interest on this home will constitute qualified residence interest. However, if the second residence is rented out to others, in order to be considered a qualified residence, the individual must use the property for more than 14 days or ten percent of the time that the home is rented out, whichever is greater. Alternatively, the second residence may be a home used free of rent by another family member.

The law divides interest on a qualified residence into two different classifications, *acquisition debt* and *home equity debt*. If the debt involved is acquisition debt (debt incurred to purchase, construct, or substantially improve a qualified residence), then the interest on such debt is fully deductible (subject to the overall reduction in most itemized deductions by high income individuals) so long as the acquisition debt on a residence does not exceed the home's value and total acquisition debt does not exceed $1 million ($500,000 in the case of a married individual filing separately).

Any mortgage debt secured by a qualified residence which was incurred on or before October 13, 1987, and was secured by the residence prior to that date, regardless of the dollar amount of the debt, will be considered acquisition debt but will reduce the $1 million/$500,000 ceiling for other acquisition debt.

Any debt which was incurred after October 13, 1987 to refinance a pre-October 14, 1987 debt will also be considered acquisition debt but only to the extent of the 1987 outstanding balance on the old debt. Thus, if you purchased your home in 1985 with an $800,000 mortgage, refinanced it in March 1987, and raised the indebtedness to $1.1 million, the debt is all acquisition debt, even though it exceeds $1 million. If this loan is refinanced again after October 13, 1987, the amount of the acquisition debt will be limited to the balance remaining on the refinanced debt.

Home equity debt is any other debt secured by a qualified residence which does not exceed the home's value. Total home equity debt may not exceed $100,000 ($50,000 in the case of a married individual filing separately).

CAUTION! If the home equity loan exceeds the above limits, then the deductibility of the interest allocable to this excess debt will depend upon the use of the proceeds, whether for personal expenditures, such as to pay off credit cards, or for investment purposes, such as to increase a stock portfolio, or for a business or passive activity.

TAX PLANNING IDEA Consider equity lines of credit or second mortgages to pay personal expenses so that the interest may be deductible. But do not overextend yourself and risk losing your home to the bank in a foreclosure proceeding.

CAUTION!   Congress has periodically considered legislation which would curtail tax deductions for qualified residence interest. Most such proposals would limit qualifying debt to a reduced number—as low as $200,000. Other proposals would alternatively eliminate home equity indebtedness or deny the deduction for second homes.

CAUTION!   Do not offer a single premium life insurance or annuity contract as additional collateral for a home loan generating qualified residence interest! As discussed in Chapter 6, interest paid to acquire or to maintain such a policy or contract is never deductible and, according to a 1995 IRS ruling, overrides the general rules on deducting home mortgage interest.

FILING POINTER   Check your year-end statements received from lending institutions to determine whether the lending institution has properly reflected the appropriate amount of interest payments that you have made throughout the year. These interest statements will normally not include a payment you made on December 31 (though they probably will include a payment you made on December 31 of the year before that). (See the discussion in Chapter 13 on audits for guidance as to how to deal with this situation.) Also, check your settlement sheet if you purchased or refinanced any real estate during the year, in order to pick up any interest paid from the date of the loan through the close of the month. The mortgage statement from the financial institution may not reflect any amounts shown on the settlement sheet.

YEAR-END REMINDER   Even though you cannot claim a deduction for interest that you pay before it is due, don't forget that most home mortgages are paid one month in arrears; that is, your January payment is really the monthly payment for December. Thus, if you make your January payment by December 31, you will be entitled to claim a deduction in the earlier year for the interest portion of the payment (subject to the limitations on qualified residence interest and overall itemized deductions discussed above). This January payment would not really be a prepayment of interest.

QUESTION: I need to take out a *bridge loan* in order to buy a new house while my present house is on the market. Is the interest on the bridge loan deductible?

ANSWER: Interest on the bridge loan may be deductible as qualified residence interest but only if it meets all criteria including securing the loan by your principal residence or by a designated second home.

However, if you own a third piece of property, which you want to maintain as your designated second home for the purpose of the qualified residence interest deduction, all or a portion of the interest on the bridge loan may not be deductible. For example, assume the bridge loan is secured by your old home, which is not sold prior to the time that you purchase the new home. Once you vacate the old home it will no longer qualify as your principal residence. If the third piece of property is maintained as the designated second home for purpose of the qualified residence interest rules, your old residence loses its character as a qualified residence and the interest on that bridge loan no longer meets the requirements for qualified residence interest.

CONTROVERSY

Should the interest cost on temporary rental of a principal residence be considered as qualified residence interest or as passive activity interest? If you continue to deduct the interest as qualified residence interest, you may benefit by decreasing passive activity loss which may be unusable. On the other hand, if you deduct the interest as passive activity interest on a rental schedule, you create a lower adjusted gross income which, in turn, maximizes your ability to deduct medical expenses, casualty and theft losses, and miscellaneous itemized deductions (see Chapter 4) as well as itemized deductions, in general, and personal exemptions (see Chapter 1).

Due to the lack of clarity in the law, some individuals renting out their principal residence temporarily are seeking to achieve a double benefit by treating the interest cost as qualifying residence interest but by deducting this expense on the rental schedule. The legislative history of these complex laws offers some support for this "best of both worlds" position.

QUESTION: My home was destroyed in the recent floods in the Upper Midwest. My insurance carrier is slow in paying, so I'm continuing to make mortgage payments. Is my interest expense deductible on my nonexistent house?

ANSWER: According to a prior IRS Information Release, as a disaster victim, you may continue to deduct interest payments as qualified residence interest so long as you intend to rebuild and reoccupy the home within a reasonable time.

QUESTION: My wife and I bought our home 30 years ago for $30,000. It is now worth about $250,000. There is no mortgage on the property at this time. However, we would like to take out a mortgage for $175,000. Will the interest on this loan be deductible?

ANSWER: The interest on $100,000 of your $175,000 mortgage will be qualified residence interest regardless of the use to which you put the proceeds. Your ability to deduct the interest on the remaining $75,000 will depend on the use to which the money is put. For example, if the excess proceeds are used to meet personal obligations such as tuition or medical bills, no portion of the interest attributable to the excess proceeds will be deductible. If you use the excess proceeds to buy an interest in a partnership or S corporation which is a passive activity, your interest on the excess loan will be passive activity interest. If you materially participate in the partnership or S corporation, that interest will be business interest. On the other hand, if you use the excess proceeds to buy an interest in a C corporation, your interest will be investment interest regardless of the nature and extent of your participation in the business.

Because your deduction of qualified residence interest is limited, you might consider selling your current home and purchasing a new one. No tax is likely to be paid on the appreciation (see Chapter 6), and you can buy the new home with a small down payment and finance the rest of it. In this circumstance, the entire interest on the mortgage on the new home up to the $1 million/$500,000 ceiling will be qualified residence interest.

QUESTION: My wife and I purchased a residential lot in the mountains many years ago. We own it free and clear. Now that my wife and I will be retiring, we plan to build a home on this lot and move away from the hustle and bustle of city life. We anticipate construction to begin in March 1998, and we should be able to move in the following year. Is the interest that we will be paying on the construction loan deductible at all? What about the permanent financing? Both loans will be secured by the lot and improvements.

ANSWER: You can treat the residence under construction as your secondary residence and, thus, the interest on the construction loan will be qualified residence interest so long as you have not elected to treat the interest on any other home (other than your current principal residence) as qualified residence interest and so long as the total acquisition debt on your current residence when added to the construction loan principal doesn't exceed the statutory limits. Homes under construction may be qualified residences for purpose of the qualified residence interest deduction for only two years from the date that construction starts. The IRS has announced that forthcoming regulations will provide that your permanent financing (if incurred within 90 days of completion) will still be deemed to be acquisition debt to the extent of the construction costs incurred within the two-year period prior to the permanent financing.

QUESTION: Every year I always seem to pay an alternative minimum tax due to some investments I have made. What is the effect of the qualified residence interest rules on me if I have to pay alternative minimum tax again?

ANSWER: For alternative minimum tax purposes, the rules governing home mortgage interest deductions are more restrictive. Only the interest on the acquisition debt is deductible in computing alternative minimum taxable income. No housing interest deduction is allowed for interest on home equity loans unless the proceeds are used to rehabilitate the existing home. Interest on any debt incurred before July 1, 1982 which is secured by your principal residence (or second home) is deductible for alternative minimum tax purposes, regardless of the use of the proceeds.

INVESTMENT INTEREST

Investment interest is any interest incurred to purchase property which is held for investment, such as raw land or property that produces interest, dividends, or annuities. A typical example of investment interest is the interest charged on a margin account by your broker. Investment interest does not include interest expense associated with the acquisition or maintenance of rental real estate or with the acquisition or conduct of any other passive activity.

Investment interest is deductible as an itemized deduction but only to the extent of net investment income. It is not subject to the reduction discussed in Chapter 1 for high-income individuals. Net investment income is the excess of portfolio (investment) income such as interest and dividends over investment expenses such as investment seminar fees. Unlike personal interest, any investment interest for which no deduction can be claimed in the current year is carried forward and deducted in a succeeding year if there is sufficient positive net investment income.

FILING POINTER   Make sure that you reduce interest income if you bought any bonds between interest payment dates. Show the reduction for the accrued interest (which you paid at the time of purchase) on Schedule B as a reduction of the gross interest figure which will be reported by the borrower on IRS Form 1099. Do not show the accrued interest as an investment interest expense on Schedule A.

CAUTION!   As discussed in Chapter 2, gain on disposition of an income-producing investment asset under usual rules would give rise to additional investment income. However, for the purpose of computing allowable investment interest, this gain will not be considered as investment income to an individual who claims a reduced tax rate for capital gain (see Chapter 5).

FILING POINTER   A high-bracketed individual who discovers that his or her investment interest expense is limited due to insufficient investment income should recompute investment interest to consider investment gains while recomputing overall tax liability with investment gains taxed at ordinary income rates. Keep in mind that, although the recomputation may save immediate taxes, it still may not be the better approach due to loss of the investment interest carryforward.

FILING POINTER   Let's say you're the sole shareholder of your C corporation and the company needs money for operations. If you borrow the funds and lend them to the corporation or contribute them as additional capital, the interest you pay the bank will not be business interest but will be investment interest subject to deduction limitations. Have the corporation borrow the money directly and let it deduct the interest in full. In contrast, interest paid by an S corporation shareholder or by a partner on borrowed funds loaned or contributed to the entity is generally characterized as business interest when that owner materially participates in the business and as passive activity interest when the owner does not. This approach in the case of an S corporation will also give the shareholder added tax basis to absorb losses.

CAUTION!   A change in status from C corporation to S corporation or vice versa should change the nature of the interest on funds loaned or contributed to the business, according to a 1997 letter ruling of the IRS.

DEDUCTING POINTS

Points are charges made by financial institutions when loans are made and are generally expressed as a percentage of a loan amount. For example, two points on a $100,000 loan would be $2,000. When the points are paid for the use of money, they will receive the same tax treatment as interest payments. Thus, points paid on a loan to purchase a principal residence will be fully deductible (subject to the overall reduction in most itemized deductions by high income individuals) in the year paid so long as all mortgage debt on qualified residences does not exceed $1 million ($500,000 for married individuals filing separately).

Points paid on a loan to purchase a second qualified residence are claimed ratably over the term of the loan so long as all mortgage acquisition debt does not exceed the $1 million/ $500,000 ceiling.

CAUTION!   A 1994 Revenue Procedure sets forth the IRS position as to when points are fully deductible in connection with acquisition of a principal residence. The points must be incurred in connection with the indebtedness and not in connection with lender services. If amounts are designated as points in lieu of normal settlement charges, these loan charges will not be deductible. The points must conform to an established business practice in the geographic area. The IRS will not allow an immediate deduction for excessive points caused by electing to "buy down" the interest rate of the loan.

An amount must be paid or applied at closing from the buyer's own funds in excess of the dollar amount of the points. In other words, the buyer may not borrow the amount of the points.

 FILING POINTER   If your seller, upon acquisition of a principal residence, is willing to pick up some of your up-front costs, you will no longer have to pay your own points and have the seller pay nondeductible costs associated with the closing. The 1994 Revenue Procedure allows a buyer to deduct points paid by a seller if all other requirements for the deduction are satisfied. The buyer is treated as having paid the points and reduces the purchase price by the amount of the points.

YEAR-END REMINDER   Closing on your principal residence by December 31 allows acceleration of any deduction for the points which you may pay at closing.

CONTROVERSY

Points paid when a mortgage is refinanced present additional issues. Since the points are a cost of obtaining the loan, the benefit of which extends over the entire period of the loan, it is the IRS position, which was upheld by the Tax Court, that such points are not currently deductible unless the refinancing proceeds are used to improve a principal residence (but not a second qualified residence). If the loan proceeds are not used to improve a principal residence, the IRS view is that the points are additional interest which may be claimed ratably over the term of the loan as qualified residence interest if the mortgage debt on all qualified residences is within the $100,000/$50,000 limit on home equity debt.

However, the Eighth Circuit Court of Appeals ruled in 1990 that the IRS and the Tax Court incorrectly barred the deduction on points paid in connection with a refinancing. The facts of the case were that the taxpayers had purchased a principal residence with a secured loan calling for a balloon payment after three years. Eighteen months later the taxpayers obtained a home improvement loan and secured that second loan with their principal residence. Less than three years after the taxpayers purchased their principal residence, they obtained a permanent 30-year mortgage and paid off the two prior loans. The taxpayers incurred points in acquiring the permanent mortgage, and the Eighth Circuit ruled that these points could be claimed in the year paid rather than ratably over the life of the loan. The Court of Appeals ruled that the 30-year permanent mortgage was clearly contemplated at the time the residence was purchased and, as such, was sufficiently integrated in the overall transaction to acquire the home that the points could be said to be "in connection with" the purchase of their principal residence.

The IRS is required to follow the decision of the Eighth Circuit only for those taxpayers who live within that Court's jurisdiction (Arkansas, Iowa, Minnesota, Missouri, Nebraska, North Dakota, and South Dakota). Pursuant to a 1991 announcement, the IRS will maintain its contrary position for residents of other states.

CAUTION!   On a refinance, besides issues related to points, be careful of earmarking portions of the new borrowing to pay off interest on the old loan with the same lender. In a 1996 decision, the Tax Court ruled that such interest was not immediately deductible.

CAUTION!   In a land contract sale, legal title remains with the seller until full payment, while the buyer assumes the responsibilities of ownership. The buyer may make a single mortgage payment to the seller (who pays existing mortgages with the funds) or may pay existing mortgages plus make an additional payment to the seller. If the buyer subsequently puts his or her own financing in place and takes legal title, this step is a refinance according to Treasury Regulations.

FILING POINTER   Points paid on other loans for business, investment, or passive activity purposes are also deducted ratably over the term of the loan subject to the respective limitations applicable to investment interest or passive activity interest.

MAXIMIZING MEDICAL EXPENSES

An itemized deduction not subject to the overall reduction for most itemized deductions by high-income individuals (see Chapter 1) exists for unreimbursed medical expenses of a taxpayer, his or her spouse, dependents, and individuals who would be dependents but who exceed the income limitation. However, the deduction is available only to the extent that the total unreimbursed medical expenses for the family exceed 7½ percent of adjusted gross income. Consequently, less than five percent of individual taxpayers claim medical expenses as itemized deductions. However, if you have high medical expenses that exceed or approach this 7½ percent figure, do not overlook any unreimbursed medical expenses. All amounts paid to physicians and other medical personnel to diagnose, treat, or prevent illness will fall within the category of deductible medical expenses.

FILING POINTER The types of medical expenses that will qualify for a deduction include payments for acupuncturists, ambulance services, capital improvements (discussed below), chiropractors, dental charges, *in vitro* fertilization costs, laboratory fees, medical travel (discussed below), nursing services, ophthalmologists, optometrists, osteopaths, prescriptions, prescription eyeglasses and contact lenses, psychiatrists, psychologists, wheelchairs, and x-rays.

QUESTION: What about marijuana? I use it legally in my state to alleviate severe chronic pain. I even have a prescription.

ANSWER: The IRS said "no" in a February 13, 1997 Revenue Ruling. It remains an illegal controlled substance under Federal law.

QUESTION: I had an abortion last year. Can I deduct the portion not paid by insurance? What about the cost of a stop-smoking program?

ANSWER: The IRS has ruled that the unreimbursed costs of a *legal* abortion are deductible. Of course, total unreimbursed medical expenses must exceed 7½ percent of your adjusted gross income to save you any taxes. In 1979 the IRS issued a letter ruling denying a deduction for stop-smoking programs not entered into to cure a *specific* ailment. It has not modified its position. Have your doctor direct you to stop smoking to alleviate an existing condition, even one in the early stages. Weight loss programs must also be prescribed for a specific ailment to qualify for a deduction.

CAUTION! Expenses for cosmetic surgery are not deductible medical expenses unless resulting from a congenital defect, an accident, or a disfiguring disease. Cosmetic surgery is defined as a procedure which "does not meaningfully promote the proper function of the body or prevent or treat illness or disease." In a 1996 letter ruling, the IRS determined that sugery to correct eyesight, an increasingly popular procedure, is *not* cosmetic in nature.

FILING POINTER You can deduct medical expenses paid on behalf of your child (or any other dependent), but these payments will be subject to a floor of 7½ percent of your income. If it looks like you won't have medical expenses that exceed that floor, or if the benefit from those deductions is modest, have the child pay the expenses personally. If the child has enough itemized deductions, the child may get to use the deductions when you wouldn't. Reason? 7½ percent of your child's income is probably much less than 7½ percent of yours. Be careful though—make sure that this move won't cost you your ability to claim the child as a dependent.

FILING POINTER   Following divorce, either parent may deduct medical expenses of their child (subject to the 7½ percent of AGI floor) to the extent paid by that parent irrespective of which parent is entitled to claim the child as a dependent.

TAX PLANNING IDEA   If your medical expenses always seem to be just under the 7½ percent of AGI floor, consider attempting to claim the deduction in alternate years by timing your payments. For example, it may make sense to pay the orthodontist or other health care professional in a lump sum rather than pay the bill over time.

YEAR-END REMINDER   If you're close to the 7½ percent floor for the year, try to accelerate planned medical and dental expenses. Remember, once you get over the 7½ percent floor, your ability to deduct further medical expenses is worth anywhere from 15 cents to 39.6 cents on the dollar.

FILING POINTER   Effective in 1997, certain amounts paid for long-term care insurance qualify as potentially deductible health insurance. The maximum payment to be considered as health insurance is $200 if the insured in under age 41, $375 if age 41–50, $750 if age 51–60, $2,000 if age 61–70, or $2,500 if over age 70 and is indexed in 1998 and succeeding years for cost of living. Benefits received are tax-free up to the greater of $175 per day indexed for cost of living or actual unreimbursed costs. The maximum exclusion is coupled with the exclusion for accelerated death benefits discussed in Chapter 2.

CAUTION!   See Chapter 3 concerning the ability of certain sole proprietors, general partners, and more than two percent shareholders of S corporations to deduct a portion of health insurance coverage irrespective of whether they itemize.

OUT-OF-THE-ORDINARY MEDICAL EXPENSES

The cost of schools may be a medical expense if the institution is for the mentally or physically handicapped and the resources of the institution for alleviating the handicap are the principal reason for attendance there. The curriculum at the school must be directed primarily at the treatment of the handicap but may also include regular educational programs. Consequently, schools that train the blind or emotionally disturbed, for example, will fall within this special classification and the cost of attendance will be deductible as a medical expense subject to the 7½ percent of AGI floor. However, only 50 percent of any cost of attending the school that is attributable to meals is deductible.

Also qualifying as a medical expense is the cost of travel to and from the physician. An individual is entitled to claim transportation expenses to and from a medical facility, at the rate of ten cents a mile if by automobile. If an out-of-town trip is for medical purposes, 50 percent of the cost of your meals and 100 percent of the lodging expenses will also be considered a medical expense.

The issue of whether the cost of capital improvements to an individual's home qualifies as a medical expense has given rise to many factual clashes with the Internal Revenue Service. The general rule is that these expenditures do not qualify for a deduction. However, a deduction can be claimed for the total cost of a medically prescribed capital improvement to the extent that the cost exceeds any increase in value of the property.

For example, if a heart patient requires the use of an elevator in his or her home, the cost of that elevator will be a currently deductible medical expense to the extent that the value of the home is not increased by the addition of the elevator. A swimming pool is a capital improvement to a residence but its cost may also qualify in part as a medical expense deduction under this rule where exercise in the pool is prescribed by a physician for treatment of a medical condition.

ILLUSTRATION

Ken has a chronic back problem and his physician instructed him to swim 30 to 60 minutes a day. Ken installed a swimming pool in his home at a total cost of $8,000. Before the pool was installed, Ken had his house appraised at $250,000. After the pool was put in, the appraiser said the house was worth $255,000. Ken has a medical expense of $3,000, the amount by which the cost of the pool ($8,000) exceeded the increase in value to Ken's home ($5,000), and, to the extent that this $3,000 medical expense and Ken's other medical expenses paid during the year exceed 7½ percent of Ken's adjusted gross income, he will have a medical expense deduction.

FILING POINTER   If your physician has prescribed the addition of an elevator or similar capital improvement to your home, or regular exercise in a swimming pool, it would be well worth your time and effort to have the home appraised both with and without the new addition in order to qualify any excess cost as a medical expense deduction.

CONTROVERSY

Whether costs associated with travel to a more favorable climate can be deducted as a medical expense is expected to be a lingering issue despite a 1990 decision by the Tax Court in favor of the Internal Revenue Service. In that case, a wife followed medical advice that she should seek a warmer climate during the winter in order to alleviate heart and lung ailments. While her husband remained in Michigan, she spent the winter in Florida. Although the court conceded that the wife "did not enjoy any significant elements of personal pleasure, recreation or vacation" due to her poor health, it took a narrow view in its first such interpretation of the law and denied a deduction for the costs associated with the travel.

QUESTION: I'm recovering from a heart attack, and my doctor has instructed me to join an exercise class for beginners and work out at least three times a week with the class. Can I deduct the costs?

ANSWER: Yes. Sometimes fees paid to a health club will fall within the category of deductible medical expenses. This is the case when an individual works out at a health club at the express direction of a physician in order to alleviate a particular physical condition. However, where the physician merely recommends regular exercise to maintain the taxpayer's general health, the health club fees will not be deductible as a medical expense. The same applies to massages, according to a 1995 decision of the Tax Court.

QUESTION: I bought a roomful of exercise equipment and work out an hour a day. I feel great, and my doctor says I've never tested better. Can I deduct the equipment?

ANSWER: You can't claim a medical expense deduction inasmuch as the exercise is not for prescribed alleviation of a particular problem. Don't try claiming a business deduction either. A certified public accountant tried this approach, alleging that the exercise maintained his stamina and allowed him to work long hours on two jobs. The Tax Court ruled in 1991 that the cost of maintaining good health is an "inherently personal" expense.

CLAIMING CHARITABLE CONTRIBUTIONS

Subject to the overall reduction in most itemized deductions by high-income individuals discussed in Chapter 1, you may claim deductions for your donations to certain charitable organizations. In order to qualify, the recipient of your donation must be organized and operated exclusively for religious, charitable, scientific, literary, educational, or certain other narrow allowable purposes. Contributions to other organizations which receive tax-exempt status do not qualify for the deduction.

If you are in doubt as to whether a gift to an exempt organization will qualify for a deduction, request a copy of the organization's IRS tax exemption letter, which will clearly indicate whether contributions will qualify for a deduction. Alternatively, the IRS publishes a list of organizations to which contributions are deductible (Publication 78).

If you donate property rather than cash to a charitable organization, the amount of the charitable contribution is generally equal to the property's fair market value. But if the property that you are contributing would have generated short-term capital gain, mid-term capital gain (see Chapter 5), or ordinary income if you had sold it, the amount of the contribution is equal to the property's cost or other tax basis. For example, if you purchase stock for $1,000 and three months later (when it is worth $5,000) you give it to your local church, the measure of your contribution will be $1,000. If, however, you wait until you have owned the stock for more than 18 months, the charitable contribution amount will be the property's value at that time. Another rule similarly limits the measure of your contribution to the property's basis if the charitable organization is expected to sell the donated property and only retain the proceeds or where the donated property is otherwise unrelated to the recipient's tax-exempt purpose such as an old car (not an antique) given to a museum.

The general rule is that the charitable contribution deduction computed prior to the overall reduction by high-income individuals cannot exceed 50 percent of your adjusted gross income; however, the deduction for contributions of appreciated property can't exceed 30 percent of your AGI. Contributions which can't be deducted because of the 50/30 percent limits can be carried forward for up to five years.

CAUTION!   No deduction for any contribution of $250 or more may be claimed unless the charity has previously provided you with written substantiation which reports the amount of the contribution, the value of any goods or services received in exchange for the contribution, and (in the case of a noncash contribution) a description of the donated property. A check is *not* sufficient to satisfy this recordkeeping requirement.

A formal appraisal of contributed property is not required unless the property is worth more than $5,000. However, an appraisal may be warranted for the donation of any significantly valued property in order to validate the claimed market value. Subject also to the overall reduction in most itemized deductions by high-income individuals, the cost of the appraisal can be claimed as a miscellaneous itemized deduction if your total miscellaneous itemized deductions exceed two percent of your adjusted gross income.

YEAR-END REMINDER   You can claim a charitable contribution for amounts charged to your credit card in the year that the charge is made even though you don't pay the credit card charge until the following year.

FILING POINTER   Does your credit card company give a percentage of your purchases to a charity? In a 1996 letter ruling, the IRS said that you get to claim the charitable contribution at least where you have your choice of several charities or a personal rebate.

FILING POINTER   Rather than donate investment property that has declined in value, sell the property first and then donate the proceeds. The loss that you realize on the sale is deductible (subject to the limitation on deductions for capital losses discussed in Chapter 5) and the gift of the sale proceeds qualifies as a charitable contribution. Say you bought stock five years ago for $4,000. Today it is worth $1,000. If you sell it for $1,000, you will have a capital loss of $3,000. If you donate the $1,000 proceeds to a charitable organization you will have a $1,000 charitable contribution deduction, as well.

YEAR-END REMINDER   Furniture, equipment, linens, recordings, books, and cookware, as well as clothing no longer worn, can be subjects of year-end donations. Always get a receipt from the charity to verify the contribution. When an appraisal is not required, have the charity indicate the value of the donated property. Your estimate of value, even when permitted, can be challenged. President Clinton took criticism for valuing used underwear at $1–$2 per pair on several of his tax returns from the 1980s which were released to the public.

CAUTION!   If you overstate the value of your charitable contribution by more than 200 percent and the overvaluation results in an additional tax liability of more than $5,000, you may owe a special penalty. The penalty is significant—20 percent of the underpaid tax that is attributable to the overvaluation of the charitable gift.

 FILING POINTER   Although you are not entitled to a charitable contribution deduction for the value of your time that you donate to a charitable organization, you may claim a contribution for reimbursed expenses made in connection with the contribution of services. For example, volunteers can deduct the cost of their uniforms and travel expenses (including actual gas and oil expenses, or at the standard mileage rate of 14 cents per mile, plus tolls and parking).

CAUTION!   The charitable mileage rate was 12 cents per mile in 1997 prior to the increase contained in The Taxpayer Relief Act of 1997.

QUESTION: I just bought a new car and want to get rid of my old car. I heard that the local vocational school needs old cars for the students to work on. Can I get a tax break if I give the car to the school?

ANSWER: Yes, you can claim the car's value as a charitable contribution if you give it to the vocational school. Take the car to your mechanic or to a couple of used car dealers and ask them to give you a written statement of the car's value. Then get a written receipt from the school which describes the vehicle.

QUESTION: Our 18-year-old son spent a year working as a missionary for our church. We put $200 each month into his checking account to support the activities and to pay for his rent, food, and transportation while serving in the mission. Can we claim a charitable deduction for our support of the mission?

ANSWER: The U.S. Supreme Court ruled in 1990 that a parent supporting a child's mission by paying his or her living expenses may not deduct these costs. However, certain of the costs may be deductible by your son in the unlikely event that he makes enough to itemize. Even if you had paid the $200 each month directly to the church, the IRS might have denied you the deduction. In a 1994 letter ruling, the IRS disallowed a deduction for a charitable contribution which parents made to a church when their son was engaged in a divinity program even though there was no formal commitment by the church to use the funds for the son's benefit.

QUESTION: Each year my husband and I have a high school exchange student stay in our home. We spend about $100 a month during the child's stay with us for his food, books, etc. Can we claim a tax deduction for these expenditures?

ANSWER: Yes, you may be able to claim a charitable contribution for these expenses up to $50 for each month that the child is a member of the household and a full-time student.

However, to qualify for the deduction, the exchange student must be living with you under a written agreement between you and the sponsoring organization. The organization must be a charitable organization. No deduction can be claimed if you are fully or partially reimbursed by the sponsoring organization for your costs. In order to claim the $50 per month charitable contribution, the exchange student cannot be claimed as your dependent.

QUESTION: We are foster parents. The foster child placement agency reimburses us for some, but not all, of our out-of-pocket costs expended for the child's support. Can we claim a deduction for our unreimbursed expenses?

ANSWER: Yes, unreimbursed out-of-pocket expenses spent to provide the support for a foster child who lives in your home can be claimed as charitable contributions so long as the placement agency is a charitable organization and the child doesn't qualify to be your dependent. For these purposes, support of the foster child would include food, clothing, medical expenses, educational expenses, recreational expenses, etc.

DEDUCTING STATE INCOME TAXES

Subject to the overall reduction in most itemized deductions by high-income individuals (see Chapter 1), state income taxes are deductible against federal tax liability in the year when they are actually paid or applied. Consequently, individuals who itemize should not deduct withholding, estimated taxes, and other payments of state taxes in the year for which they are to be credited by the state. Deduct these taxes in the year that your employer withholds or you write the check.

YEAR-END REMINDER   If you expect to owe taxes when you file your state return, pay the difference before December 31. That way, you won't wait a year to deduct your state tax payment. For example, if you will owe $3,000 in state taxes and you are in a 36 percent bracket, you will reduce your federal taxes by $1,080, and the cost will be just a few months' interest on the $3,000 which would otherwise be due on April 15.

PROPERTY TAX DEDUCTIONS

Subject to the overall reduction in most itemized deductions by high-income individuals (see Chapter 1), itemizers may claim a deduction for state and local real property taxes which are paid during the year. In order to qualify for this deduction, the real property tax must be imposed by the taxing jurisdiction and levied for the general public welfare. Taxes assessed for a local benefit are deductible as a tax only to the extent that the charge is allocable to interest and maintenance costs. For example, no deduction can be claimed for taxes imposed to provide a local improvement such as a sidewalk if there is no breakdown showing interest and maintenance charges. These nondeductible fees are added to the basis of the property to reduce future gain.

When you own property together with another person, each of you is entitled to claim whatever portion you pay of the real property taxes assessed against the property, even if you pay more than your proportionate share.

If you own a condominium, you are treated as owning your particular unit outright. In contrast, if you have an interest in a cooperative, you do not own the property outright but rather own stock in a corporation which owns the real property. As the shareholder in a cooperative corporation, you are entitled to occupy a particular apartment unit. Regardless of whether you own the residence in a condominium form of ownership or in a cooperative form of ownership, for tax purposes you are treated in the same manner as the owner of any other real property. Condominium owners are assessed real property tax directly, and cooperative apartment owners make monthly payments to the corporation for their proportionate share of the real estate taxes. The taxes may be claimed by both condominium owners and cooperative owners.

QUESTION: I bought my new house in August 1997. My year-end statement from the lender shows no payment of taxes though I am required to pay $225 per month toward property taxes. Can I deduct the $1,125 that I paid in 1997 for these taxes?

ANSWER: If you finance the acquisition of real property through a financial institution, the lender may require you to pay your property taxes directly to the institution as part of your monthly mortgage payment. You may claim these property taxes included in your payment only when the financial institution pays the taxing authority.

YEAR-END REMINDER   If your property taxes are not escrowed, pay the bill for current taxes prior to year end in order to accelerate the deduction.

CAUTION!   Look for increased scrutiny of property tax deductions. Local assessments of user fees, for such services as sewer, water, and trash, are often included in property tax bills. Nearly half of the largest jurisdictions do not separately state these nondeductible user fees. The General Accounting Office believes that taxpayers are improperly deducting almost $2 billion each year in "property taxes."

DEDUCTING THE COST OF YOUR EDUCATION

The cost of your tuition, books, supplies, and the like not available for an education credit (see Chapter 3) or the Education IRA exclusion (see Chapter 2) will be deductible when you itemize your deductions if the educational course is required by your employer or by law so that you can keep your job or if the course maintains or improves your skills at your existing job. No deduction can be claimed if the educational course is required to meet the minimum requirements to qualify you for a new job. For example, continuing professional education courses attended by accountants, doctors, and lawyers are deductible but the costs of an accountant attending law school are treated as nondeductible because a law school degree qualifies an individual for a new trade or business.

Educational expenses are deductible as miscellaneous itemized deductions but only to the extent that, together with any other miscellaneous itemized deductions, they exceed two percent of adjusted gross income. They are further subject to the overall reduction in most itemized deductions by high-income individuals (see Chapter 1).

(See Chapter 2 concerning a possible exclusion for employer-paid educational expenses.)

YEAR-END REMINDER   If you will be taking a deductible course in the term beginning in January and your miscellaneous itemized deductions will exceed two percent of your adjusted gross income, pay for it in December.

QUESTION: I am currently a third grade teacher at the local public school. I would like to move out of elementary school teaching and begin to teach at the high school level. I was a math major in college, and our school system needs math teachers desperately. However, before I can teach in high school, I need to take a couple of courses in secondary school education, although these courses are not required by the school system for high school teachers. Can I deduct the cost of these courses?

ANSWER: You will be able to claim a tax deduction for these courses, subject to the adjusted gross income limitations. Although going from elementary to secondary school teaching may appear to be a new business, Treasury Regulations specifically provide that a move by an elementary school teacher to the secondary school system does not constitute a new trade or business.

OTHER MISCELLANEOUS ITEMIZED DEDUCTIONS

In addition to educational expenses, you may claim a deduction for certain other miscellaneous expenses that you incurred during the year, but only to the extent that the aggregate of the educational and miscellaneous expenses exceeds two percent of your adjusted gross income and subject again to the overall reduction in most itemized deductions by high-income individuals (see Chapter 1). Examples of these miscellaneous itemized deductions are legal fees to the extent related to taxable income, investment fees, safe deposit box fees, tax return preparation fees, tax consulting fees, uniforms, professional subscriptions, the cost of looking for a new job, union dues and other professional organization membership fees, and other unreimbursed employee business expenses.

Only a few types of miscellaneous itemized deductions are not subject to the two percent floor including, most importantly, gambling losses of a nonprofessional (see Chapter 2) and certain employee business expenses of a handicapped worker (see Chapter 11). Itemized gambling losses are also not subject to the overall reduction by high-income individuals.

YEAR-END REMINDER   If you're close to the two percent floor for your miscellaneous expenses (or just over it), be on the lookout to accelerate other expenses from early 1998 into 1997. That way, you'll be sure to get a deduction for them.

FILING POINTER   Allocate tax preparation and consulting expenses, when appropriate, to the Schedule C or (in the case of rental real property) to the Schedule E in lieu of claiming the entire cost on Schedule A as a miscellaneous itemized deduction subject to the two percent limitation. The IRS sanctioned a division of costs in a 1992 ruling. The Tax Court in 1994 even allowed an individual to claim his entire $55 tax preparation fee on a Schedule C when the business schedule constituted most of the line items on the return.

CAUTION!   The Tax Court did not explain its decision; instead, it criticized the IRS for litigating over $15 in taxes. If the case is broadly read, no allocation is required when return preparation charges relate primarily to a single schedule. Even with this interpretation, indiviuals who itemize are probably looking at allocating charges.

FILING POINTER   Because of these limitations on the deduction for employee business expenses, you should take the opportunity to negotiate with your employer so that the employee business expenses are reimbursed by your employer.

QUESTION: I am a financial officer with a local company and earn $50,000 per year. Each semester I teach a financial accounting course at the local community college and am paid a salary of $3,000. This past semester my work schedule prevented me from teaching a couple of the classes, so I got a substitute and paid her $800 to teach those classes for me. Can I claim this $800 as a deduction on my tax return, and if so, where? If you need to know, my adjusted gross income for the year, including the salary I receive for teaching, will be about $60,000.

ANSWER: Unfortunately, it is unlikely that you will be able to claim a deduction for the $800 you paid your substitute teacher, even though that was a direct cost of producing the $3,000 of teaching income. The $800 you paid the substitute teacher would qualify as a miscellaneous itemized deduction, but miscellaneous itemized deductions may only be used to the extent that the aggregate exceeds two percent of your adjusted gross income (in your case, 2% × $60,000 = $1,200). Consequently, no deduction is available to you for the $800 unless you have more than $400 of other expenses which qualify as miscellaneous itemized deductions. Before you face this situation again, see if you can negotiate with the school so that it will pay your substitute teacher directly and reduce your salary payment by the substitute's fee.

CAUTION!   Employee business expenses must be reasonable in nature. Here's a situation which probably didn't even come close. In a May 5, 1997 decision the Tax Court agreed with the IRS that a mathematics professor who served as advisor to a comic book club could not deduct the cost of 16,000 comics which he purchased over a three-year period.

QUESTION: My husband and I just purchased a computer system which will be set up in our family room. To what extent, if any, can we deduct the $5,000 cost of the system? I will be using the computer in my catering business which I operate as a sole proprietor and my husband will be using it to complete projects for his employer, a government contractor. Of course, we will also keep track of our investments on the computer and the children will be using the system for school projects.

ANSWER: You must determine how much time the computer is being utilized for each of the different functions which you have identified including business use, investment use, and personal use. If you use the computer more than half of the time in your business, then you will be able to either write off the percentage of the cost attributable to your use (see Chapter 10 for a discussion of expensing the cost of tangible personal property used in business) or you may elect to depreciate the percentage allocable to your use on an accelerated basis over five years. If the computer is used fifty percent or less in your business, you may only depreciate the allocable percentage on an equal basis over the five-year life. The election to expense the allocable percentage of the cost in the year of purchase would not be available.

Your husband's use of the computer would probably not be considered business use. An employee's use of a home computer is considered business use only if it satisfies a stringent two-prong test that it be "for the convenience of the employer" and "as a condition of employment." The IRS and the courts have been very reluctant to find that an employee's use of a home computer is for an employer's convenience.

To the extent the computer is used for tracking your investments, you are entitled to a depreciation deduction over five years calculated on an equal basis each year. However, this depreciation is a miscellaneous itemized deduction and is deductible only to the extent it and any other miscellaneous itemized deductions exceed two percent of your adjusted gross income and is further subject to the overall reduction in most itemized deductions by high-income individuals (see Chapter 1).

The personal use of the computer is not deductible.

CAUTION!   The IRS doesn't like employees to claim business expenses, and consequently these itemized deductions are heavily scrutinized (see Chapter 13). The IRS especially seeks tax returns on which the two percent floor is avoided by claiming employment-related expenses on a Schedule C as expenses offsetting small amounts of self-employment income. One tact of the IRS, especially when the employee owns the business, is to claim that the expenses belonged to the business and should have been reimbursed rather than deducted. However, the Tax Court in a 1996 decision determined that, especially when the employee owns the business, it is the employee who sets the conditions for reimbursement and, as such, he or she can deduct those reasonable expenses which are not reimbursed.

FILING POINTER   *Statutory employees*, meaning independent contractors treated under the law as employees for Social Security purposes only, are unaffected and may deduct business expenses on a Schedule C. Full-time life insurance salespersons (see Chapter 11) and certain other outside salespersons constitute the largest groups of statutory employees whose numbers also include food, beverage (except milk), and laundry drivers as well as certain home workers. Eligible workers may wish to seek reclassification as statutory employees to avoid the two percent floor.

FILING POINTER   While employees other than statutory employees, including apparently S corporation owners who receive an IRS Form W-2 from their business, must deduct unreimbursed business expenses as miscellaneous itemized deductions subject to the dual limitation, partners in an unincorporated business may deduct without limitation any *unreimbursable* expenses.

QUESTION: I am a partner in a large unincorporated law firm. While the partnership pays certain of our business expenses such as bar dues, we are each responsible for expenses such as our own automobile and business entertainment. Can I deduct these costs?

ANSWER: An IRS technical advice memorandum in 1993 confirms that partners in a partnership may deduct business expenses which are not subject to reimbursement by the entity. Of course, automobile related expenses are limited based on the percentage of business use, and only one-half of the costs of business entertainment is deductible. Claim the deductible costs as an adjustment on Schedule E to your share of the income reported by the partnership.

CAUTION!   The adjustment for partner-paid business expenses will reduce self-employment income for purposes of Social Security contributions *and* allowable retirement plan contributions.

CASUALTY AND THEFT LOSSES

If you suffer a loss of property as a result of a sudden, unexpected, or unusual event and that loss is uninsured, or if you are the victim of theft, you may be able to claim a loss measured by the lesser of the property's adjusted basis or fair market value (or decline in value if the casualty isn't total).

However, unlike a casualty or theft of business or income-producing property which is fully deductible beyond insurance recovery, such a loss of personal use property is only potentially deductible as an itemized deduction. In such case, the loss in excess of $100 will be deductible to the extent (when aggregated with any other casualty or theft losses of personal use property less separate $100 deductibles) it exceeds ten percent of your adjusted gross income. Casualty and theft losses are not subject to the overall reduction in most itemized deductions by high-income individuals (see Chapter 1).

QUESTION: Over the course of the past month all of my ornamental pine trees that served as a buffer between my home and the neighbor's home died. My arborist has identified the problem—an attack by a swarm of pine beetles. Can I claim the cost of replacement as a deduction on my tax return?

ANSWER: There is no clear cut answer for you. If you can establish that the attack was "sudden" and had not previously occurred on your property or in the area, you will have a good argument for claiming a casualty loss. The courts and even the IRS approve of a casualty loss deduction in cases such as yours so long as the loss of the trees was sudden and unexpected and the loss occurred over a relatively short period of time. In one case, however, the IRS ruled that a loss of trees as a result of an attack of pine beetles was not deductible where it took the insects nine months to destroy the trees. In your case, it appears as though your loss would be deductible because of the relatively short period of time involved.

Assuming the loss falls within the definition of a casualty loss for tax purposes, the measure of your loss is the lesser of your cost basis (see Chapter 5) in the trees or the decline in your property's value. The cost of replacing the trees is a factor which may provide evidence of the decline in value.

QUESTION: I forgot to winterize my car and the engine blew up. Can I claim a casualty loss?

ANSWER: Personal neglect does not give rise to a casualty loss. So spoke the Tax Court in a 1996 decision. A business taxpayer would not get a casualty loss either but would be able to deduct the repair bill if actual expenses are deducted rather than optional mileage (see Chapter10).

FILING POINTER   The IRS follows state law as to the definition of "theft." Consequently, courts reach different results (generally pro-IRS) in cases involving alleged misrepresentations of stockbrokers and corporate management. (See Chapter 5 as to securities losses other than by theft.) In other situations, the Tax Court ruled in 1990 that payments to a fortune teller under New York law gave rise to a tax deduction for theft loss. And both an Oklahoma federal district court and the Tax Court (applying New York law) in separate cases determined in 1994 that a woman who was swindled by her new "companion" could claim a theft loss.

CAUTION!   A casualty loss must be deducted in the year of loss to the extent of the portion for which there is no further reasonable prospect of recovery. Additional loss, or gain if recovery is greater than expected, may be claimed in a subsequent year upon receipt of insurance or other recovery. (See Chapter 6 for a discussion of avoiding gain following a casualty.) A theft loss is deductible in the same manner; however, a theft loss that is not immediately discovered may be claimed no earlier than the year of discovery of the loss.

QUESTION: Over the past few years my car stereo has been stolen three or four times. As luck would have it, my car was broken into again last week and the stereo system was taken.

In the past, I have always submitted a claim to my insurance company, but I can't afford to have my car insurance rates go up any more as a result of these continued claims against my policy. Since I will have fairly low income this year, should I claim the loss of the stereo system as a casualty loss on my tax return?

ANSWER: Unfortunately, you are not allowed to claim a casualty loss deduction of personal use property if the loss is covered by insurance and you simply fail to make the insurance claim. The law allows a deduction for uninsured losses only and not for losses in which no insurance claim is made.

QUESTION: I backed my car into my boss' Cadillac this past January. I submitted the claim to my carrier and it paid all except my $500 deductible, which I paid out-of-pocket. My wife started a new business this year, and I don't think we'll have much income after applying her losses against my salary. Can I claim the $500 as a loss?

ANSWER: Even if the $400 loss after subtracting the $100 floor exceeds ten percent of your adjusted gross income, you are not permitted to deduct losses to the property of others (even if you caused the loss).

FILING POINTER   Insurance proceeds reimbursing an individual for increased living expenses following a casualty to his or her home are tax-free provided they are not in excess of the actual increase in living expenses.

GET AN IMMEDIATE REFUND FOR "DISASTER" LOSSES

If you suffer a loss as a result of a *disaster*, you are given the option of deducting that loss in the year in which the disaster occurred or in the preceding tax year. A disaster loss is any loss (whether to personal property or to property used in a trade or business or held for investment purposes) which is attributable to a disaster occurring in an area which has been declared by the President of the United States to be a disaster area entitled to federal assistance. The IRS lists the designated disaster areas each year.

If you suffer a loss to personal use property as a result of a disaster, the loss is deductible only if it would otherwise qualify as a casualty loss, that is, the loss was the result of a sudden or unexpected event. For example, you may suffer damage to your landscape around your personal residence as a result of a drought, and you live in a county which the President has declared a disaster area. However, drought damage more often than not does not qualify for casualty loss treatment since the drought generally causes damage through a progressive deterioration rather than as a result of a sudden and identifiable event. Consequently, the damage to the landscaping around your residence would not be deductible as a casualty loss or under the disaster loss rules. On the other hand, if the damage had been to a rental property, for example, then the disaster loss rules would apply and a loss could be claimed either in the year in which it occurred or in the preceding year.

If you do suffer a disaster loss to personal use property and the disaster loss qualifies as a casualty loss (for example, hurricane damage to your home and the President has declared the area to be a disaster area), the loss is deductible in the current year or the preceding year but subject to the same limitations as would have applied to a casualty loss. In other words, no loss is deductible except to the extent it exceeds $100 and (with other casualties and thefts above the separate $100 floors) exceeds ten percent of your adjusted gross income.

ILLUSTRATION

Steven lives in a county which has been declared a disaster area because of flooding. Steve's house was flooded in the storms, and he suffered $5,000 damage for which he carried no insurance. In 1997, the year of the loss, Steve's adjusted gross income is $40,000. In 1996, Steve's adjusted gross income was $25,000.

Steve would be entitled to a larger deduction if he amended his 1996 return and claimed the disaster loss deduction in that year rather than in 1997.

	1997 Loss	1996 Loss
	$5,000	$5,000
	(100)	(100)
	$4,900	$4,900
10% AGI	(4,000)	(2,500)
Deduction	$ 900	$2,400

The election to claim a disaster loss deduction in a year prior to its occurrence is made by filing the return (or an amended return if the prior year's return has already been filed) and attaching an election statement to the return. The original return (or the amended return) claiming the disaster loss in the year before its occurrence must generally be filed on or before April 15 of the year following the year in which the disaster actually occurred. For example, if a disaster loss was actually suffered in 1997, the election to claim the disaster loss on the 1996 return must generally be made by April 15, 1998.

See Chapter 6 for a discussion of avoiding gain in a disaster, caused when the insurance recovery exceeds your tax basis in an asset. See Chapter 1 for a discussion of net operating loss arising from a disaster.

5

GAINS--AND LOSSES

CAPITAL ASSETS AND SECTION 1231 ASSETS—SPECIAL TREATMENT

Most assets owned by individuals are capital assets. Exceptions include ordinary income property such as inventory and accounts receivable, as well as Section 1231 property discussed below.

The distinction between capital gain and ordinary income is important in that capital gain on qualifying assets held more than one year is taxed at lower rates than ordinary income. (See Chapter 4 concerning an option to waive the lower rates to receive a larger investment interest deduction.)

Additionally, the distinction between ordinary income assets and capital assets is significant due to the fact that individuals are limited in deducting capital losses to the amount of capital gains plus $3,000 ($1,500 in the case of a married individual filing a separate return). Unused amounts carry forward to subsequent years until the loss is fully utilized.

Most depreciable property as well as land held long-term and used in a trade or business, including rental activity, is Section 1231 property. If an individual's gains from Section 1231 sales exceed the losses from such sales, then all of the gains and all of the losses will be treated as long-term capital gains and losses. In contrast, if Section 1231 losses exceed Section 1231 gains, then all of the gains and losses will be ordinary in nature. Section 1231 net gain, however, will be ordinary and not capital to the extent of any net Section 1231 losses deducted in the five preceding years.

Section 1231 is overridden by the *recapture* rules. Under these rules, all gain is ordinary on the disposition of personal property to the extent of depreciation previously claimed. As discussed below, for individuals the gain attributable to all depreciation previously claimed on real property held long-term will be subject to a 25 percent maximum rate.

CAUTION! For sales by individuals prior to May 7, 1997, only a portion of certain accelerated depreciation claimed on real property did not receive regular capital gain treatment. However, that portion was taxed at ordinary income rates up to 39.6 percent.

QUESTION: During the past year, I have, in two separate transactions, sold equipment and real estate used in my business. All of the property was acquired in 1988. The transactions resulted in the following gains and losses:

$25,000 gain from the sale of equipment used in business

$50,000 loss from the sale of unimproved land used in business

How should I treat these gains and losses on my tax return?

ANSWER: Assuming no depreciation recapture, these transactions will be lumped together to compute your net Section 1231 gain or loss for the year. Your Section 1231 losses ($50,000) exceed your Section 1231 gains ($25,000). Therefore, the gains will be treated as ordinary income and the loss will be treated as an ordinary loss. If your 1231 gains had totaled more than $50,000, then all of the gains would have been treated as long-term capital gain and the loss would have been treated as a long-term capital loss.

LONG-TERM, MID-TERM, AND SHORT-TERM CAPITAL GAIN

Capital gain on assets held for more than 18 months generally enjoys long-term treatment at a maximum tax rate of 20 percent. In the event the gain would have been taxed at the lowest individual tax bracket of 15 percent if it were ordinary income, the long-term capital gain rate is instead generally ten percent. These same rates also apply in computing an individual's alternative minimum tax (see Chapter 1).

Capital gain on assets held more than one year but less than 18 months receives mid-term treatment and a maximum rate of 28 percent.

CAUTION!   For dispositions prior to May 7, 1997, there was no mid-term rate. Long-term capital gain was taxed at a maximum rate of 28 percent. For dispositions prior to July 29, 1997, long-term capital gain required a holding period of greater than one year. Consequently, individuals who sold qualifying assets in 1997 between one year and 18 months after acquisition pay a 20 percent rate if the sale was after May 6, 1997 but before July 29, 1997.

CAUTION!   Certain assets are not eligible for the maximum 20 percent/10 percent rate on long-term capital gain. Collectibles such as art, jewelry, stamps, and coins remain taxed at a maximum rate of 28 percent on long-term capital gain. Small business stock (see Chapter 7) eligible for a 50 percent exclusion if held more than five years also remains taxed at a maximum rate of 28 percent on long-term capital gain; the exclusion effectively creates a maximum tax rate of 14 percent. Long-term capital gain attributable to prior depreciation on real property is taxed at a maximum 25 percent rate.

TAX PLANNING IDEA   For qualifying capital assets and Section 1231 assets acquired after 2000 and held more than five years, the maximum rate of tax will

be 18 percent. For such qualifying assets held more than five years irrespective of acquisition date, the rate of tax after 2000 will be eight percent in the event the gain would have been taxed at 15 percent if it were ordinary income. Individuals will be permitted to start the new millennium by electing to treat eligible assets in their possession on New Year's Day 2001 as having been sold and reacquired on that date at fair market value.

CAUTION! A "fresh-start" election will work to your benefit only in very limited circumstances. All but the lowest bracket taxpayers will need to hold the asset until January 2, 2006 to enjoy any saving. Even then, it will be difficult to come out ahead if an asset went materially up or down in value between its date of acquisition and January 1, 2001. If the asset went up in value, you will pay taxes prematurely in order after five years to possibly save two percent on future appreciation. If the asset went down in value, you must permanently forego the loss to possibly save the two percent.

COMPUTING GAIN OR LOSS CORRECTLY

In order to calculate gain or loss on the sale of any asset, whether it is a capital asset, Section 1231 asset, or otherwise, you need to know:

1. The selling price;
2. The expenses of sale; and
3. The adjusted basis.

Your selling price in a transaction is the amount of cash and the fair market value of other property received including the amount of mortgages on which your liability is discharged. For example, if the property is sold subject to an existing mortgage or if the buyer assumes an existing mortgage, the selling price includes the principal balance of that mortgage. You must reduce your selling price by expenses of sale. This determines the amount realized on the sale.

Your adjusted basis in the property which is being sold will depend on how you acquired the property. Generally, your basis will be the amount you paid for it plus all capital expenditures which you made with respect to the property. In the real estate area, capital expenditures would include improvements to the property, surveying costs, and legal fees paid at the time the property was purchased.

If you acquired the property by gift, your basis will be the same as your donor's basis (in other words, the basis of the person who gave the property to you), increased generally by any gift tax paid and increased further by any capital expenditures which you made with respect to the property. If you inherited the property, your basis will be its fair market value at the time of the death, increased by your subsequent capital expenditures.

In any of these situations, if you were entitled to claim depreciation with respect to the property, then your basis is reduced by the depreciation allowed or allowable to determine your adjusted basis. To the extent that the amount realized exceeds your adjusted basis, you have a realized gain. To the extent that the amount realized is less than your adjusted basis, you have a realized loss which may or may not be deductible.

All realized gain is recognized unless deferred under a specific provision of the law. All recognized gain is taxed unless excluded under a specific provision of the law. (See Chapter 6 as to the important exclusion of gain on sale of a principal residence. See other deferral strategies in this chapter and in Chapter 6.)

Except for casualty and theft losses (discussed in Chapter 4), individuals are only entitled to recognize losses incurred in their business or investment transactions.

If property is held for business purposes, rather than for personal purposes, any loss is deductible in full in the year of sale as an ordinary loss. If property is held for investment purposes, any loss is deductible in the year of sale to the extent of capital gains and a $3,000 limitation ($1,500 in the case of a married individual filing a separate return) on offsetting ordinary income with capital losses; unused amounts are carried forward to subsequent years until the loss is completely utilized.

QUESTION: I listed some land costing $200,000 for sale with a broker for $450,000. After 18 months on the market, I sold the property for $430,000. I paid the broker a commission, and incurred advertising and legal fees related to the sale of the property totaling $25,000. What will this mean to me in taxes?

ANSWER: The amount realized on this sale is $405,000 and the gain realized is $205,000.

$ 430,000	Selling Price
– 25,000	Commissions and Fees
$ 405,000	Amount Realized
– 200,000	Adjusted Basis
$ 205,000	Gain Realized

All of the gain on the sale will be taxed as a capital gain unless you defer gain through a tax-free exchange (discussed in Chapter 6). The $205,000 in capital gain will mean an additional tax of $41,000 at 20 percent.

QUESTION: My late wife and I bought a second home at the beach in 1978 at a price of $110,000 plus $5,000 in closing costs. In 1979, we added a screened porch at a cost of $6,000. My wife died in 1989, and this property in Delaware was valued at $200,000 on the federal estate tax return which we had to file. I have a contract to sell the house at $255,000 and my selling costs will be $14,000. What is my gain on the sale?

ANSWER: One-half of the property received a step-up in its basis in 1989 upon the death of your wife. The other half did not. Consequently, it is easiest to compute your basis by looking at the house as two separate halves.

On the one-half of the property which you have always owned, your cost was $55,000 plus closing costs of $2,500 and improvements of $3,000, giving you a basis of $60,500 on this portion. On the one-half interest which you acquired through inheritance from your wife, your basis is the $100,000 value of the fractional interest at the time of death. Improvements prior to this date are disregarded, inasmuch as they are reflected in the fair market value.

Consequently, your adjusted basis in the property as a whole is $160,500. Your amount realized will be $241,000, reflecting the selling price of $255,000 less $14,000 in commissions and fees. Your gain is $80,500.

CONTROVERSY

Had the spouse's death occurred before 1977, or before 1982 in the case of joint interests created before 1977, the step-up in basis would not necessarily be on one-half of the property. Under prior law, husband-wife jointly held property with right of survivorship (that is, assets passing automatically to the surviving spouse by operation of law, outside of the will) was included in the estate of the deceased spouse to the extent that the decedent contributed to the acquisition of the property. When the decedent was the only working spouse during the course of the marriage, the entire property in such cases may be entitled to a step-up in basis. If a federal estate tax return were filed, both the date of death value and the degree of contribution from the spouse who died could be determined from the return. If no return had to be filed, this information would have to be obtained from local probate records, other documentation, or recollection.

Had the spouse's death occurred after 1981 in the case of joint interests created before 1977, the step-up in basis would have been unclear. The IRS position is that the step-up in basis would be on one-half of the property. However, the Sixth Circuit Court of Appeals in 1992 followed by the Fourth Circuit Court of Appeals on June 26, 1997 ruled that the degree of step-up in basis in such cases is also determined by the contribution of the decedent to the acquisition of the property.

FILING POINTER   Under a quirk in the law, surviving spouses domiciled in community property states get to step up their tax basis in inherited community property (except real estate in non-community property states) to the full fair market value on date of death. The same 100 percent step-up in basis is available to all surviving spouses as to real estate in community property states. See Chapter 1 for a list of the nine community property states.

CAUTION!   One of the great tax shelters remaining today is that capital gain on the rise in value of assets is, in essence, forgiven at death. Although less likely than several years ago, future tax legislation may bring about an end to this step-up in basis, causing the estate or heirs to pay a capital gain tax on disposition of appreciated property. Appreciation prior to enactment would likely be "grandfathered" and not taxed.

TAX PLANNING IDEA   It is crucial that all records related to the purchase price of real property (plus improvements), stocks, and other assets be retained indefinitely. In the event of audit, you are required to prove your tax basis for assets which you sold. On his 1992 tax return, President Clinton reported a $1,000 gain on sale of an interest in an unsuccessful land development corporation for $1,000. A spokesperson indicated that, even though the President had lost "thousands of dollars" on the investment, he was unable to establish basis and declined to show the loss.

FILING POINTER   In computing basis in a mutual fund, remember that reinvested dividends constitute part of your basis. You have paid taxes each year on the dividends.

HOW TO DETERMINE THE BEST YEAR FOR RECOGNIZING GAIN OR LOSS

Non-tax considerations often control the timing of sales of assets. For example, sales of securities are often made solely for investment purposes in order to diversify your portfolio or to liquidate a stock when you believe it has reached its zenith. However, tax considerations, whenever possible, should be part of your sales analysis.

Here are some of the factors that you should keep in mind before making any dispositions that will involve significant taxable gains or losses:

1. Your marginal tax bracket in the current year vis-à-vis your marginal tax bracket next year. Will the contemplated transaction add sufficient income or loss to your federal taxable income to raise or lower your marginal tax bracket?

2. Sales earlier in the year. Prior sales generating capital losses allow subsequent sales of appreciated property in the same year with no additional taxable income. Prior sales of appreciated property can be offset by year end sales of capital assets in a loss position.

3. Likelihood of congressional activity affecting tax rates. Although the chance of congressional activity affecting tax rates is often difficult to assess in a timely manner, it should not be overlooked.

YEAR-END REMINDER   As year end approaches and sales of stock, real estate, or other investments are contemplated either in the current year or in the next year, an overall assessment of comparative tax brackets and the nature of already existing transactions should be made to determine the impact of additional taxable transactions on your overall tax liability.

CONTROVERSY

The Taxpayer Relief Act of 1997 left unclear the manner in which capital losses are netted against various rates of capital gain from same-year transactions. A technical correction is expected.

DEFERRING GAIN THROUGH CONDITIONAL SALES

Gain or loss is generally recognized in the year in which the transaction is completed for tax purposes. Generally, a sale will be closed when the title has been transferred from the seller to the buyer or when all of the benefits of ownership are transferred to the buyer. A sale will not be closed and the gain or loss will not be recognized when the sale is subject to conditions which have not been fulfilled. These conditional sales are generally handled through escrow arrangements, with the escrow agent being instructed to dismantle the "sale" should the conditions not be fulfilled by returning the consideration to the buyer and the subject property to the seller.

A conditional sale will not be closed for tax purposes until the condition has been fulfilled only if the condition is a condition precedent. This is a condition allowing either of the parties to turn its back on the transaction. For example, parties to a real estate contract can transfer the deed and purchase money to an escrow agent with the condition that the sale not be completed until the title is examined and determined to be marketable. For tax purposes, there will be no completed transaction and no gain or loss recognized until the condition precedent—the examination of and finding of a marketable title—has been completed. But if the condition involved is a condition subsequent to the sale, then the transaction will be closed and gain or loss recognized in the earlier year.

YEAR-END REMINDER   Utilization of a condition precedent, especially for sales near year end, can delay taxation of a transaction until the close of the escrow in the succeeding year.

QUESTION: I've been trying to sell my house and there is a prospective buyer who has his eye on the house. However, I've heard rumors that the swim and tennis club located in the neighborhood may be closing and the property sold to a developer. The swim and tennis club is a big attraction for the buyer and he would not be interested in the house if the club were not there. I understand that the current membership of the club will be voting in early January on the issue of whether to sell the club property to the developer.

I'm happy with the price that I have been offered but I would like to enter into a deal with the club and sell the property with that of the club's should the membership vote to sell to the developer. What can the buyer and I do to protect our interests under these circumstances?

ANSWER: One suggestion is that your contract to sell the house to the buyer be conditioned on the club's membership voting against selling the club property to the developer. If the condition is satisfied, you will sell the house for the price and under the terms of the contract to which you and your buyer have agreed. If the membership votes to sell the property to the developer, you are relieved of the obligation to sell the property to your buyer and can join the club and sell the property to the developer if that is your desire.

For tax purposes, if you enter into such a contract, the sale of the property will not be closed, if at all, until next year, when the membership takes its vote on this issue. Should they decide in favor of selling the property to the developer, you do not go through with the contract to sell the property. On the other hand, if the membership votes against selling the club property to the developer, then your sale will be closed for tax purposes next January rather than in the year you entered into the contract.

DEFERRING GAIN THROUGH INSTALLMENT SALES

Whenever an individual sells property (other than such items as inventory or marketable securities) and receives all or a portion of the payment after the year of sale, in the absence of an election to the contrary, he or she will report the realized gain as payments are received from the buyer—in other words, on the installment basis. If the individual realizes any depreciation recapture income on the sale, however, all of the recapture must be reported in the year of sale, and any remaining gain is reported as payments are received from the buyer. Recapture income is all gain from the sale of depreciated personal property up to the seller's original cost. When applicable, it constitutes only a portion of the gain up to the seller's original cost on the sale of depreciated real property.

If any property other than farm property is sold on the installment basis and the selling price is more than $150,000, a special rule may apply. Under a complex provision, the seller will be required to pay interest to the IRS on the deferred tax if the seller's total outstanding obligations from sales during the year exceed $5 million.

Should an installment obligation be used to secure a loan made to the taxpayer, then the loan amount is considered to have been a payment on the installment note, accelerating gain recognition to the taxpayer.

QUESTION: I own a tract of land that I bought a couple of years ago for $300,000. I've just signed a contract to sell the tract for $500,000, payable $100,000 at closing, and the buyer is giving me his promissory note for $400,000 to cover the remainder of the purchase price. The promissory note will be paid off in eight years in equal amounts of $50,000 and the buyer will be paying me the market rate of interest. How can I report this gain?

ANSWER: You can report the gain realized on this transaction on the installment method. Your gain on the property is $200,000, and a portion of this $200,000 gain will be taxable to you in the year of sale as well as in the eight years during which you receive payments on your buyer's promissory note in accordance with the following ratio:

$$\frac{\text{profit}}{\text{contract price}} \quad \times \quad \text{payment} \quad = \quad \text{reportable gain}$$

$$\text{Year of Sale:} \quad \frac{\$200,000}{\$500,000} \quad \times \quad \$100,000 \quad = \quad \$40,000$$

$$\text{Subsequent Years:} \quad \frac{\$200,000}{\$500,000} \quad \times \quad \$50,000 \quad = \quad \$20,000$$

QUESTION: How do the installment sales rules work if my buyer assumes the mortgage on the property? I own an apartment building that is worth $500,000. My buyer will be assuming the existing mortgage of $200,000 and will be giving me $100,000 in cash at closing. The remaining $200,000 will be paid in equal annual installments over the next five years. In addition, the buyer will be paying me the going rate of interest. My basis in the apartment building is $300,000.

ANSWER: If the buyer assumes a mortgage on the property, or takes the property subject to a mortgage, the calculation of the amount of gain that you must report each year is different. The contract price, the denominator of your profit ratio, is reduced by the amount of the mortgage to which the property is subject or the amount of the mortgage assumed by the buyer except to the extent that such liabilities exceed your basis in the property.

In the year of sale, you will be required to recognize a gain of $66,667 ($200,000/$300,000 × $100,000) and in each of the next five years you will be required to report $26,667 of gain on the sale ($200,000/$300,000 × $40,000 note payments).

Now let's assume that your basis in the property was only $150,000. Your gain of $350,000 ($500,000 – $150,000) can be reported on the installment method, but the calculation changes because the mortgage assumed by the buyer exceeds your basis in the property by $50,000. The $50,000 excess amount will be included in the denominator of your profit ratio and will also be considered a payment in the year of sale.

$$\text{Year of Sale:} \quad \frac{\$350,000}{\$350,000} \quad \times \quad \$150,000 \quad = \quad \$150,000$$

$$\text{Subsequent Years:} \quad \frac{\$350,000}{\$350,000} \quad \times \quad \$40,000 \quad = \quad \$40,000$$

As you can see, whenever the buyer assumes a mortgage which is in excess of the seller's basis, the full amount of each payment on the promissory note as well as the full amount of the down payment and the excess of the mortgage over basis will be taxable income.

QUESTION: My brother wants to buy my apartment building. Can I report the gain on the installment method?

ANSWER: Yes, but special rules will apply if your brother sells the apartment building within two years after he purchased it from you and before he had made all of the payments on your installment obligation. If this occurs, there will be an acceleration of the reporting of your gain. This acceleration rule is designed to prevent tax avoidance by having the related party pay the initial owner of the property on an installment basis while the related party buyer turns around and sells the property at little or no gain in a conventional sale, receiving the full market value of the property immediately.

For purpose of this related party rule, spouses, children, grandchildren, parents, siblings, and certain corporations and partnerships are considered as related. The related party sale rule applies only for two years after the initial installment sale. Once two years have passed, the related party buyer can dispose of the property which was the subject of the installment sale without accelerating gain recognition on the initial transaction. Furthermore, the related party sale rule will not apply upon a disposition by the related party buyer if the Internal Revenue Service can be convinced that neither the first installment sale nor the second sale was entered into for a tax avoidance purpose.

TAX PLANNING IDEA In-laws do not come within the definition of a related party. Thus, if there is a bona fide sale to an in-law, for example, to a son-in-law, installment reporting is still available. However, if the true buyer of property was in fact the related party (in our example, the daughter), the IRS will view the transaction as a sale between the related parties and disregard the terms of the contract listing the in-law as the purchaser.

MINIMIZING TAXABLE GAIN ON SALES OF SECURITIES

Gain on the sale of marketable securities is reported in the year of the sale even though payment for the stock is not received until the following year. Under rules governing the

New York Stock Exchange, payment is received on the settlement date, which is generally five full business days after the date of the sale. Despite this difference in the sale date and the settlement date, the seller must report the gain in the year of the sale rather than in the year of the settlement. For example, if the individual sells stock on December 31, 1997, payment will not be received until 1998. However, inasmuch as installment reporting is not available for marketable securities, the gain from this transaction will be reported in 1997 even though no payment is received until 1998.

TAX PLANNING IDEA   Although installment reporting is not available for stock sales, you can still postpone paying taxes on the sale of securities from one year to the next by using a technique known as a short sale. In a short sale you enter into a contract to sell stock that you do not currently own. (You may also sell short even if you own the stock by "selling short against the box.") In order to go through with the sale, you borrow shares from your broker to deliver to your buyer. At a later date, the short sale will be closed by your delivery of stock of the same company that you just sold.

For tax purposes, if you close the short sale by January 30 and you continue to own identical stock for at least 60 days after you close the transaction, the gain is reported that year upon repayment the borrowed stock and not in the prior year when you sold the borrowed stock. For example, in December, you enter into a contract to sell 100 shares of XYZ stock. In order to complete this transaction, you borrow 100 shares of XYZ stock for delivery to your buyer. Later, by January 30, you close this short sale by delivering another 100 shares of XYZ stock (shares that you either own or that you purchase on the market) to the lender, usually your broker. For tax purposes, the transaction is closed in January and the gain is reported in that year and not in the preceding year if you continue to own at least 100 shares of XYZ stock for at least 60 days after closing.

CAUTION!   The requirements of closing the short sale by delivery of stock no later than 30 days after year-end and of holding identical stock for at least 60 days after closing are newly created by the Taxpayer Relief Act of 1997.

CAUTION!   Using short sales merely for tax purposes without considering the economic volatility of the stock market is one-sided and could lead to a disaster if the stock market takes off and you've locked in your profit at a lower level.

FILING POINTER   When an individual has acquired stock holdings over a period of time and does not dispose of all holdings at the same time, he or she must specifically identify which shares of stock are being sold in the transaction in order to properly compute gain. If the individual is unable to identify the lot from which the sold shares are derived, Treasury Regulations require that person to treat the shares to be sold as coming from the oldest lot first. The seller can adequately identify the securities to be sold by delivering a certificate or by specifically identifying the securities to the broker who holds the certificate. This allows disposition of the higher basis shares, thereby reducing gain.

YEAR-END REMINDER   Suppose you have a substantial profit on a stock and you want to shift your taxable gain into next year. You can guarantee your present profit by buying a put (an option to sell) on your stock at its current price, good for a long enough period to carry you into the next year. If the stock keeps climbing, don't exercise the put. Instead, sell the stock at a higher price.

YEAR-END REMINDER   Mutual fund trading poses special tax issues; the timing of purchases and sales of shares is important. Many funds distribute capital gains to shareholders in December, and a shareholder of record must report the entire gain even if he or she just acquired the shares. Make purchases of mutual fund shares after the record date.

QUESTION: I told my broker last year to sell 400 shares of stock but he sold 4,000 shares. By the time I discovered his error and bought 3,600 shares back, the stock had climbed $4 per share. Following arbitration early this year, the brokerage firm "split the difference" with me and gave me $7,200 (one-half of what the error cost me) and dropped the commission charges. However, my accountant says I have to report a gain on the "sale" of all 4,000 shares. Isn't this really a correction of my broker's error?

ANSWER: Not according to the Tax Court in a 1996 decision. According to the Court, a rescission requires that you be restored to your exact original position, generally through mutual consent or court order, in the same tax year. You met none of the conditions. Rather, through arbitration you were awarded damages in the following year (see Chapter 2). Under the Court's reasoning, it is virtually impossible for an error by a brokerage firm to be rescinded because you can't typically get back the exact shares.

MAXIMIZING TAX LOSS ON SALES OF SECURITIES

If you sold any stocks or bonds at a loss or if you own any stocks or bonds that become totally worthless during the year, you are entitled to claim a capital loss deduction. As with other capital losses, these losses will offset any capital gains recognized during the year and will offset up to $3,000 of ordinary income. Any unused capital loss can be carried forward.

However, a special rule applies with respect to the disposition of certain small business stock, known as Section 1244 stock. While gains from Section 1244 stock are taxed as capital gains, losses are deductible as ordinary losses. The maximum ordinary loss from Section 1244 stock in a single tax year is $50,000 ($100,000 on a joint return) but no more than your basis in stock. The stock must be issued by a domestic corporation for money or other property (not services) and the total of capital stock and paid-in surplus must not be in excess of

$1 million. For the five tax years ending before the loss, more than 50 percent of the corporation's gross receipts must have come from the active conduct of a trade or business. No formal corporate action is now required for a shareholder to benefit under this special rule but, if the stock was issued before November 7, 1978, the corporation had to formally adopt a written plan for issuance of such stock.

TAX PLANNING IDEA Section 1244 treatment is not available if you receive your stock from another shareholder rather than from the corporation itself. In certain situations, it is possible to structure a stock issuance in either manner. Original issuance of the stock by the corporation will ensure desirable ordinary loss treatment, provided all criteria have been met.

TAX PLANNING IDEA When funding a new corporation, it is often desirable to lend needed funds rather than to commit to an equity contribution. However, the loss on a worthless loan will be ordinary in nature only if the obligation can be characterized as a business bad debt. As discussed later in this chapter, such a characterization is difficult to show. The result is that favorable tax treatment if you don't get your money back may be lost by structuring the corporate funding as debt.

CAUTION! In general, financing a corporation with debt carries multiple hazards. A proper debt-equity ratio must be maintained or IRS can recharacterize debt on the books as disguised equity. Additionally, if you transfer property with a value in excess of its tax basis to a corporation, you will pay taxes on the rise in value if you take back any debt from the corporation.

CAUTION! A wash sale of stock occurs when, within a 60-day period, beginning 30 days before the sale of securities, the seller replaces the sold stocks with substantially identical stocks or securities. If the wash sale results in a loss, the loss cannot be recognized. The wash sale rules are designed to prevent an individual from disposing of the stock to create a tax loss but preserving a position in the market by a quick replacement of the sold shares.

FILING POINTER To avoid the application of the wash sale rules without changing your basic investment position, replace the securities sold with securities in the same or a related industry.

QUESTION: I have been dabbling in the stock market this year and among other transactions have had four transactions dealing with some XYZ stock. Here are the four transactions. Please explain to me what impact the tax rules are going to have on these transactions:

June 1—bought 100 shares at $10 per share

August 1—sold 20 shares at $8 per share

August 27—bought 40 shares at $7 per share

October 1—sold 50 shares at $9 per share

ANSWER: Your sale of the 20 shares of XYZ stock on August 1 resulted in a loss of $2 per share. However, because you acquired 40 shares of XYZ stock (at $7 per share) within 30 days of that loss sale, you will not be able to deduct the $2 per share loss which you realized on the August 1 sale. Your basis in 20 of the 40 shares that you bought on August 27 will be their cost basis, $7 per share, but the remaining 20 shares will have a basis equal to $9 per share (the $10 basis of the 20 shares sold on August 1 less the $1 difference between the August 1 sale price and the August 27 purchase price).

The sale on October 1 is not subject to any wash sale rule assuming that no other XYZ transactions took place before November 1. If you identified that the 50 shares of stock that were sold on October 1 came from your June 1 lot, then you will recognize a loss of $1 per share ($9 less $10 cost basis). If you identified that 40 of the shares that were sold on October 1 came from your August 27 purchase, then 20 of the 50 shares will have been sold at a gain ($9 less $7 cost basis), 20 at no gain or loss ($9 less $9 cost basis), and 10 at a $1 loss ($9 less $10 cost basis). If you failed to identify from which lot the 50 shares that were sold on October 1 came, then you will automatically be deemed to have sold 50 of the shares that you bought on June 1 under the first-in, first-out rule discussed above.

FILING POINTER   In contrast with the usual three-year statute of limitations discussed in Chapter 13, a claim for refund attributable to a worthless security can be submitted up to seven years after the original due date of the return for the year that the security became worthless.

YEAR-END REMINDER   In the absence of an identifiable event such as a bankruptcy to show worthlessness of a security, you may be able to sell the equity or debt instrument to a third party for a small amount prior to year end and claim the loss.

CONVERT YOUR PERSONAL LOSSES TO DEDUCTIBLE LOSSES

Individuals are entitled to claim a tax loss on the sale of an asset only if the property was used in business or was investment property. As a result, if you sell your personal residence at a loss, the loss will not be deductible. Similarly, when you sell your 1980 Chevrolet for less than what you paid for it, the loss is not deductible unless the car was used in a business.

If you convert property that had been used in strictly personal activities to use in a trade or business, or for use in an investment activity, the property loses its personal character and assumes the business or investment character. For example, if you move out of your personal residence and rent it, you have converted it so that the loss suffered on its sale will be deductible to the extent it is attributable to the decline in value after you rented it.

TAX PLANNING IDEA   If the housing market in your area is depressed and you anticipate that the sale of your personal residence will result in a loss, consider renting the property prior to the sale so as to clearly establish that the home is no longer your personal residence. When the house is sold at a loss, the decrease in value since its conversion to rental property will be a Section 1231 ordinary loss; whereas, if you had sold it without converting it from personal use, the loss would not be deductible.

CONTROVERSY

The courts are split as to the level of rental activity required to treat the rental property as a trade or business, thus giving rise to Section 1231 treatment. In the most recent case of significance, the Tax Court in 1993 disallowed a Section 1231 loss claimed by an individual who was transferred by an employer to another state and who leased his home to the original builder for a low rental. The builder maintained the property and showed it to prospective buyers. The Tax Court held that the lease was a caretaking arrangement lacking a primary rental or investment purpose.

QUESTION: When my mother died, the terms of her will provided that I was to inherit her home. Very shortly after her death, the real estate market in the area where the home was located collapsed and the property declined rapidly in value. If I sell this property, can I claim a loss?

ANSWER: If you never use the inherited property as your residence (personal loss) and never rented the property (Section 1231 loss), any loss suffered on its sale will be a capital loss of limited benefit from sale of investment property.

 CAUTION!   Congress has periodically considered legislation which, if enacted, would allow an individual to claim a capital loss on sale of a principal residence.

WRITING OFF YOUR UNCOLLECTIBLE LOANS AS LOSSES

When you have lent someone money and you are unable to collect the debt because it is worthless, you are entitled to claim a bad debt deduction on your personal tax return. If the loan was made in a nonbusiness context, meaning any debt other than one created or acquired in the course of a business, then you are entitled to claim a short-term capital loss in the year that the debt becomes worthless. The short-term capital loss will offset capital gain income recognized in the same tax year and will offset ordinary income to the extent of $3,000. Any capital loss which is not deductible as a result of these limitations can be carried forward to subsequent years.

Like a security, an uncollectible loan can be claimed as a deduction only in the year in which it is totally worthless. So long as there is some expectation that the debt will be repaid, it is not totally worthless and therefore is nondeductible unless the debt paper is sold at a loss.

FILING POINTER   Like a refund claim because of a worthless security, a refund claim on account of a worthless debt can be made up to seven years after the original due date of the return for the year that the debt became worthless.

FILING POINTER   Loans to family members which become worthless during the year will also qualify for the bad debt deduction even though the debtor is a member of your family. However, you must be able to establish that the loan to the family member was in fact a loan and not a gift. The IRS will strictly scrutinize any transaction between related parties to determine whether the advance of money was a loan or a gift. In order to establish that the advance was a loan, you should document the advance with a promissory note which establishes an interest rate and a fixed time for repayment. The more businesslike the transaction, the more likely it is that, should the debt become worthless because of the debtor's insolvency or other inability to repay, you will be entitled to a bad debt deduction. For example, a dad who lent his daughter $37,000 to open a skating rink was permitted to claim a bad debt when business dried up and went bust. The Tax Court in its 1995 decision cited a long history of family loans and repayments.

QUESTION: Several years ago I set up a corporation for the purpose of maintaining a kennel for dogs and cats. A number of veterinarians promised that they would make me referrals, so I put $5,000 of my own money into the corporation and guaranteed a corporate obligation to the bank of $50,000. The veterinarians promised me that I could make a lot more money than what I had been making as an animal trainer. The business has gone under, and I had to sell everything that I owned in order to pay off the bank as well as the IRS for payroll taxes and the state for payroll and sales taxes. Can I write this off?

ANSWER: As to the loan, you are entitled to claim a bad debt deduction on payments made as a result of your guarantee. The issue is whether the loss is a nonbusiness bad debt, in which case it will be a capital loss (which you will have to use at $3,000 per year over a number of years in the absence of capital gain from the sale of your assets) or a business bad debt, in which case it will be an ordinary loss (which is usable in full this year).

The test which is used to make the distinction centers on whether the loan (or, in this case, the guarantee of the loan) was connected with a business of yours as opposed to a business of a corporation owned by you. This subtle distinction is very important. The IRS and the courts take the position that a shareholder's loan to a corporation, even one which is 100 percent owned by the shareholder, is a nonbusiness bad debt when the motivation is to make or protect an investment. However, it appears as if your dominant motive was to give you a better income. The courts view a loan which is for the purpose of earning a higher income as being business motivated—meaning in your case the business of being an employee of the kennel. Claim the business bad debt.

As to the unpaid taxes to the IRS which you paid personally, you cannot deduct this "penalty" which is imposed when a corporation defaults. (See the discussion in Chapter 10 on the Trust Fund Recovery Penalty.) However, the Ninth Circuit Court of Appeals ruled in 1995 that an individual who personally pays a tax obligation when state law makes him or her a *co-obligor* with the corporation for the liability, as opposed to a guarantor, can claim a nonbusiness bad debt upon payment.

FILING POINTER   If you must personally pay corporate state withholding or sales tax, check whether you were equally liable for payment from the beginning under state law. If so, you may be able to claim a deduction, although both the IRS and the Tax Court may take a different position outside of the Ninth Circuit (California, Oregon, Washington, Idaho, Montana, Alaska, and Hawaii).

The alternative, or your only choice if you will be required to pay federal withholding taxes or state withholding or sales taxes for which you are not automatically liable as a co-obligor, is to lend money to the corporation to make payment—and then claim a bad debt on the loan.

CAUTION!   If you lend money when it is clear that you will not be repaid, the IRS will challenge your claim of a bad debt.

CAUTION!   See Chapter 10 as to the need to be careful to designate corporate payments for only those portions of the total tax debt for which there is personal liability.

QUESTION: My former husband is thousands of dollars behind in child support. Can I claim a bad debt? He'll never catch up.

ANSWER: Even if the obligation is totally worthless, you have no basis in the debt which would allow a write-off according to a 1993 Revenue Ruling reiterating a prior Tax Court decision.

6

REAL ESTATE—THE MOST TAX-FAVORED INVESTMENT

OWNING AND TITLING REAL ESTATE FOR TAX ADVANTAGE

The owning of real estate offers the most tax-favored investment. As discussed in Chapter 4, in the case of real estate held for personal use, taxes, interest in most instances, and borrowing costs (points) paid to acquire a principal residence remain deductible. In contrast, nondeductible today are other personal interest payments, certain taxes which were formerly deductible (sales, gasoline), and points paid on other asset acquisitions. As discussed later in this chapter, individuals may in most cases exclude gain recognition on disposition of a principal residence.

In the case of real estate held for investment purpose, numerous tax advantages exist as well which are also discussed later in this chapter. Ownership of real estate offers exceptions to the passive activity rules discussed in Chapter 2 while often allowing deductible losses in excess of outgoing cash or generating incoming cash in excess of generated income. Further exceptions discussed in Chapter 11 apply for real estate professionals.

An individual can own real property either in his or her own name or as the sole shareholder of a corporation which owns the property. Real estate held for personal use should be held in your personal name. But whether real estate held for investment purpose should be owned individually or in corporate form will depend in part on tax considerations as well as non-tax considerations such as limited liability.

From a tax point of view, any profit or loss generated by the investment property will be reported on the personal tax return if the individual owns the property in his or her own name. Any operating losses suffered by the individual may be subject to disallowance on account of inadequate basis (see Chapter 5), or "at risk" limitations (see Chapter 7) or on account of not being an activity entered into for profit (see Chapter 10). More often, operating losses will be subject to the passive activity rules which allow losses from such activities to be deducted only to the extent of the income generated from such activities. However, if the investment real estate is rented, up to $25,000 of the losses incurred by the individual from the rental activity may be deductible if he or she actively participates in the rental activity. (See the discussion of rental activity losses later in this chapter.)

If the investment real estate is owned in corporate name, then the individual shareholder of the corporation will obtain no personal tax benefits from that ownership unless the corporation elects to be an S corporation. If such an election is made, the individual shareholder will be able to report the income or losses from the corporation's ownership of the real estate on his or her personal return. Losses incurred by the S corporation are deductible by the individual shareholder to the extent of tax basis, meaning investment in the company either in the form of an equity investment or in the form of loans to the corporation. The limitation on passive losses will still apply.

The passive loss limitation also applies to personal service C (regular) corporations such as incorporated medical, legal, and accounting practices. The passive loss limitation applies to other C corporations in modified form. Passive losses incurred by non-personal service C corporations can offset net active income but not portfolio income.

If two or more individuals invest in real estate, they can do so by owning the property in corporate name, jointly (either with a right of survivorship or as tenants in common), or through a partnership. If the investment real estate is merely rented out, a partnership in the tax sense need not exist. Each co-owner may report his or her respective share of the rental income or loss on a personal return. On the other hand, if services (such as attendant parking) are provided, then a partnership does exist for tax purposes. If a partnership exists, each partner reports his or her share of the partnership income or loss on a personal return. Once again, the rules on passive losses will affect the ability of individual co-owners or partners to claim losses. (See Chapter 10 for a further discussion of alternative types of entities, in the context of an active trade or business.)

TAX PLANNING IDEA   A limited liability company, now recognized in all states as a means of enjoying protection from creditors without incorporating (and its variation in a number of states, the limited liability partnership), is generally treated for tax purposes as a partnership. Thus, an LLC, where available, often offers the best of both worlds to real property owners—limited liability protection from creditors in the event of lawsuit and partnership tax treatment with its pass-throughs and flexible ownership options.

TAX PLANNING IDEA   While there is no requirement of filing a partnership return when multiple individuals share passive ownership of real property through a general partnership as opposed to a limited partnership or limited liability company, this approach is easier than reporting percentages of each income and expense item for each of the separate properties on the rental income schedule of your tax return. However, opting not to file a formal partnership return allows greater flexibility in tax planning. For example, a partnership interest in real property cannot be swapped tax-free (see the subsequent discussion in this chapter on tax-free exchanges) for a similar partnership interest or for real property itself. In contrast, a fractional interest in real property through co-ownership can be swapped for a whole or fractional interest in other realty.

QUESTION: Two friends and I are planning to acquire rental properties. We hope to acquire several of them in order to minimize our exposure in the event that one stays vacant for a long period of time. We are looking for break-even cash flow during the year and for appreciation to make an above average rate of return on the cash down payment. How should we own the properties?

ANSWER: Utilization of a regular C corporation is clearly inadvisable. Because a regular corporation is taxed on its profit at the corporate level, it will be difficult to avoid double taxation—once at the corporate level on any operating profit or upon sale of a property and then again at the individual level upon distribution of the operating cash flow or sale proceeds to you and your co-owners. Additionally, a C corporation will not be able to take advantage of the provision that allows deductions for up to $25,000 of rental losses in excess of passive income. An S corporation is a possibility; however, unless there is going to be a significant cash contribution by the three of you, you may not have enough tax basis to use the losses likely to arise as a result of depreciation.

In a partnership or co-ownership context not constituting a formal partnership, you will receive additional basis (unless you are a limited partner and the financing is recourse) from your share of partnership liabilities. Consequently, partnership or co-ownership is probably best for you. If your state recognizes limited liability companies, you can have the benefits of favorable tax treatment and of maximum protection from creditors.

CAUTION!   See the discussion in Chapter 10 on an important 1994 Tax Court case applying the "hobby loss" rules to real property ownership in two component parts, the first as to the property rental and the second as to the holding for potential appreciation.

EXCLUDING GAIN ON THE SALE OF A PRINCIPAL RESIDENCE

Most gain on home sales is free of tax as a result of a new $250,000 exclusion available once every two years to an individual irrespective of age who has owned and lived in the property as a *principal residence* for at least two of the previous five years. Married couples filing jointly get a $500,000 exclusion if both individuals lived in the house for two years even if only one owned the house for the required period.

Even if the two-year ownership or occupancy period is not satisfied, or even if another principal residence has been sold within two years, a pro rata portion of the would-be exclusion may be tax free (based on the portion of the two years which has been satisfied) if the change of residence is on account of changed employment, health, or other circumstances which may be provided by future regulation.

What qualifies as your principal residence for purposes of this rule? The law does not define "principal residence." For this purpose a residence includes a condominium or a cooperative and even a houseboat or a mobile home, so long as it is equipped with cooking, sleeping, and sanitation facilities. The residence can include vast acreage around the home if the land usage is consistent with residential use. However, a retirement home or lifecare facility, even though an individual may purchase the right to exclusive lifetime occupancy, cannot qualify in the absence of a legal interest in the underlying property.

When an individual has two homes, the question arises as to which is his or her principal residence. This is a fact-and-circumstance analysis and will involve an investigation of various factors including voting residence, the amount of time spent in each home, and the domicile of the family.

FILING POINTER   The two of five year ownership and occupancy rules are not applicable for sales of a principal residence owned on August 5, 1997 and sold within two years thereafter.

FILING POINTER   If an individual actually occupies a home as a principal residence for at least one year, time in a nursing facility may count toward the second year of occupancy.

FILING POINTER   Ignore sales before May 7, 1997 in applying the "once every two years" rule.

TAX PLANNING IDEA   If a husband and wife each sell qualifying properties within two years of each other, even in the same year, they may each claim maximum $250,000 exclusions on their respective sales.

TAX PLANNING IDEA   Use of the exclusion is optional. Under certain circumstances, it may be desirable not to claim the exclusion on an earlier sale in order to have the full $250,000/$500,000 exclusion available on a subsequent sale within two years.

TAX PLANNING IDEA   Two *tacking* rules facilitate use of the exclusion. To avoid inequities to divorcing taxpayers, an individual's home occupancy includes periods in which the property was occupied by the spouse pursuant to a written agreement or court order. To benefit a surviving spouse who was not on the title, a widow or widower's home ownership or occupancy includes periods in which the property was owned or occupied by the deceased spouse.

CAUTION!   Except for sale of a remainder interest to an unrelated party, which gives full title to the purchaser following the seller's death, the sale of any interest of less than the entire ownership interest does not qualify for the exclusion.

CONTROVERSY

What if you have been claiming a depreciation deduction for your office-in-home (see Chapter 10) or on account of a rental of a portion of your home? First, gain will be recognized to the extent of depreciation attributable to periods after May 6, 1997. Second, all depreciation ever claimed will reduce the basis of property (see Chapter 5). However, will the office-in-home or partial rental cause loss of the exclusion on a portion of the principal residence? The answer is unclear, but it appears as if disqualifying use of one or more rooms should be limited to no more than three of the five years preceding sale.

CAUTION! The $250,000/$500,000 exclusion did not apply to sales before May 7, 1997. Instead, prior to that date (or for closings or binding contracts prior to August 5, 1997 at the election of the taxpayer), if you sold your principal residence and bought and used a new principal residence within a four-year period beginning two years before the date of the sale and ending two years after the date of the sale, and you spent at least as much as the adjusted sales price (the amount realized after commissions and fees but before payoffs of mortgages) of the old home, then none of the gain realized on the sale of the residence was recognized. Instead, your basis in the new principal residence was reduced by the amount of gain which was not recognized so that, when the new home was ultimately sold and no reinvestment was made, the gain realized on the sale of the first principal residence was taxed at that time.

Additionally, you could elect to exclude up to $125,000 of gain ($62,500 if married filing separate) realized on the sale of your principal residence if you were at least 55 years old before the house was sold and you owned and used the house as your principal residence for a total of three of the previous five years before the sale. In other words, the gain was permanently forgiven and never recognized. If you elected to exclude the gain generated by the sale of a principal residence, you could not make another election even if the gain realized on the sale of your residence did not amount to $125,000. It was a one-time election which was permanently noted by the IRS. If you were married at the time of the sale, one of you must have satisfied each and every requirement for the exclusion. Additionally, you could not make the election to exclude gain if your spouse had previously used the election—this was known as the "tainted spouse" rule.

FILING POINTER Few individuals who sold principal residences from May 7, 1997 to August 4, 1997 will come out ahead by electing to apply prior law. Certain individuals who will sell a principal residence again within two years and others with gain in excess of $250,000/$500,000 are possible exceptions.

MAKE FULL USE OF THE $25,000 WRITE-OFF FOR RENTAL REAL ESTATE

As discussed earlier in this chapter, except for certain individuals in a real property trade or business whose special treatment is discussed in Chapter 11, rental real estate is automatically considered a passive activity. Under the general rule, losses arising from such rental activity can only offset passive income and cannot be used to offset active income (salary and self-employment income, for example) or portfolio income (interest and dividends, for example).

However, the statute carves out an exception to this general rule, allowing individuals to offset up to $25,000 of active or investment income with losses generated by rental of real estate in which the taxpayer actively participates. The $25,000 ceiling is reduced to $12,500 in the case of a married individual filing a separate return who lives apart from the spouse for the entire year. For spouses who live together during any part of the year but who file separate returns, the $25,000/$12,500 rule does not apply.

For those taxpayers with higher levels of income, the $25,000/$12,500 amount is reduced one dollar for every two dollars that the taxpayer's modified adjusted gross income (AGI excluding passive losses, taxable Social Security, and IRA deductions) exceeds $100,000 ($50,000 in the case of a married individual filing a separate return). Thus, if the taxpayer's (other than a spouse filing a separate return) modified adjusted gross income is $150,000 or more, the rental activity loss will not be able to offset active or investment income. The $12,500 amount of a spouse who files a separate return and is eligible for the deduction is completely phased out if his or her modified adjusted gross income is at least $75,000.

In order to qualify under the $25,000/$12,500 rule, the individual must actively participate in the rental activity both in the year the loss arose and in the year the loss is allowed. To be considered an active participant with respect to the rental real estate, the individual must own at least a ten percent interest in the property and, unless also a general partner, generally may not own the interest as a limited partner.

The active participation requirement may be satisfied without continuous and substantial involvement in the operations of the rental activity so long as the individual is involved in a significant way (such as making management decisions involving approval of tenants, terms of the rental contract, or capital expenditures). Alternatively, the individual should be able to engage a management company which undertakes supervision of the rental property, as long as the individual exercises independent judgment over the recommendations of the management company. Although regulations haven't yet been issued, it appears that an individual will not satisfy the active participation rule if all significant management decisions are left to a management company.

YEAR-END REMINDER   Prior to year end, make sure that you are structuring your rental activities in an appropriate manner in order to maximize the use of your $25,000 write-off. Ascertain that you can satisfy the active participation test by maintaining an appropriate rein on the management decisions. Watch the timing of year-end expenditures with respect to the property. When necessary and when possible, structure the timing of your income to keep your modified AGI below $100,000.

CAUTION!   A single individual with modified adjusted gross income in the $100,000 to $150,000 range and losses from rental properties can be in the highest marginal tax bracket of any taxpayer. The individual falling within this range can lose more than 55 cents on each additional dollar of earnings when caught in the phaseout of the $25,000 deduction for rental real estate, the phaseout of itemized deductions, and the phaseout of personal exemptions. Married couples caught in phaseout fare only slightly better.

QUESTION: What can I do if my income as a corporate executive is over $150,000 and I don't have the option to write off $25,000 in rental losses? I expect my adjusted gross income to be about $225,000 before losses. In 1987, I purchased an apartment building that produces $40,000 of gross income. The mortgage on the apartment house requires an interest payment of $15,000 per year. My depreciation is about $20,000 a year and my other expenses on the property, such as insurance, management fees, and repairs, are about $15,000. I expect a loss of about $10,000. What are my options?

ANSWER: If you don't have any passive income, you will lose the ability to claim your $10,000 loss. Your best choice is to reduce or pay off the mortgage on the apartment building so as to reduce your interest expense. You might do this by securing a second mortgage on your principal residence and using the proceeds to pay down the apartment building's mortgage. The interest on the second mortgage on your principal residence will be deductible so long as the amount of the second mortgage doesn't exceed the lesser of the home's equity or $100,000 ($50,000 if you're married and file a separate return). This qualified residence interest will either be fully deductible or a small portion may be lost, depending on the extent of your other itemized deductions, as you must reduce most itemized deductions by three percent of the amount by which your AGI exceeds the threshold ($121,200 in 1997, $60,600 if you are married filing separately), subject to a maximum loss of 80 percent of affected deductions. (See Chapter 1 for a further discussion of the phaseout of itemized deductions.)

CAUTION! On multiple occasions, the Tax Court has upheld the IRS's position that the $25,000/$12,500 exception to the passive loss rule for rental real estate is not applicable to short-term rentals (seven days or less; 30 days or less if services are provided).

MAXIMIZE YOUR DEPRECIATION AND AMORTIZATION DEDUCTIONS

If real property is residential in nature, the adjusted basis of the building portion (as opposed to the land portion) is recovered ratably over 27½ years. If the real estate is nonresidential real estate, meaning it is used for commercial purposes including rentals normally 30 days or less, then the write-off is over a 39-year period. In either case, first-year depreciation does not give a full-year write-off, inasmuch as a proration of a full year's depreciation is used depending on the month of acquisition. The IRS publishes tables for use in computing depreciation.

After the property's acquisition, the owner will undoubtedly make any number of expenditures with respect to that property, some of which will be currently deductible and some of which must be added to the property's basis and then cost recovered through depreciation. If the expense is a repair or maintenance cost, the owner receives an immediate benefit from the expenditure by being able to currently deduct the expense. On the other hand, if the expenditure materially enhances the value of the property or prolongs its life, it is considered a capital expenditure and must be capitalized and then cost recovered over time, 27½ years in the case of residential property or 39 years in the case of nonresidential property.

The following are examples of the various types of expenditures which might fall into the repair category or the capital expenditure category:

Repairs	Capital Expenditures
Painting	Plumbing system installation
Maintenance on furnace	New furnace
Patching leaking roof	New roof

FILING POINTER   Don't forget to include the costs of acquiring real property in your basis. Most such costs, including construction period interest and taxes, transfer taxes, and recordation fees, are added to the basis of property and, to the extent that the property is depreciable (meaning the extent to which (1) costs can be allocated to the building rather than the raw land and (2) the building is used in a trade or business or for investment purposes), will be recovered through depreciation deductions. Points, loan origination fees, and loan commitment fees are not added to the basis of property. Rather, they are amortized over the term of the loan.

FILING POINTER   With the real estate, investors often acquire interest in personal property such as furnishings and appliances. These items of personal property can be written off over a shorter period, generally seven years.

YEAR-END REMINDER   Where a cash outlay will be a repair as opposed to a capital expenditure, a repair at your end will offer a valuable deduction unless you will have unusable losses. In fact, all bills related to rental properties should normally be paid in December.

RENTING TO FAMILY MEMBERS AT A LOSS

You can provide housing to your family members at a reasonable cost and still get a tax break. If a property is rented at its "fair rental value" and the home is the family member's principal residence, you will be able to claim a rental loss deduction with respect to the property, subject, of course, to the usual limitations on deducting rental losses. For example, a couple can purchase a home, rent it to their daughter as her principal residence, charge her the full market rent on the property, and be eligible to claim a rental loss deduction with respect to that property. On the other hand, if a couple purchases a home and lets their daughter use the property rent free or if the property does not constitute the daughter's principal residence, then the daughter's use of the property will be attributed to the couple and no loss can be claimed.

QUESTION: I own a piece of investment property near the location where my parents want to retire. When my current tenant's lease expires, can I rent the property to my parents and get the same tax breaks that I am getting now from my tenant?

ANSWER: Yes. So long as you charge your parents the same amount of rent that you would charge an unrelated party, the fact that your parents are your new tenants will not change your tax treatment of the rental losses that have been generated. However, you must apparently limit your visits as well as the visits of other family members to your parents to no more than the greater of 14 days or ten percent of the number of days that the property is rented at fair value.

QUESTION: My son and his wife have found their "dream home" but cannot afford the necessary down payment. I am able to lend them the money for the down payment, but I would like to get some tax breaks from this loan. Any suggestions?

ANSWER: Rather than lending the couple money, you and your son and his wife should consider a shared equity arrangement. In a shared equity arrangement you and your son and his wife will each own a share of the "dream home." So long as your son and his wife pay you for the fair rental value of your fractional share, you will be able to offset the income not only with the interest, taxes, and other expenses that you pay but also with the depreciation of your percentage interest in the property. The passive activity rules, including the $25,000/$12,500 rule, will be applicable to your ownership interest.

If your son and his wife itemize deductions, they can write off the taxes and interest, subject to the qualified residence interest rules, that they pay.

RENTING, USING, AND WRITING OFF YOUR VACATION HOME

Any residence which you own as an investment may fall within the definition of a vacation home. This is a generic term that is applied to property which an individual or members of the individual's family use personally to an extent. In addition to the traditional home, the term "vacation home" includes condos, apartments, boats, and mobile homes equipped with living accommodations. If there is any personal use of the home by the individual or by family members, write-offs with respect to that property are limited.

If a vacation home is rented for 14 days or less during the year and there is any personal use, the individual gets to pocket the rental income. The individual does not have to report the income; however, he or she is permitted to claim no expenses other than mortgage interest (if the property is treated as the second residence under the qualified residence interest rules) and property taxes.

If a vacation home is rented for more than 14 days and personal use does not exceed the greater of 14 days or ten percent of the days that the property is rented at fair value, expenses must be prorated based on the number of rental days and the number of personal days. The rental income is compared to the expenses allocable to the rental days. Any loss offsets other passive income and, as discussed earlier in this chapter, can offset other types of income in the case of certain real estate professionals and in the case of individuals eligible to utilize the $25,000/$12,500 write-off. However, as discussed earlier in this chapter, few vacation home landlords qualify for a write-off under the $25,000/$12,500 rule inasmuch as it does not apply to short-term rentals according to the IRS.

In such case, the personal portion of the property taxes may be claimed as an itemized deduction; however, the personal portion of the mortgage interest is not eligible for treatment as qualified residence interest.

If a vacation home is rented for more than 14 days and personal use exceeds the greater of 14 days or ten percent of the fair rental days, expenses must also be prorated based on the number of rental days and the number of personal days. However, an individual is penalized in that no loss is permitted to be claimed in connection with the rental aspects of the property. As regards the personal use aspects, property taxes may be claimed as an itemized deduction, as may the mortgage interest if the property is treated as the second residence of the individual.

CAUTION!   A home with multiple bedrooms, one of which is occupied by the homeowner and the others of which are rented to housemates, is treated as one home. The owner has made personal use of the home and no rental loss is allowed. In contrast, if the home had separate cooking facilities, bathrooms, and entrances such as in a duplex, the owner's occupation of one portion of the building would not taint the other portion and the rental loss would be allowed subject to the $25,000/$12,500 rule.

YEAR-END REMINDER   Care should be exercised if significant tax benefits would be lost by allowing personal use to exceed the greater of 14 days or ten percent of the number of rental days. In some cases it may be possible to reduce the number of personal days.

CAUTION!   Personal use by an individual includes not only his or her own use of the premises but also use by family members, by any individual if less than the fair rent is charged, by a co-owner, or by any person under an arrangement in which that person's investment property is made available for use. Consequently, if you rent your beach house to your grandchild's family for three weeks, that time will be considered your personal use of the beach house even if you charge your grandchild the same rate that you charge the general public. Similarly, if you let your next-door neighbor use the beach house and only charge one-half of the going rate, your neighbor's time at the beach house will be considered as your personal use of the property.

FILING POINTER   Use of a property during a period substantially devoted to full-time repair and maintenance does not count as personal use of the property. Under a 1993 Tax Court decision, the period of repair and maintenance includes the time expended in capital improvements.

CONTROVERSY

The Tax Court backs up the IRS's position that you may count only days of actual use as rental days and not days in which a unit is in a rental pool, even if the rental agent gives you a fixed or minimum annual fee. However, in a decision binding the IRS and the Tax Court only in Michigan, Ohio, Kentucky, and Tennessee, the Sixth Circuit Court of Appeals determined in 1996 that the total number of days that a unit is available in the rental pool counts as rental days, at least when fair rental value is received for the year.

TAX PLANNING IDEA Individuals with homes in seasonally desirable locations (such as Louisville during Derby Week or New Orleans during Marti Gras) should consider taking advantage of the tax-free windfall of legally putting cash in their pockets for up to 14 days' rent. Owners of beach homes or ski resort properties may fare best by renting their units for seven weekends and keeping the cash, especially in light of the IRS position that short-term rentals do not qualify for the $25,000/$12,500 exception to the passive loss rule for rental real estate.

CAUTION! Congress has periodically considered legislation which, if enacted, would end the 14-day rule, requiring property owners to account for income and expenses of all rentals irrespective of duration.

CONTROVERSY

The IRS takes the position that mortgage interest and property taxes are prorated between the rental activities and personal activities based on the number of days of each use. However, the courts have rejected the IRS approach, instead prorating just these two expenses based on the number of rental days and the number of other days in the year (reasoning that interest and property taxes accrue even when the property sits vacant). The effect is to increase the interest and property taxes allocable to the personal days and to decrease the interest and taxes chargeable to the rental days.

QUESTION: I own a beach house and rented it 160 days during the year. My family and I used the house for 20 days; it is vacant the remainder of the year. I received $16,000 in rent. The mortgage interest was $5,000, I paid $3,000 in property taxes, and my insurance and repair costs totaled $4,000. My depreciation allowance for the year based on the total cost of the structure itself (ignoring the land) would be $8,000. How is all of this handled on my tax return?

ANSWER: Since your personal use of the property (20 days) exceeds the ten percent of the number of days that the house is rented, you will not be able to claim a tax loss on the property. First, however, determine whether the position of the courts or the IRS position gives you a better result. Using the favored allocation method of the courts, limit your deductions chargeable to the rental activity by applying a fraction (160/365 to interest and property taxes and 160/180 to other expenses) to the whole amounts of the expenses as shown below:

	Rental Portion	Personal Portion
Mortgage Interest	$ 2,192	$2,808
Property Taxes	1,315	1,685
Insurance & Repairs	3,556	N/D
Depreciation	7,111	N/D
	$14,174	$4,493

Because the portion of the expenses attributable to the rental period is less than the $16,000 of rental income, all of the $14,174 in expenses will be deductible. The remaining property taxes and mortgage interest (if the interest is treated as qualified residence interest on a second home) will be used as itemized deductions.

Using the IRS method of allocating interest and taxes between rental portion and personal portion, interest and taxes charged to the rental days would be $4,444 and $2,667, respectively. Rental expenses would total $17,779; thus $1,779 of expenses would be disallowed with the depreciation deduction for the year reduced by that amount.

MAXIMIZE PASSIVE INCOME BY MAXIMIZING YOUR RENTAL RECEIPTS

Individuals with passive losses from nonrental activities or passive losses from rental activities in excess of the amount deductible to them, if any, need to try to generate passive income. One way to do this is to maximize rental income which is considered passive income against which passive losses can be offset. Review rental contracts to be certain that the rent being charged is the maximum that the market will bear.

CAUTION! When the landlord and tenant are related parties (such as an individual taxpayer leasing real estate to a family-owned corporation), special care should be taken. While you can increase rent (as long as it remains a fair amount) in order to wipe out losses, Treasury Regulations state that positive net income arising from a leasing arrangement to an entity in which the taxpayer materially participates will not generate passive income capable of offsetting passive losses from other activities.

TAX PLANNING IDEA If a property owner rents to his or her family-owned corporation, the owner should consider a rent increase within the limits of "fair rent" and a decrease in salary payments. This will save Social Security taxes if the decrease reduces the salary below the Social Security base of $65,400 (before 1998 increases for cost of living) and will help to reduce passive losses. Before taking this step, however, consider the impact on reduced retirement benefits.

QUESTION: I am leasing an office townhouse which I own personally to my professional corporation in which I conduct a psychiatric practice. The rental income pays the eight percent mortgage and other expenses associated with the property; however, I always end up with losses on the property each year on my tax return due to depreciation. I have no other passive activities, and I expect my income to be over $150,000. What should I be doing to avoid unusable losses?

ANSWER: Determine whether you are charging your professional corporation a below-market rent. If you are charging too little, raise the rent to avoid unusable passive losses. If you cannot avoid passive losses by raising the rent to the highest possible fair rental amount, you may wish to pay off a portion of the mortgage with available cash or by borrowing against your home. It makes little sense to have idle cash earning about four percent in a certificate of deposit and paying taxes on this income while you are carrying a mortgage of eight percent and not enjoying the deduction for the full mortgage interest.

FILING POINTER Can your sole proprietorship rent space from you personally? No, because your unincorporated business is your *alter ego*. However, on August 5, 1997, the Eighth Circuit Court of Appeals agreed with the Tax Court that a sole proprietorship can rent one-half of property owned jointly by the sole proprietor and his wife, allowing the couple to enjoy 50 percent of the advantages of rental property. Had the real estate been in the spouse's name alone, the Court would apparently have allowed the full tax benefit to the couple.

DEFERRING GAIN BY EXCHANGING PROPERTIES

A taxpayer who owns investment or business real property can exchange it for like-kind investment or business real property and the gain realized on the exchange (the difference between the value of the property received and the adjusted basis in the property exchanged) will not be recognized. Rather, the taxpayer's basis in the exchanged property will carry over and become the basis of the newly acquired property. If the taxpayer, in addition to receiving investment or business real property, receives personal property, cash, or other consideration, collectively referred to as "boot," the taxpayer's gain will be recognized to the extent of the value of the boot received. Deferred gain is taxed upon subsequent sale of the property received in the exchange.

A very simple tax-free exchange transaction involves two parties, each of whom owns a piece of real estate that the other party desires to acquire. The parties simply exchange the real estate and, if necessary, equalize the values by the addition of boot.

However, in everyday life it is quite unusual to find two parties who wish to acquire each other's property. The more likely transaction involves three or more parties. Assume Alex wants to dispose of Tara and wishes to acquire Twin Oaks, which is owned by Betty. Charles wishes to acquire Tara. In order to best effectuate a tax-free exchange, Alex will need Charles to purchase Twin Oaks from Betty and then swap Twin Oaks with Alex in exchange for Tara.

The law permits some delay in the exchange of properties so long as the property to be received in the exchange is identified within 45 days after the date on which the taxpayer transferred property. Additionally, the closing on the acquired property must take place within 180 days after the date of transfer or, if earlier, the due date of the return, including extensions, for the year of the transfer. This 45-day/180-day provision now permits taxpayers to contract for an exchange of properties without having a particular replacement property in mind and allows some flexibility with respect to the identification and closing on the new property. In order for the multiexchange situation to work, there must be contractual interdependence in the transactions.

Mortgages are a reality in today's real estate market. The existence of mortgaged property on either side of the exchange will have an impact on the tax-free nature of the exchange. If the other party to the exchange assumes a taxpayer's mortgage, this assumption is also considered boot and the taxpayer's gain will be recognized to the extent of this and any other boot. However, if the taxpayer receives property subject to a mortgage in the exchange or pays some cash for the new property, either will reduce or eliminate the taxpayer's gain recognition. In other words, any mortgage that is assumed or cash that is paid out will be netted against any mortgage of which the taxpayer is relieved. Only to the extent that a taxpayer is relieved of a mortgage greater than that which he or she assumes plus the cash that he or she pays will gain be recognized. Use IRS Form 8824 to report the exchange.

CAUTION!   If you exchange depreciable real estate in whole or in part for depreciable real estate, you will not be able to avoid all gain recognition. The depreciation recapture rules (see Chapter 5) override the general nonrecognition of gain rules in these situations.

QUESTION: I'm interested in this tax-free exchange. I own a rental property in Houston worth $250,000. I've found a buyer who is willing to assume my existing $50,000 mortgage and pay me $200,000 for the property. I'd like to buy another rental property in California. I've found a number of possibilities in the San Francisco area. What do I do next?

ANSWER: You should engage an attorney in Texas to draft the appropriate contract language to effectuate an exchange. You will have to determine which California property or properties you want within 45 days after you close on the Texas property, and you must close on the California property within 180 days after the Texas closing. Unless you assume a mortgage on the California property of at least $50,000 or pay at least $50,000 in cash (or a combination of the two), you will be required to report your gain to the extent of the $50,000 mortgage assumed by your buyer. Let's say the California property which you find is worth $300,000. You must necessarily assume a mortgage of $100,000 or pay cash of $100,000 (in addition to the $200,000 received from your buyer) or a combination of the two in order to equalize the equities of the two properties.

An independent escrow agent who is unrelated to you and has not served in a professional or agency role for you during the most recent two years would hold the $200,000 proceeds from the Texas property's closing and then use those funds pursuant to your written instruction to acquire the California property for you. Your access to the proceeds from the Texas property must be substantially limited in order to qualify for the tax-free exchange treatment. What will not work is for you to sell the Texas property in a conventional sales transaction and then take possession of and use the proceeds to reinvest in other property. The tax-free exchange treatment for investment or business property differs in this material respect from the deferral of gain rules on the sale of a principal residence.

DEFERRING GAIN FROM INVOLUNTARY CONVERSIONS

The law permits taxpayers whose property (business, investment, or personal) has been taken by the government or involuntarily converted (seizure or destruction, for example) to defer gain by using the condemnation or insurance proceeds to reinvest in property that is similar or related in service or use to the property which was condemned or otherwise destroyed. If all of the condemnation or insurance proceeds are reinvested within the replacement period, no gain will be recognized.

The replacement period generally ends two years after the close of the tax year in which the condemnation or other conversion occurred. The replacement period is extended an additional year for business or investment real estate which has been condemned and an additional two years for a principal residence which was involuntarily converted as the result of a disaster. (See Chapter 4 for the tax treatment of "disasters" and other casualties causing tax losses.)

The similar or related in service or use standard is a very strict test. A more lenient replacement test applies if the transaction involved is the condemnation of business or investment real estate. In these circumstances, the taxpayer can satisfy the law if mere like-kind property is the replacement. Under this latter test unimproved realty would qualify as an appropriate replacement for improved real estate. An even more lenient rule applies for business or investment property converted as the result of a disaster loss. It may be timely replaced by any tangible *business* property.

Where the converted property is rental property, the replacement property's use is viewed at the landlord level; so long as the landlord is providing similar services, the test will be satisfied. For example, the IRS has ruled that a landlord/investor can qualify for the deferral of gain on the conversion of warehouse property by using the conversion proceeds to build a gas station which would then be leased to an oil company.

In lieu of acquiring replacement real estate, an individual who has received conversion proceeds can acquire at least an 80 percent interest in a corporation owning the appropriate replacement property. However, if the individual is seeking to replace the real estate with like-kind property instead of property that is similar or related in service or use, then he or she must acquire the property directly. The individual cannot acquire an 80 percent interest in the corporation that owns real estate in order to satisfy the like-kind test.

CAUTION! The reinvested proceeds of any involuntary conversion must be used to acquire the replacement property from an unrelated person if the gain realized exceeds $100,000 or if the taxpayer is a C corporation (see Chapter 10) or a partnership with one or more C corporations owning more than one-half of the partnership interests.

FILING POINTER If a principal residence is condemned or otherwise involuntarily converted, the realized gain will usually not be recognized under the general $250,000/$500,000 exclusion applicable to sales of principal residences discussed earlier in this chapter. If the realized gain exceeds the amount of the available exclusion, gain recognition requires reinvestment of the conversion proceeds less the excluded gain.

QUESTION: I don't understand how I can have an income tax gain when my apartment building is destroyed by fire. Please explain.

ANSWER: It does seem unfair to tax you after such a catastrophe, but that's what will happen if you don't act. Here's the reason for the tax. Let's say you receive $200,000 from the insurance company but your basis in the building is $90,000. Because you received proceeds in excess of your basis, you have realized a gain. The gain of $110,000 can be deferred by timely purchasing (or reconstructing) a qualifying replacement property for at least $200,000. Note that, if your destroyed building were mortgaged and you received only your equity in cash from the insurance company, the mortgage amount plus the cash you receive is the amount that must be spent on the replacement property.

LOW-INCOME HOUSING—A HIGH-INCOME SHELTER

Although investing in low-income housing projects presents substantial economic risks, many individuals are interested in this type of investment since it is one area still offering some real tax breaks. Before investing in such projects, however, consider not only the tax ramifications but also the economic risks of the investments and the fact that you may not be able to receive your cash contributions back as a result of an inability to dispose of the property at an appreciated value.

Taxpayers who construct or substantially rehabilitate low-income housing are permitted to claim the low-income housing credit. In the case of nonsubsidized housing, the credit is an amount equal to 70 percent (91 percent in high cost areas) of the construction and rehabilitation costs. In the case of subsidized housing, the credit is an amount equal to 30 percent of the construction and rehabilitation costs.

This credit is claimed over a ten-year period of time, and the amount of the credit that can be claimed each year is determined by the IRS so that the present value of the ten credit amounts will equal the applicable percent of the qualified costs. For low-income housing projects placed in service during 1997, the maximum credit available in each of the ten years is approximately 8.5 percent for nonsubsidized housing and approximately 3.6 percent for subsidized housing. The actual percentage is tied to the month in which the project is opened.

To qualify for the credit, the acquisition or rehabilitation costs must involve low-income housing as determined under a complex definition.

Once an individual makes an investment in a low-income housing project and a credit is made available, it can only be used to offset the tax generated by the passive income and to provide a credit equivalent of the $25,000 deduction. If you are in the 28 percent tax bracket and have no passive income, this credit equivalent rule would allow you to claim up to a $7,000 low-income housing credit (28 percent multiplied by $25,000). The credit increases to a maximum of $9,900 in a 39.6 tax bracket. In other words, investors in low-income housing projects are in essence subject to the $25,000 rental real estate rule previously described.

Two important differences exist, however, for low-income housing project investors. First, there is no requirement that you actively participate in the low-income housing project in order to be eligible for the credit. Consequently, investors who are limited partners will still qualify for the low-income housing project credit. Second, the credit is available for all individuals irrespective of modified adjusted gross income.

For married individuals who live apart for the entire year and who file separately, the credit is an equivalent of the $12,500 deduction. Married individuals who file separately but who do not live apart for the entire year do not qualify for the credit equivalent of the $25,000/$12,500 deduction.

The amount of the credit, unlike the rehabilitation tax credit subsequently discussed, does not cause a reduction in the tax basis of the housing project. Consequently, the full cost of the building is eligible for depreciation. The building's basis will be depreciated on a straight-line basis (equal depreciation every 12 months) over 27½ years.

CAUTION!   If the project does not remain qualified as a low-income housing project for 15 years, then the low-income housing credit is subject to recapture. A sale of the project or of an interest in the project will also trigger a recapture of the credit unless the seller furnishes a bond to the IRS and it is reasonably expected that the project will continue to meet the definition of a low-income housing project.

TAX PLANNING IDEA   An additional benefit is provided for investors in low-income housing projects. If the project is sold in a qualified sale, the investor can elect to defer recognition of the gain realized on the disposition if he or she timely reinvests the sales proceeds in another low-income housing project. The reinvestment must occur within a two-year period beginning one year before the disposition.

To qualify for the deferral of gain on the sale of a low-income housing project, the project must be sold to the tenants of the project or to a cooperative or other tax-exempt organization established solely for the benefit of the tenants. In addition, the sale must be approved by the U.S. Department of Housing and Urban Development.

CAUTION!   Once again, this rule provides for the deferral of gain recognition and not for its exclusion from income. This deferral is accomplished by requiring the taxpayer to reduce his or her basis in the new project by the amount of the gain that is deferred, so that when the new project is sold, and no election is made to reinvest in another low-income housing project, the deferred gain is then taxed.

THE REHABILITATION TAX CREDIT FOR AGED AND HISTORIC BUILDINGS

Taxpayers who incur rehabilitation expenditures with respect to commercial buildings constructed before 1936 are eligible for a tax credit equal to ten percent of the rehabilitation costs. For those taxpayers who invest in certified historic structures (both commercial and residential rental), the credit amount will be 20 percent of the rehabilitation expenditures.

To qualify for the credit with respect to certified historic structures, all expenditures must be certified by the U.S. Department of the Interior as being in character with the property in the area in which the property is located. With respect to rehabilitations on any property not a certified historic structure, a taxpayer must:

1. Retain at least 50 percent of the existing external walls of the building as external walls;

2. Retain at least 75 percent of the existing external walls as either internal or external walls; and

3. Retain at least 75 percent of the internal structure framework of the building.

In addition, to qualify for the credit, a taxpayer must, during a 24-month period, make rehabilitation expenditures at least equal to his or her adjusted basis in the building (or $5,000, if that is greater). For example, if your adjusted basis in a building is $80,000, to qualify for the rehabilitation credit you must spend at least $80,000 to renovate the building while complying with the wall retention rules described above.

As with the low-income housing credit, the rehabilitation tax credit is subject to the rules on passive activities. But once again, Congress has provided a tax break for those investors who qualify for this credit. There is no requirement that the taxpayer actively participate in the management of the project. As a result, you can invest in the project as a limited partner and still qualify for the rehabilitation credit, the phaseout of the $25,000 equivalent does not begin until modified adjusted gross income exceeds $200,000, rather than at the general phase-out level of $100,000 applicable to rental losses. For a taxpayer with modified adjusted gross income between $200,000 and $250,000, the rehabilitation tax credit is phased out. A taxpayer with modified adjusted gross income in excess of $250,000 cannot use the rehabilitation tax credit.

Remember, the credit equivalent rule does not mean that you can offset $25,000 of tax. What it means is that you can offset your tax liability to the same extent that a $25,000 deduction would have reduced your tax liability. If you are in the 28 percent tax bracket, this means that you will be able to claim a tax credit equal to $7,000. If you are in the 31 percent tax bracket, the credit equivalent will be $7,750. In a 36 percent bracket, the credit equivalent rises to $9,000. For married individuals who live apart for the entire year and who file separately, the credit is an equivalent of the $12,500 deduction and the phaseout levels are one-half of the levels for other taxpayers. Married individuals who file separately but who do not live apart for the entire year do not qualify for the credit equivalent of the $25,000/ $12,500 deduction.

 CAUTION!   Unlike the low-income housing credit, the taxpayer is required to reduce basis in the rehabilitated building by the full amount of the tax credit claimed. For example, if you purchase a building which qualifies as a certified historic structure for $100,000 and spend $150,000 to renovate the structure, the rehabilitation credit for which you would be eligible is $30,000 (20% × $150,000). For the purpose of depreciation, your basis in the building would be $220,000 (the $100,000 cost of the building plus $150,000 in rehabilitation expenditures less the $30,000 rehabilitation tax credit), written off over the applicable recovery period depending upon whether it is used for residential rental or commercial purposes.

CAUTION!   If the building is sold within five years, a ratable portion of the rehabilitation tax credit is recaptured. There is no recapture of the credit after five years.

7

OTHER TAX-FAVORED INVESTMENTS

IS THE TAX SHELTER DEAD OR BREATHING?

It has been a dozen years since the Tax Reform Act of 1986 took away much of the desire and most of the means to shelter income. Given the Act's maximum effective individual tax bracket of 28 percent as of 1988, investors chose to pay taxes and keep 72 cents on the dollar rather than risk the full dollar on speculative sheltering investments. Additionally, the passive activity rules, discussed in Chapter 2, coupled with the existing basis rules and at risk rules, imposed additional obstacles.

The basis rules limit your ability to claim losses beyond your unreturned investment in a venture plus your share of the venture's liabilities if it is unincorporated. The at risk rules further limit your ability to claim losses to the extent that your "investment," irrespective of basis, is based on nonrecourse financing (that is, financing for which you are not personally liable). Your loss is limited to what you have put on the line. However, in the real estate field your at risk amount will include nonrecourse financing, so long as the financing was provided by a commercial lender. The passive activity rules generally limit your ability to shelter business and portfolio income with passive losses.

So what remains of tax shelters a dozen years after the Tax Reform Act of 1986?

The real estate lobby convinced Congress to retain some of the benefits of real estate investments and, as described in the preceding chapter, you will still be able to find a tax shelter by investing in a second home, rental real estate, low-income housing, or rehabilitation of older buildings or certified historic structures. Of course, your own primary residence is the best tax shelter.

Investing through an Individual Retirement Account or employer-sponsored retirement plan, discussed in Chapter 9, is an excellent way of sheltering income while securing your future.

Notwithstanding the Tax Reform Act of 1986, passive activities can still be tax-favored investments—if leveraging is eliminated or reduced or if investments producing passive losses are coupled with those producing passive income. Additionally, oil and gas, insurance, and annuity investments continue to be tax-favored.

The Revenue Reconciliation Act of 1993, with its maximum marginal individual tax bracket of 39.6 percent, has rekindled the desire to shelter income. Despite its expressed purpose of deficit reduction, the Act created two new significant tax favored investments, small business stock and empowerment zones.

QUESTION: My investment in a video store is $5,000. The remainder of the capital for the business was made available to me by a financial institution. I've signed a commercial note which my attorney tells me is a nonrecourse note in the amount of $20,000. I work every day in the store. Am I limited in the losses I can deduct?

ANSWER: Yes. You may claim deductions with respect to the video operations beyond the income generated by the venture only to the extent of $5,000. If you are personally liable on the bank loan, your initial at risk amount would be $25,000.

Any net loss for which a deduction is denied under these at risk rules may be deducted in a subsequent year during which the business venture produces income or additional contributions of capital are made by you.

REDUCE LEVERAGED INVESTMENTS

The old rule of thumb with respect to passive activities was leverage the deal to the greatest extent possible. In other words, make your investment with as much borrowed money as possible. There were two advantages to the leveraged passive activity. First, the investor could obtain significant write-offs with minimal cash on his or her part. Second, the interest paid on the borrowed funds was fully deductible by the investor so that the cost of the mortgage money was significantly reduced.

As a result of the institution of the passive loss rules, the rule of thumb is to minimize leverage in a passive activity so that it at least breaks even from a tax point of view. When the activity produces write-offs such as depreciation in the case of real estate or depletion in the case of natural resources that don't require a cash expenditure, the activity may generate positive cash flow.

ILLUSTRATION

The cost of a small apartment building is $200,000 of which $140,000 is allocable to the building. You put up $75,000 and finance the rest over 30 years at ten percent. Projections for the property indicate that you can expect to receive $21,500 in income. Real estate taxes and insurance could run $4,000. Your annual mortgage payment will be just over $13,000. Here are the specifics for the first year:

$21,500	Rent		$21,500	Rent
(3,000)	Taxes		(3,000)	Taxes
(1,000)	Insurance		(1,000)	Insurance
(13,164)	Principal & Interest Payments		(12,469)	Interest Payments
			(4,879)	Depreciation
$ 4,336	Cash Flow		$ 152	Passive Income

As the illustration reveals, this investment would produce an annual positive cash flow, of which virtually all is sheltered for tax purposes.

FILING POINTER   If you presently have highly leveraged passive activities generating unusable passive losses, curtail the debt with any available cash. Not only do you reduce or eliminate passive losses, but also in many cases you rid yourself of debt typically at a higher interest rate than the rate of earnings on your idle money.

PIGS—PASSIVE INCOME GENERATORS

If you have existing passive activities generating unusable losses, rather than curtail existing debt, you can buy a PIG—a passive income generator. A PIG is designed to give you the passive income to use existing passive losses. You may buy a PIG, often through an "all cash" deal, or an existing investment may become a PIG.

If you invested in a tax shelter some years ago, you may find yourself holding what is often known as a burned-out shelter. A burned-out shelter is one that produced tax write-offs in its early years of operation but these write-offs diminished over the years and the investment is now producing taxable income. If the shelter is not making cash distributions, the investors find themselves with increased taxable income resulting from their investment in the shelter but no cash distributions. This kind of taxable income is known as phantom income because the investor has no cash in his or her pocket to go along with the increase in income.

TAX PLANNING IDEA   Certainly being in a position of an investor with phantom income is not good. However, the phantom income investment will likely be a PIG, allowing use of passive losses.

Your PIG will be fatter, however, if your gain on disposition of a passive activity is accompanied by receipt of cash. For example, if you have unusable passive losses, you can create a PIG by selling a rental property at a gain on an installment basis if sufficient principal can be collected each year. Rather than amortizing the obligation, consider having the purchaser curtail equal amounts of principal each year while paying interest on the unpaid balance. This creates more passive income and less portfolio income in the early years.

CAUTION!   If you buy a PIG, don't work it more than 100 hours per year. Income otherwise passive in nature will be recharacterized as nonpassive under the significant participation activity regulations to prevent individuals from structuring activities in such a way as to generate passive income in order to shelter passive losses from other activities.

A significant participation activity is one in which an individual taxpayer is involved for more than 100 hours per year but in which he or she does not materially participate. (See Chapter 2 for a discussion of material participation.) If an individual engages in significant participation activities during the year and the gross income from these activities exceeds the deductions from these activities, then Treasury Regulations will treat the net income as income from a nonpassive activity. The result of this recharacterization is that an individual has less passive income against which to offset passive losses.

QUESTION: A friend of mine told me that he's been able to use something called a "master limited partnership" as a tax shelter. What is a master limited partnership? How does it work?

ANSWER: A master limited partnership (MLP), also known as a publicly traded partnership, is an unincorporated entity offered on a public exchange or a secondary market which is generally designed to distribute significant tax-free return of capital and long-term capital gain along with ordinary income. Such interests are much more marketable (and potentially more liquid) than in the case of other partnerships. MLPs have been instituted in all sorts of businesses. You can even buy an interest in the Boston Celtics pro basketball team through an MLP.

Master limited partnerships formed after December 17, 1987 are generally taxed as corporations. Thus, income and loss will not pass through to the partners. However, partnership treatment will apply if 90 percent or more of the MLP's gross income is from interest, dividends, real estate rents, gains from the sale of capital assets, income or gains from certain oil and gas activities, and gains from the sale of certain business assets. The MLP must have met this passive income requirement for each year after 1987. In any event, corporate tax treatment will not apply until 1998 to any MLP publicly traded on December 17, 1987 (or any MLP which filed either a registration statement with the SEC or certain agreements with a state regulatory commission by December 17, 1987).

Under special rules, a partner's share of net business income from an MLP treated as a partnership cannot be used to offset losses from other MLPs or other passive loss activities. A partner's share of loss from such an MLP is suspended and carried forward until the MLP generates net business income. The MLP loss may not be used against passive income from any other MLP or passive business interest. Suspended losses not offset by future net business income are deductible when the partner completely disposes of the MLP interest. (See Chapter 2 for a discussion of suspended losses from passive activities.) In any event partners in an MLP taxed as a partnership may claim tax credits for rehabilitation expenses and low income housing expenses in each case up to the $25,000/$12,500 deduction equivalent (discussed in Chapter 6).

THE BENEFITS OF OIL AND GAS INVESTMENTS

If you are willing to assume some risk with respect to investments in the oil and gas industry, consider investing in a working interest in an oil and gas property as other than a limited partner or shareholder in a corporation. Working interests in oil and gas properties are excluded from the definition of a passive activity so long as the investor's liability in the working interest is not limited.

Although most investments in the oil and gas field were previously structured as limited partnerships, many deals are now being structured as general partnerships in which the investor becomes a general partner. Since there is no material participation requirement for such working interests, meaning the investor need not be involved in the management of the property, the losses generated by the partnership will flow through to the investor general partner and be deductible on his or her personal return subject only to the at risk rules. However, as a general partner the investor would be individually liable for the partnership's debts, even if they exceed the amount of investment, so there is a significant degree of risk in this kind of deal.

QUESTION: What sort of write-offs are available if I buy a working interest?

ANSWER: Investment in the oil and gas industry can provide an immediate write-off of intangible drilling costs, should the partnership elect to expense rather than capitalize these costs. If the partnership elects to capitalize the costs, then they are recovered through depletion and depreciation. More than likely, however, the partnership will elect to expense the intangible drilling costs and then each partner can elect to either expense his or her proportionate share of the intangible drilling costs personally or amortize them over a ten-year period of time. If the partner elects to expense the intangible drilling costs, to the extent that they would be considered excess intangible drilling costs, they are a tax preference item, and the alternative minimum tax may be triggered. Excess intangible drilling costs are those costs incurred in drilling productive wells, which exceed the amount of the deduction for the intangible drilling costs, had the taxpayer elected to amortize them over a ten-year period of time.

Depletion is the second incentive attracting investors to the oil and gas industry. The depletion deduction allows the investor who has purchased an interest in a producing well to shelter the cash distributions. This deduction is either computed on a cost basis or a percentage basis.

Cost depletion allows the investor to deduct each year a ratable portion of his or her cost basis in the producing well, determined by the number of barrels of oil sold, until the basis is fully recovered. Percentage depletion allows annual write-offs generally of 15 percent of the gross income derived from the property and continues to be available to the taxpayer even though the basis in the producing well has been recovered. However, to the extent that the taxpayer's percentage depletion deduction exceeds his or her basis in the well, the depletion allowance will be a tax preference item which may trigger application of the alternative minimum tax.

INSURING YOUR FUTURE

Now more than ever, the key to your investments should be the economic return available to you and not the tax benefits derived from the investments since, in most cases outside of the real estate area, there will be little or no tax benefits available. Life insurance is an investment that continues to receive favorable tax treatment although it produces no write-offs or tax credits.

Investing in whole life insurance or universal life insurance allows you to obtain both life insurance protection and a savings vehicle. The savings vehicle in the life insurance contract, the cash surrender value, accumulates tax-free until the policy is surrendered. If the policy is never surrendered but the insurance company pays the death benefits to the beneficiary, the payout will generally be tax-free.

QUESTION: Is my understanding of life insurance products correct? I can pay my premiums under the contract, have the premiums accumulate in value tax-free, and get my money back tax-free.

ANSWER: Your understanding is basically correct; however, the definition of a life insurance contract has been more strictly written than was the case in the past. For life insurance contracts entered into after June 20, 1988, if the contract does not meet a strict definition, then withdrawals from the contract's cash surrender value and loans against the policy will be taxable to you as income. Only if withdrawals and loans exceed the earnings under the contract would they be tax-free. All taxable amounts received under the contract prior to death would be subject to a ten percent penalty unless received after you reached age 59½, became disabled, or the distribution was one of a series of payments to be paid each year over your life expectancy.

A contract will not meet the new strict definition of a life insurance contract if, at any time during the policy's first seven years, the cumulative amount paid under the contract is greater than the net level premiums that would have been paid prior to that time if the contract had provided for paid-up future benefits at the end of seven years. This revised definition hurts those life insurance products that were designed and purchased primarily as investment vehicles rather than for life insurance protection.

◈ **CAUTION!**   Future tax legislation may bring about a change, even an end, to the general tax-free "inside build-up" of life insurance contracts. See Chapter 2 as to the tax-free surrender by terminally ill individuals of all or portions of life insurance contracts without causing income tax liability.

ANNUITIES AS INVESTMENTS

Commercial annuity contracts are another investment enjoying tax-favored treatment. You purchase the annuity contract either in a lump sum or over a period of time. The contract will then provide you with a fixed payment at a specified age (for example, beginning at age 65). As with life insurance contracts, the earnings generated by the annuity contract build up tax-free. Only when the annuitant begins receiving distributions from the contract will taxes be due.

Payment under an annuity contract will be subject to a ten percent penalty on the taxable portion if made prior to age 59½ unless the payment is on account of disability or is one of a series to be paid over the life expectancy of the recipient. If you borrow from the annuity contract, the loan amount will be considered a taxable cash withdrawal, to the extent of the interest buildup, and will be subject to the ten percent penalty rule. If the loan exceeds the interest buildup, then this excess is a tax-free recovery of your investment.

Once you begin receiving the annuity, a portion of each payment will be tax-free to allow you to recover your investment in the contract. Once your investment in the contract has been recovered, then the entire annuity payment will be taxable as ordinary income.

A private annuity is simply an individual's promise to pay a fixed amount to another (the annuitant) for life in return for the annuitant's transfer of property or cash to the person paying the annuity. The tax rules governing the taxation of a private annuity are somewhat different from those governing a commercial annuity where there has been a transfer of property (as opposed to cash) to purchase the annuity. The annuitant will be deemed to have sold the property in exchange for the private annuity so that the annuity payment will consist of three elements: the recovery of basis in the property, the gain element, and the annuity element.

As with a commercial annuity, a portion of the private annuity payment will be tax-free until the basis in the transferred property has been recovered. The gain portion of the annuity is determined by subtracting the basis of the property from the present value of the annuity, using insurance tables. If the present value of the annuity is less than the value of the property, the excess will be considered a gift by the annuitant to the person paying the annuity, and compliance with the federal gift tax laws will be required.

QUESTION: I am 69 years old and I want to sell my business to my son. He has offered to pay me over ten years. The sales proceeds and my Social Security will be my only retirement income. I am scared about how I will live when my son has finished paying for my business. Can I sell my business to him and receive an annuity instead of payments for a fixed time period?

ANSWER: Yes, you can sell your business and take back an annuity. However, depending on how many years you live, your son may pay for your business a couple of times over or he could get a "windfall."

SMALL BUSINESS STOCK—EXCLUDE ONE-HALF OF YOUR GAIN

Individuals investing in certain C corporations (see Chapter 10) after August 10, 1993 and holding on to their Section 1202 small business stock for more than five years will ultimately be able to exclude one-half of their gain from income. Consequently, in late 1998 when the exclusion will first apply to stock acquired in late 1993, your gain on sale of your stock will be taxed at no more than 14 percent in that small business stock has a maximum 28 percent rate and not the general 20 percent rate on the capital gain which is not excluded (see Chapter 5).

Your excludable gain is limited to the greater of ten times your basis in the stock or $10 million. Forty-two percent of your excluded gain is a tax preference item for alternative minimum tax purposes. See Chapter 1 for a discussion of the AMT.

Your stock must be of original issue by the corporation, whether acquired for cash, property, or services. If acquired for services, the five-year holding period commences when you report income on receipt of the stock. (See Chapter 2 for a discussion of stock received for services.) The corporation must not be engaged in certain activities, including professional services, financial and brokerage services, consulting, or any other business where the "principal asset" is the reputation or skill of one or more employees.

The issuing corporation must not have a basis of more than $50 million in its assets; neither real property nor portfolio securities may constitute more than ten percent of assets. During the five-year period, the corporation must use at least 80 percent (by value) of its assets in the active conduct of a business.

QUESTION: I am a general partner in a family partnership which has a number of investments, mostly in publicly traded stocks. Can the partnership invest in small business stock? If I make an additional investment personally, can I give it to my children during the five-year holding period?

ANSWER: Yes, partnerships and S corporations (see Chapter 9) can invest in a qualifying corporation; a partner or shareholder must hold his or her interest in the entity during the entire investment period in order to share in the exclusion of one-half of the gain. A recipient of a gift or inheritance of small business stock gets to add the time the stock was held by a transferor to his or her own holding period in order to determine whether the five-year requirement has been met.

 TAX PLANNING IDEA   If you sell small business stock which you owned for more than six months, you have a 60-day period thereafter in which to reinvest at least as much as the sales price in order to avoid gain recognition. If you acquire new small business stock for less than the sales price but for more than the basis of the stock (see Chapter 5), you will avoid recognition of a portion of the gain. Any gain not recognized is deferred until sale of the replacement stock.

CAUTION!   No deferral of gain is available for sales of small business stock before August 6, 1997.

CAUTION!   The term "small business stock" is also utilized as another name for Section 1244 stock, discussed in Chapter 5. Section 1244 small business stock is eligible for ordinary loss treatment upon its worthlessness or sale at a loss. However, the criteria for small business stock under Section 1244 are significantly different than the criteria for exclusion of gain under Section 1202.

INVESTMENTS IN SELECT LOCALITIES—EMPOWERED WITH TAX ADVANTAGES

Businesses that operate in certain designated areas of the country qualify for certain tax breaks. The first $15,000 of wages paid to a resident of a designated empowerment zone who also works in the empowerment zone will qualify the employer for a 20 percent tax credit.

Additionally, an empowerment zone business can write off up to $37,500 per year of the cost of tangible personal property purchased for use in the business. As discussed in Chapter 10, other businesses are limited to $17,500 per year. The phaseout of the ability to expense this tangible personal property at $200,000 of qualifying purchases is computed by counting only one-half of the cost of such property used in the empowerment zone.

QUESTION: What is an empowerment zone?

ANSWER: The Secretary of Housing and Urban Development and the Secretary of Agriculture have designated certain urban and rural areas of the country as empowerment zones. These designated areas meet certain statutorily prescribed criteria, including size, population, and poverty level. State and local governments assist in the development of empowerment zones by providing funding for businesses. The interest from bonds, the proceeds of which are invested in businesses located in empowerment zones, are exempt from federal income tax.

 FILING POINTER   Did you ever want to live in the nation's capital? The Taxpayer Relief Act of 1997 created many tax benefits for the District of Columbia empowerment zone, provides a tax credit for "first-time homebuyers" of $5,000 upon purchase of a princial residence anywhere in the city. A "first-time homebuyer" is defined as an individual or, if married, a couple who has not owned another principal residence in the District of Columbia during the year leading up to the date of contract or construction. The credit is phased out at modified adjusted gross income levels of between $110,000 and $130,000 for married couples and $70,000 and $90,000 for single individuals. Reduce your tax basis by the amount of the credit. Any unused credit carries forward indefinitely.

CAUTION!   The D.C. Homebuyer Credit was not available for purchases before August 6, 1997 and expires at the end of 2000.

8

MARRIAGE—AND DIVORCE

PLANNING YOUR WEDDING—DON'T FORGET TAXES

When two working people marry, they usually discover that they will pay more taxes as husband and wife than they did as two single individuals. Many of these couples marry in December, causing them to be treated for tax purposes as married for the entire year. By waiting a few weeks until January, they might have saved enough in taxes to pay for their honeymoon.

QUESTION: John and I are planning a holiday wedding. For the year coming to an end, John has income from wages and interest in the amount of $60,000. He has itemized deductions of $16,000. I have income from wages and interest of $22,000. My itemized deductions of $1,500 are insufficient to itemize. Should we get married in December or wait a few weeks?

ANSWER: You will save at least $543 by putting off the wedding until January. Or schedule a New Year's Eve bash but recite your vows after midnight.

Computations below do not reflect the scheduled indexing of brackets, the standard deduction, and the personal exemption for 1998.

	John	Mary
Wages and Interest	$60,000	$22,000
Itemized/Standard Deduction	(16,000)	(4,000)
Exemptions	(2,650)	(2,650)
Taxable Income	$41,350	$15,350
Tax	$ 8,374	$ 2,303
Total Tax as Single Individuals		$10,677

	John and Mary
Wages and Interest	$82,000
Itemized Deductions	(17,500)
Exemptions	(5,300)
Taxable Income	$59,200
Tax as a Married Couple	$11,220

YEAR-END REMINDER   Couples planning to marry should typically wed before year-end if either of the couple has little or no income but are typically better off waiting until next year if both have a high income. The table below illustrates the "marriage tax penalty" for two high income individuals and the equally significant disadvantage of being unmarried when one-half of a couple has little or no income. It is based on adjusted gross income and assumes no dependents, itemized deductions of 15 percent of AGI, and no other tax benefits limited as a result of income level. Computations do not reflect the scheduled indexing for inflation of the lowest three tax brackets, the standard deduction, and the personal exemption for 1998.

Individual 1 Income	Tax as Single	Individual 2 Income	Tax as Single	Tax as Married Filing Jointly	Marriage Penalty (-) or Bonus (+)
$ 0	$ 0	$ 50,000	$ 7,954	$ 5,580	+$2,374
$ 0	$ 0	$ 25,000	$ 2,730	$ 1,920	+$ 810
$ 15,000	$ 1,230	$ 25,000	$ 2,730	$ 4,170	- $ 210
$ 25,000	$ 2,730	$ 50,000	$ 7,954	$11,010	- $ 326
$ 50,000	$ 7,954	$ 50,000	$ 7,954	$16,960	- $1,052
$ 75,000	$13,945	$ 50,000	$ 7,954	$22,986	- $1,087
$ 75,000	$13,945	$ 75,000	$13,945	$29,806	- $1,916
$100,000	$20,625	$ 75,000	$13,945	$36,626	- $2,056
$100,000	$20,625	$100,000	$20,625	$44,517	- $3,267

THE FILING STATUS TRAP UPON SEPARATION

If a marriage sours and there are children involved, the custodial parent (this means the spouse with primary actual custody when there is legal joint custody) becomes eligible to file as head of household prior to divorce or legal separation under a decree of separate maintenance. However, the noncustodial parent is forced into utilizing the highest tax brackets for individuals—those for married individuals filing separately. (See Chapter 1 for a detailed discussion of filing status alternatives.)

QUESTION: My wife, Jane, and I separated in June 1997, and Jane has custody of our four-year-old daughter. What are the alternatives concerning our filing status for 1997?

ANSWER: Under a special rule, Jane will be considered as unmarried and eligible for head of household status since you were not a member of her household for the last six months of the year, provided the household is the principal residence of your daughter (irrespective of whether Jane claims the dependency exemption or passes it to you). In contrast, unless you can persuade Jane to file a joint tax return, you will be forced to file as married filing separate until such time as your divorce is final or there is a legal decree of separate maintenance (a court decreed separation—not just a signed separation agreement between the parties).

You should negotiate with Jane to get her consent to a joint return. She may require that the tax liability be divided in a way that she pays nothing more than what she would have paid filing as head of household. You should still come out ahead despite this guarantee; the premium that you would have to pay Jane will probably be made up by retention of lower marginal tax brackets. To illustrate, in 1997 the 28 percent tax bracket for married individuals filing jointly begins at $41,200 of taxable income while the 28 percent tax bracket for married individuals filing separately begins at $20,600 of taxable income. The 31 percent marginal tax bracket for married couples filing jointly begins at $99,600 of taxable income, while it begins at $49,800 for married individuals filing separately.

The higher marginal tax brackets of 36 and 39.6 percent begin at $151,750 and $271,050 of taxable income respectively for married couples filing jointly but, as in the case of all tax brackets, begin at one-half of these amounts for married individuals filing separately.

CAUTION!   Because the IRS can collect from whichever individual it chooses on a joint return, as a divorcing individual with little or no separate tax liability, you should not sign a joint return if your spouse is insolvent, is fiscally irresponsible, or is unwilling to give you the return to mail with a certified check attached for any unpaid tax liability. In any event, you should obtain written indemnification from your spouse against liability arising from his or her unstated income or overstated deductions although the indemnification is not binding on the IRS.

Unfortunately, if you sign a joint return, the IRS can come after you for many years—first with a tax deficiency and then with the bill for you to pay. If you failed to inform the IRS of your last known address, you may have to pay first and then contest the liability if you can. (See Chapter 13 for a discussion of these other procedural topics.)

In a 1994 case, the Tax Court was unsympathetic to an abused ex-wife's claim that her signature on two joint returns during their marriage was provided under duress. Despite testimony that she was verbally and physically abused, the former wife was found liable for more than $1 million in taxes arising out of a financial scam. The Court ruled that the taxpayer failed to prove that she was under duress at the precise time when the tax return was signed and that she would not have otherwise signed the return. On a couple occasions, most recently in a January 14, 1997 decision, the Tax Court determined that a former spouse "intended" to file a joint return and allowed the other spouse the benefit of the joint filing.

Pursuant to the Taxpayer Bill of Rights-2 (see Chapter 13), the Government is studying proposals to further limit a spouse's liability on a joint return in certain circumstances.

FILING POINTER   The *"innocent spouse"* rule, under which the IRS would not hold you responsible for a tax deficiency arising from your spouse's errors on a joint return, may apply. Unfortunately, this relief statute is narrow in scope. You must not have had any reason to know of the errors and must show that it would be inequitable to hold you liable. The additional tax liability must exceed $500 and, in the case of overstated deductions, must exceed 25 percent of your adjusted gross income (ten percent if your AGI was $20,000 or less) for the year immediately prior to the issuance of a statutory notice of deficiency by the IRS. If you've remarried, you get hurt a second time. Your AGI includes the income of your spouse. In 1996 the Ninth Circuit Court of Appeals ruled that the innocent spouse rule is not to be applied in an all or nothing manner—partial relief is available.

FILING POINTER If you feel that you're an innocent spouse because your husband or wife agreed to indemnify you against tax liability on a joint return but you didn't meet the standard for being off the hook with the IRS, there may be added hope for recovery. In 1995, the U.S. Supreme Court declined to hear an appeal from a decision of the Fourth Circuit Court of Appeals holding that a spouse's indemnification to the other spouse is not dischargeable in bankruptcy.

SEPARATION AND THE DEPENDENCY ALLOWANCE

A controversial issue over the years has involved the question of who gets to claim the children as dependents on a separate return. Given that personal exemptions may be utilized in full without phase-out by individuals in some cases with marginal tax brackets as high as 36 percent, an exemption in 1998 may itself be worth as much as $954 (even prior to that year's indexing for inflation) irrespective of any state tax savings. Add the child credit of $400 in 1998 or $500 thereafter or an educational tax credit if you are eligible (see Chapter 3). The right to claim a child as a dependent, from birth through college years, can be worth over $30,000 in tax savings. For that reason, dependency allowances are usually an issue in negotiating a separation agreement.

Present law awards the exemptions automatically to the custodial parent (again, that parent who has actual custody of the child for the greater part of the year) unless the custodial parent releases the right to claim the benefit. This release can be claimed by having the custodial parent sign IRS Form 8332 on an annual basis, an indefinite basis, or for a specific number of years. The noncustodial parent attaches Form 8332 to his or her tax return.

TAX PLANNING IDEA Noncustodial parents are well-advised to have a specific provision placed in the separation agreement requiring the custodial parent to execute Form 8332 or, even better, get the Form signed with the separation agreement. The Tax Court ruled in 1995 that a noncustodial parent can't claim the exemption without an executed Form 8332 even if the custodial parent signed an agreement or is under court order to pass the exemption on to the noncustodial parent.

CAUTION! The passing of one or more exemptions to the noncustodial parent can be agreed by the parties; however, a state court can probably not require a custodial parent to waive the right to claim a child as a dependent inasmuch as federal law overrides conflicting state law. However, the Maryland legislature in its 1994 session considered (but tabled) a bill which would have required a custodial parent in most cases to waive the exemption in favor of a noncustodial parent providing a majority of the support.

Form 8332. Release of Claim to Exemption for Child of Divorced or Separated Parents.

Form **8332** (Rev. June 1996) Department of the Treasury Internal Revenue Service	**Release of Claim to Exemption for Child of Divorced or Separated Parents** ▶ **ATTACH** to noncustodial parent's return **EACH YEAR** exemption claimed.	OMB No. 1545-0915 Attachment Sequence No. **51**

Name(s) of parent claiming exemption	**Social security number**

Part I   **Release of Claim to Exemption for Current Year**

I agree not to claim an exemption for_____

Name(s) of child (or children)

for the tax year 19_____ .

Signature of parent releasing claim to exemption	Social security number	Date

If you choose not to claim an exemption for this child (or children) for future tax years, complete Part II.

Part II   **Release of Claim to Exemption for Future Years** *(If completed, see **Noncustodial Parent** below.)*

I agree not to claim an exemption for_____

Name(s) of child (or children)

for the tax year(s)_____ .

(Specify. See instructions.)

Signature of parent releasing claim to exemption	Social security number	Date

General Instructions

Paperwork Reduction Act Notice.– We ask for the information on this form to carry out the Internal Revenue laws of the United States. We need it to ensure that you are complying with these laws and to allow us to figure and collect the right amount of tax.

You are not required to provide the information requested on a form that is subject to the Paperwork Reduction Act unless the form displays a valid OMB control number. Books or records relating to a form or its instructions must be retained as long as their contents may become material in the administration of any Internal Revenue law. Generally, tax returns and return information are confidential, as required by Internal Revenue Code section 6103.

The time needed to complete and file this form will vary depending on individual circumstances. The estimated average time is: **Recordkeeping**, 7 min.; **Learning about the law or the form**, 5 min.; **Preparing the form**, 7 min.; and **Copying, assembling, and sending the form to the IRS**, 14 min.

If you have comments concerning the accuracy of these time estimates or suggestions for making this form simpler, we would be happy to hear from you. See the instructions for the tax return with which this form is filed.

Purpose of Form.– If you are a **custodial parent**, you may use this form to release your claim to your child's exemption. To do so, complete this form and give it to the **noncustodial parent** who will claim the child's exemption. Then, the noncustodial parent must attach this form or a similar statement to his or her tax return EACH YEAR the exemption is claimed.

You are the **custodial parent** if you had custody of the child for most of the year. You are the **noncustodial parent** if you had custody for a shorter period of time or did not have custody at all.

Instead of using this form, you (the custodial parent) may use a similar statement as long as it contains the same information required by this form.

Children of Divorced or Separated Parents.– Special rules apply to determine if the support test is met for children of parents who are divorced or legally separated under a decree of divorce or separate maintenance or separated under a written separation agreement. The rules also apply to children of parents who did not live together at any time during the last 6 months of the year, even if they do not have a separation agreement.

The general rule is that the custodial parent is treated as having provided over half of the child's support if:

1. The child received over half of his or her total support for the year from both of the parents, **AND**

2. The child was in the custody of one or both of his or her parents for more than half of the year.

Note: *Public assistance payments, such as Aid to Families with Dependent Children, are not support provided by the parents.*

If both **1** and **2** above apply, and the other four dependency tests in your tax return instruction booklet are also met, the custodial parent can claim the child's exemption.

Exception. The general rule does not apply if **any** of the following apply:

● The custodial parent agrees not to claim the child's exemption by signing this form or similar statement. The noncustodial parent **must** attach this form or similar statement to

his or her tax return for the tax year. See **Custodial Parent** later.

● The child is treated as having received over half of his or her total support from a person under a multiple support agreement (**Form 2120**, Multiple Support Declaration).

● A pre-1985 divorce decree or written separation agreement states that the noncustodial parent can claim the child as a dependent. But the noncustodial parent must provide at least $600 for the child's support during the year. This rule does not apply if the decree or agreement was changed after 1984 to say that the noncustodial parent cannot claim the child as a dependent.

Additional Information.– For more details, get **Pub. 504**, Divorced or Separated Individuals.

Specific Instructions

Custodial Parent.– You may agree to release your claim to the child's exemption for the current tax year or for future years, or both.

● Complete **Part I** if you agree to release your claim to the child's exemption for the current tax year.

● Complete **Part II** if you agree to release your claim to the child's exemption for any or all future years. If you do, write the specific future year(s) or "all future years" in the space provided in Part II.

Noncustodial Parent.– Attach Form 8332 or similar statement to your tax return for the tax year in which you claim the child's exemption. You may claim the exemption **only** if the other four dependency tests in your tax return instruction booklet are met.

Note: *If the custodial parent completed Part II, you **must** attach a copy of this form to your tax return for each future year in which you claim the exemption.*

CAUTION!   Pre-1985 instruments are governed by prior law, allowing the exemption to the non-custodial parent when authorized in the instrument and where the noncustodial parent provides at least $600 per year in child support.

CAUTION!   In a May 13, 1997 decision the Tax Court determined that the general rule giving the dependency allowance to the custodial parent in the absence of a waiver is not applicable in the year of separation when the separation occurs in the second half of the year and there is no divorce or court decreed separation by year-end. Rather, the dependency allowance goes to the spouse providing majority support of the dependent. See the discussion on court decreed separations later in this chapter.

TAX PLANNING IDEA   As discussed in Chapters 1 and 3, personal exemptions, the child credit, and educational credits are phased out and become unavailable for high-income individuals. If one parent may have adjusted gross income over the level where the benefits would be unavailable, it may be advisable to provide in the separation agreement for transfer of the benefits to the parent who will be able to utilize them.

SEPARATION AND CREDIT FOR TAX PREPAYMENTS

With the filing of a separate return for the first time following marital separation, along with the issue of who gets to claim the children as dependents, there may be a short-term larger issue of who gets credit for tax prepayments.

Prepayments take one of three forms:

1. Withholding at the source (generally on wages);
2. Application of a prior year's tax refund to estimated taxes; and
3. Other estimated tax payments.

Withholding is credited to the spouse who earned the underlying income, equally in community property states (see Chapter 1) where the spouses each report 50 percent of the income. While estimated taxes caused by application of a prior year's separate tax refund or by payment with one name on the voucher are credited solely to that individual, it is unclear who receives the credit on the separate return for these tax prepayments when they arise by application of a prior year's joint tax refund or by payment with both names on the voucher.

CONTROVERSY

The IRS position is that, in the absence of an agreement between the spouses, estimated taxes are credited based on their proportionate tax liabilities. However, the courts have tended to look to the source of the funds, i.e., whose prior year's income and payments caused the prior year's tax refund and whose money was paid in with the joint voucher? These questions raise additional issues as to the ownership of cash, and ownership issues are generally determined by state law. In a May 2, 1997 decision, the Ninth Circuit Court of Appeals ruled that ownership of estimated taxes under state law may require examination of a prenuptial agreement.

PLANNING YOUR DIVORCE—MORE TAX CONSIDERATIONS

The timing of a divorce has tax considerations similar to the timing of a marriage.

QUESTION: My wife, Paula, and I will soon be divorcing but, if advisable, we can finalize the divorce after year-end. Paula has been a housewife and has had no income of her own while raising our two young children. My income, exclusively from wages, is $80,000. Our itemized deductions, all belonging to me or paid by me, are $11,000. Should the divorce become final this year or next?

ANSWER: Look at the numbers and you see a tax savings of more than $2,900 by waiting until after year-end.

	As Married Filing Jointly	As Single
Wages	$80,000	$80,000
Itemized Deductions	(11,000)	(11,000)
Exemptions	(10,600)	(7,950)
Taxable Income	$58,400	$61,050
Tax After Credit of $400 per Child	$10,196	$13,129

These computations do not reflect the scheduled indexing of brackets, the standard deduction, and the personal exemptions for 1998. It is also assumed that the separation agreement gives the dependency allowances for the children to you.

More than $2,900 is saved by delaying the divorce until after December 31. In the succeeding year, your increased tax liability may be mitigated if you are required to make deductible alimony payments to Paula.

YEAR-END REMINDER When a marriage is terminating, the timing of the divorce or court decreed separation needed to be unmarried for tax purposes is flexible in light of the local court calendar, and both spouses have significant income, it is usually best to be unmarried before year-end. However, when one spouse has little or no income, it is usually best (from a tax perspective) to delay divorce or court decreed separation until after year-end.

CAUTION! A court decreed separation has different meanings in different states. In any event, the mere signing of a separation agreement does not make a couple unmarried in and of itself.

MAXIMIZING THE ALIMONY DEDUCTION

Alimony constitutes income to the recipient and is deductible to the payor irrespective of whether the payor itemizes. Alimony means any payment in cash if:

1. The payment is received by or on behalf of a spouse under a divorce or separation instrument;

2. The divorce or separation instrument does not designate the payment as an amount other than alimony (e.g., property settlement or child support);

3. In the case of an individual legally separated from his or her spouse under a decree of divorce or of separate maintenance, the spouses are not members of the same household at the time the payment is made; and

4. Liability to make future payments as alimony or otherwise stops by agreement or by law upon the death of the recipient spouse.

Cash payments of rent, mortgages, life insurance premiums on the payor's life where the recipient spouse is the owner of the policy, and other obligations of the payor spouse are examples of payments received on behalf of a spouse which qualify as alimony. In the case of mortgage payments, the payor spouse would deduct the entire amount of the mortgage as alimony if it otherwise qualifies, and the recipient spouse would report this amount as income. The recipient would then be able to deduct mortgage interest and property taxes paid on behalf of the recipient spouse to the extent otherwise permitted under the tax law. (See Chapter 4 concerning limitations on qualified residence interest and Chapter 1 concerning the phase-out of most itemized deductions by high-income individuals.)

If the payor spouse continues to have an ownership interest in the property for which payments are made, the payor would not receive an alimony deduction. Instead, the payor would continue to deduct the home mortgage interest and property taxes as itemized deductions to the extent otherwise allowable. The recipient spouse would report no income and would have no deduction.

ILLUSTRATION

Payments on the marital home of Jack and Jill are $1,000 per month. Of the $12,000 paid on the mortgage during the year, the hazard insurance escrow is $500, the property tax escrow is $1,000 (actually paid out during the year), and the reduction in principal is $1,500 with the remaining $9,000 constituting mortgage interest. If Jill remains in the marital home and the property is to be transferred to her, Jack will be able to deduct $12,000 per year in alimony if he makes the mortgage payments directly. Jill will pick up this amount as income but will be able to deduct the $1,000 in property taxes and the $9,000 in mortgage interest, subject to the statutory limitations. In contrast, if Jack is to maintain co-ownership of the property, he will then deduct the $10,000 in combined property taxes and mortgage interest, again to the extent otherwise permitted under the law. Jill picks up no income and receives no deduction.

TAX PLANNING IDEA When a joint return cannot or will not be filed following separation, the after-tax costs of spousal support to the payor will be increased in the absence of a written instrument compelling payment. The payor of marital support should strive to obtain a written agreement or court order in order to get the deduction. Otherwise, support payments will be treated as "voluntary" and nondeductible.

YEAR-END REMINDER In general, make your current alimony payment by December 31 to get the tax deduction in the year coming to an end. However, prepayment of more than one month in advance may be challenged by IRS as nondeductible.

AVOID RAPID DECLINES IN ANNUAL ALIMONY PAYMENTS

In the third calendar year of alimony payments, the payor spouse must pick up income under a complicated recapture provision for excess payments from year two to the extent that the amount of alimony payments paid during the second year of alimony exceeds the amount paid during the third year by $15,000. Additionally, there is recapture in year three when the amount of payments during the first year exceeds the average of the payments in years two (after that year's recapture) and three by more than $15,000.

ILLUSTRATION

Bob pays Susan $1,500 per month in alimony for each of the twelve months of 1998 and 1999. Alimony ceases with the December 1999 payment under the terms of the agreement. There are $3,000 in excess payments for the second year, since the $18,000 paid in 1999 exceeds by $3,000 the amount paid in 2000 ($0) plus the $15,000 base. There are no excess payments for 1998, the first year. The $18,000 paid in 1998 does not exceed by $15,000 the average of $15,000 and $0, the former being the 1999 payments less the $3,000 excess for that year and the latter being the 2000 payments.

Consequently, Bob will report $3,000 in income from the recomputation and Susan will get a deduction of $3,000 from the recomputation, with the taxable event occurring in 2000 in each case.

TAX PLANNING IDEA To avoid the recapture rule, alimony payments should not drop by more than $15,000 between the second year of payments and the third year of payments. Additionally, while the drop in alimony from the first year of payments to the third year of payments can exceed $15,000, payments for year one should not be more than $15,000 larger than the average of the payments for years two and three.

QUESTION: I have agreed to pay rehabilitative alimony to my wife for three years to enable her to complete her education. We have agreed on $3,000 per month as alimony for each month of calendar year 1998, $2,250 per month during calendar 1999, and $1,500 per month during calendar 2000. Will all of the payments be fully deductible to me as alimony without any recomputation required in 2000?

ANSWER: Yes, there are no excess payments for 1999, since the difference in payments between 1999 and 2000 is only $9,000. Also, there are no excess payments for 1998, because the $36,000 to be paid during that year exceeds the average payments for 1999 and 2000 by only $13,500.

CAUTION! This recapture rule is not applicable to court-ordered support during the pendency of litigation for divorce or separate maintenance. The rule is also not applicable if either spouse dies before the close of the third year of alimony or the recipient spouse remarries before the close of that third year, when the alimony payments cease by reason of the death or remarriage. Similarly, this rule is not applicable where payments are contingent based upon a percent of compensation or business income.

CONVERT CASH PAYMENTS INTENDED AS PROPERTY SETTLEMENTS INTO ALIMONY

The purpose behind the excess front loading rule requiring recapture of certain purported alimony payments was to discourage characterizing property settlements as alimony. However, it is still possible to set up payments arising from property settlements as deductible alimony to the payor, provided the payments are made over three calendar years (in as little as 14 months) and do not reduce from year to year in a manner giving rise to liability on the excess payments. The payments would have to cease upon death of the spouse receiving alimony.

QUESTION: I have agreed to pay my wife $500 per month as alimony for five years. Additionally, I am going to remain in our house, but my wife wants $12,000 for her equity in the property. I cannot afford to pay her the payments in a lump sum. Is there any way that I can deduct these additional payments?

ANSWER: If the payments on account of the house are made part of the alimony package where, for example, you would pay her $700 per month as alimony, or perhaps a bit more to take into account an interest factor on the equity, you would be permitted to deduct these additional payments provided they are labeled as alimony or spousal support and otherwise meet all of the criteria for deductibility. Your wife, however, would be taxed on the payments. If she is in a much lower marginal tax bracket than you, this approach could be particularly valuable.

FILING POINTER Just because a state court considers payment under a separation agreement as constituting a property settlement doesn't necessarily mean that the payment isn't alimony for tax purposes. In 1989, the Tax Court ruled that monthly payments labeled as combined alimony and property settlement were deductible alimony to the payor husband despite a prior state court's determination that the payments represented a property settlement under state law. Similarly, the Court held in 1994 that it could determine based on all facts and circumstances whether monthly payments labeled as alimony and enforced by a state court were really a property settlement.

CONVERT CASH PAYMENTS INTENDED AS CHILD SUPPORT INTO ALIMONY

Until ten years ago, a spouse making combined payment for the support of the other spouse and children could get a deduction for the entire amount by using such terminology as "for the support of my wife and children." Unless an amount was specifically allocated to child support, nondeductible to the payor and tax-free to the recipient, the payments had to be treated as alimony, even when they declined as a result of a child reaching adulthood, for example. This was known as the Lester rule, named after a famous 1961 U.S. Supreme Court case.

The ability to Lesterize payments is diminished today; however, there are still available opportunities. When the intention is that both alimony and child support be paid, amounts conceived by the parties to be child support can be labeled as alimony provided the reduction not occur on the happening of a contingency related to the child such as the child's attaining a certain age, marrying, dying, or leaving school.

Temporary Regulations provide that a reduction within six months before or after the date when a child attains the age of 18, 21, or the local age of majority is presumed to be clearly associated with a contingency relating to the child unless the reduction is a complete termination of payments made in at least six calendar years. Additionally, the presumption applies when payments are to be reduced on two or more occasions within one year before or after different children of the payor spouse attain a certain age between 18 and 24. These presumptions are tricky; computations are based on years, months, and days.

ILLUSTRATION

John's older child was born on January 1, 1981 and his younger child was born on October 12, 1983. He and his wife have agreed on a combination of alimony and child support, both of which will first be reduced and will terminate several years thereafter. Assuming a legal age of 18 or 21, the first presumption will jeopardize an alimony deduction if the initial decline in alimony occurs between July 1, 1998 and July 1, 1999, between April 12, 2000 and April 12, 2001, or between July 1, 2001 and July 1, 2002. If the initial decline in alimony occurs during either window, July 2, 1999 to April 11, 2000 or April 13, 2001 to June 30, 2001, the second presumption will also jeopardize the deduction if elimination of alimony occurs before April 13, 2005.

Why? If a reduction in alimony occurs when the older child is between 18½ and 20½, no further reduction or elimination may occur when the younger child is within this age range. Two reductions would exist within one year before or after different children attained a certain age between 18 and 24. Here that age would be 19½; one reduction would have occurred within one year before that age (18½) and the other would have occurred within one year after that age (20½).

If elimination in alimony is desired before April 13, 2005, the first reduction must occur before July 1, 1998, when the older child reaches age 17½. Then a window is created for eliminating alimony before the year 2005. Assuming a first reduction in alimony on June 30, 1998, elimination of alimony may occur between April 13, 2003 and April 11, 2004 (when the younger child is between age 19½ and 20½) without running awry of either presumption which could convert deductible alimony to nondeductible child support.

QUESTION: My wife and I have one son, who is age 13. The age of majority in my state is 18. I wish to maximize my tax deduction over the four years that I have agreed to pay alimony to my wife and the five years for which I am obligated to pay child support. How can I maximize my tax benefit?

ANSWER: Do little or no allocation specifically to child support. Make the preponderance of payments for the benefit of your wife, and have these payments terminate on a specific calendar date that is not within six months of your son's eighteenth birthday or within six months of his twenty-first birthday.

CAUTION!   Despite the favorable tax considerations of an allocation to alimony, be careful of a legal issue. In many states, alimony may be made nonmodifiable under the terms of a separation agreement. However, the general rule is that child support cannot be made nonmodifiable. Consequently, too low an allocation to child support could have your spouse asking a court for an increase in payments.

ENSURING THE TAX-FREE NATURE OF PROPERTY SETTLEMENTS

One of the most widely heralded changes in the tax law in recent years was to make the transfer of appreciated property between spouses tax-free upon the termination of their marriage. Prior to the law change, when appreciated property was transferred to a spouse in consideration for a reduced alimony payment or for no alimony payment at all, not only did the transferor spouse give up the property or an interest in the property, but also that spouse could be taxed on the appreciation.

Now interspousal property transfers are generally not taxed if they occur during the course of a marriage or thereafter, but only if the transfer occurs within one year after divorce or can otherwise be shown to be "related to cessation of the marriage." Where interest on a delayed transfer of property is not stated, none will be imputed under the rules set forth in Chapter 10. However, stated interest is taxed to the recipient.

Under Temporary Regulations, a transfer of property is related to the cessation of the marriage if it occurs not more than six years after the date on which the marriage ceases and is pursuant to a written instrument. Transfers occurring more than one year after divorce and which are not made pursuant to a written instrument or transfers occurring more than six years after divorce are presumed not to be related to the cessation of the marriage; however, even this presumption may be rebutted based upon the facts and circumstances.

CAUTION!   Transfers to nonresident alien spouses and transfers of installment obligations or property with liabilities in excess of the tax basis in the underlying property into trust are exceptions to the general nontaxability rule.

CAUTION!   The importance of proper wording of a separation agreement to place any tax burden where intended cannot be overstated. Poor wording can cost dollars, even hundreds of thousands of dollars. Even a court judgment can be both ambiguous and costly as a New Jersey woman found out in a 1994 decision of the Third Circuit Court of Appeals which reversed a Tax Court decision in her favor.

A state court had previously awarded the woman a "one-third interest in the business operation of the sole proprietorship. . . ." This "non-management interest" was to be "solely held for the purposes of receiving the plaintiff's one-third interest at the time the property may be sold. . . ." The state court didn't make it clear whether it created an "ownership interest" in the wife (making her share of the cash proceeds taxable to her) or a "payment of money contingent as to time and amount" (leaving the entire cash proceeds taxable to the husband). The federal appeals court found that the wife, in fact, received an ownership interest and had to pay her own taxes.

CONTROVERSY

Sometimes the IRS gets "whipsawed" and loses tax cases both against the wife and the husband on the same facts and legal issue. It happened in 1994 when the Tax Court decided that a husband wasn't taxable on a corporate buyout of his wife's shares in a hamburger franchise owned 50 percent by each when the separation agreement stated that the parties "shall cause the corporation to pay wife. . .for wife's stock in the corporation." The Ninth Circuit Court of Appeals had determined two years previously that the wife wasn't taxable either.

Thus, under a property settlement, when a payment for the benefit of one spouse is made by a corporation owned by the other spouse, is the transaction a taxable redemption to the first spouse or is it constructively a taxable redemption to the second spouse followed by a tax-free transfer to the first spouse? The law is unclear at least where the separation agreement is unclear.

TAX PLANNING IDEA   When a separation agreement is clear and the parties agree to report consistently, the likelihood of both audit and challenge by the IRS is reduced.

QUESTION: My former husband and I purchased some land in 1979 for $25,000. When we divorced in 1986, it was worth $75,000, and he transferred the property to me under the terms of our separation agreement. I have a contract to sell the land for $100,000. Will I pay taxes on gain of $25,000, $75,000, or $25,000 plus an additional amount representing my share of the appreciation while we were married?

ANSWER: You will pay taxes on a gain of $75,000 in that your tax basis in the property is $25,000, reflecting a carryover of the original basis (see Chapter 5) in the property that you had with your former spouse. Because the transfer of his interest in the property to you in 1986 was not taxable to him, you are not entitled to adjust your basis upward. If the transfer of the house to you had occurred before July 19, 1984 and the transfer was in consideration for a reduction or elimination in alimony, you probably could have added one-half of the appreciation during the marriage to your original $25,000 basis (unless the transfer occurred in 1984 before July 19 and you agreed that the transfer would be nontaxable).

QUESTION: My ex-wife and I have agreed to divide the proceeds on sale of a rental property 75 percent to her and 25 percent to me even though we own the property equally. I've gotten scared. Could the IRS tax me on 50 percent?

ANSWER: Your fears are well-founded. In a May 13, 1997 decision, the Tax Court determined that gain on property sales between divorcing spouses must be divided based on percentage ownership. If you hadn't gotten scared, you might have walked away with nothing.

 FILING POINTER   Change the percentages of legal ownership by deed prior to sale to shift the tax burden to parallel the distribution of proceeds.

CAUTION!   If the spouse who receives the greater proceeds is in a lower tax bracket than the other spouse, the IRS could view any transfer of title at or shortly before closing as a "sham." However, if the spouse receiving the larger share keeps the extra amount, a successful challenge by the IRS would probably be unsuccessful.

QUESTION: My husband and I will be getting a divorce within the next few months and we are in the process of negotiating a property settlement. As part of that settlement, my husband wants his share of the equity from the marital home, but I want to continue living in the house. If I take out a loan to buy his share of the house, can I deduct the interest on my tax return?

ANSWER: The IRS has announced that, under forthcoming regulations, debt incurred to acquire your husband's interest in the house will be considered acquisition debt (see Chapter 4). However, the interest may be deductible as qualified residence interest only if the house remains your principal residence (or is your second residence), the total acquisition debt does not exceed the lesser of the home's value or $1 million, and, finally, the loan which you take out to buy your husband's interest is secured by the home.

Let's say your house is currently worth $100,000, and the mortgage incurred to buy the property has been paid down to $40,000. This would mean that you would need $30,000 to buy your husband's equity in the property. This $30,000 loan, together with the $40,000 existing mortgage would both constitute acquisition debt, and the interest on both of these debts would be qualified residence interest.

(See Chapter 6 concerning each spouse's ability to exclude $250,000 of gain if the principal residence is sold rather than transferred to one spouse.)

QUESTION: I had to pay my former wife $45,000 in interest on a judgment representing a marital monetary award which I appealed unsuccessfully. Can I deduct the interest?

ANSWER: While there is no specific authority for such a position, you might be able to successfully argue that the interest is other than nondeductible personal interest when the marital monetary award was for the purpose of dividing business, investment, or passive activity assets (see Chapter 2). Your situation is arguably analogous to tax preparation costs which may be allocated among schedules or to interest paid on a tax deficiency which may arguably be allocated. (See Chapter 4 as to both issues.)

CUTTING THE RETIREMENT PIE WITH A QDRO

Until 15 years ago, there was no statutory provision requiring that a retirement plan account balance or an accrued benefit be divided between the employee and the spouse upon a marital termination. Courts now have this authority as to qualified retirement plans (see Chapter 10) in domestic relations matters, and the trustee of a plan must comply with a proper Qualified Domestic Relations Order (QDRO). Each spouse becomes taxable on amounts that he or she ultimately receives from the retirement plan. A QDRO requires more than a separation agreement between the spouses. It must be submitted to the local court in order to obtain a judgment, decree, or order.

The QDRO must set forth the following:

1. The name and last known mailing address of the participant and alternate payee;

2. The amount or percentage of benefits to be paid to the alternate payee, or the manner in which a computation of the amount or percentage is to be determined;

3. The number of payments or period to which the order applies; and

4. A designation of each plan to which the order applies.

 CAUTION! The taxability of a nonqualified plan of deferred compensation (see Chapter 2) cannot be shifted by a QDRO or otherwise in any circumstance.

QUESTION: My husband and I are divorcing and we have entered into a separation agreement. For so long as my husband has been employed, he has been a participant in his employer's retirement plan and has accrued benefits of approximately $200,000. As part of the property settlement, my husband has agreed that I am entitled to one-half of his retirement benefits. What are my options when I receive the $100,000?

ANSWER: A Qualified Domestic Relations Order will have to be signed by a judge from your local court awarding you the $100,000 from your husband's retirement plan. Once the Order is signed, the Order will be submitted to the administrator of your husband's retirement plan for compliance. The timing and form of payment to you will be governed by the terms of your husband's plan. If you receive the $100,000 in a lump sum, you will be eligible for favorable income tax treatment in lieu of ordinary income if your husband met the requirements. (See Chapter 9 concerning Retirement Plans.) In any event, you won't have to pay the usual ten percent penalty for premature withdrawal even if you haven't reached the age of 59½. If you have the $100,000 transferred directly into an IRA, you won't be subject to withholding or income tax liability until you withdraw the funds.

TAX PLANNING IDEA   A QDRO is not needed to divide an Individual Retirement Account. A written agreement to transfer all or a portion of an IRA from one spouse to another upon separation or divorce suffices to direct the trustee to comply and shifts future taxation of the transferred balance to the recipient spouse.

CAUTION!   According to a 1994 Tax Court case, if an Order fails to meet the requirements for a QDRO, the tax liability caused upon payment to the non-employee spouse remains with the employee spouse. Similarly, IRA transfers must meet the requirements of the law in order to shift taxation to the recipient spouse. One of these requirements is that the IRA transfer must be pursuant to a marital termination—separation or divorce. According to an IRS letter ruling, any other IRA transfer causes tax liability to the original owner. Must a QDRO be pursuant to separation or divorce? There is no specific authority; however, the IRS is expected to take such a position.

9

RETIREMENT PLANS

PLANNING FOR YOUR RETIREMENT

Planning for your retirement makes sense not only from a tax point of view but also from a financial and economic point of view. Social Security benefits will probably not be sufficient to meet your living expenses after retirement, so planning is needed to augment any government provided retirement benefits with other retirement money. Retirement plans come in many types: those which we usually fund ourselves (Individual Retirement Accounts), those which are typically funded by our employers (profit sharing plans, money purchase plans, defined benefit plans, and simplified employee pension plans), and those which are often funded both by our employers and ourselves (401(k) plans and "Simple" plans).

CAUTION!   Retirement plans are currently being scrutinized and reassessed on several fronts. The IRS has stepped up its audit program of employer plans to enforce required filings and to curtail perceived abuse. Employers are cutting back company contributions or even eliminating plans in order to control costs. While 83 percent of employers with 100 or more workers sponsor one or more retirement plans, less than 20 percent of employers with 25 or fewer workers sponsor such a plan. And Congress is perpetually looking at possible changes in the law.

TRADITIONAL IRAs

Individual Retirement Accounts (IRAs) are government sanctioned savings vehicles for workers and recipients of alimony. The traditional IRA has been supplemented by the Roth IRA discussed later in this chapter and the Education IRA discussed in Chapter 3. The traditional IRA and the Roth IRA are primarily designed for individual retirement, while the Education IRA is primarily designed for the higher education of the individual and his family. Contributions to a traditional IRA may be made until the year an individual reaches age 70½ and are deductible up to $2,000 per year subject to limitations discussed below, and the earnings generated by the contributions accumulate tax-free. When withdrawals are made from the IRA either at or before retirement, the owner pays tax not only on the amount of the contributions but also on the earnings that have been accumulating.

 YEAR-END REMINDER You may open an IRA and make a contribution for the previous year until April 15 of the succeeding year. If you are eligible for a deductible IRA, this is one of the very few steps which you can take after year-end to reduce your taxes of the previous year.

 CAUTION! Note that filing an extension on your tax return does not extend the April 15 deadline for making IRA contributions.

 TAX PLANNING IDEA If your tax return information is completed early, you can file your tax return showing a deductible contribution, obtain your refund (hopefully by April 15), and then make the contribution.

QUESTION: I am married and will be working only for a few weeks during 1998, making only $1,500. Can I set up a deductible IRA? My income will go way up in 1999. Just what are all of the rules?

ANSWER: Although the deduction limitation for IRAs is generally $2,000, that is the maximum deduction. If you made less than $2,000, you can contribute all of it but no more to an IRA and claim a full deduction for your contribution, subject to rules limiting IRA deductions for workers who are active participants or whose spouses are active participants in employer-sponsored retirement plans. Consequently, if you made $1,500, your IRA contribution can be no more than $1,500. What you made includes your earned income reported on your W-2s and self-employment as well as any alimony payments that you received. Unearned income such as interest, dividends, and rents does not count for this purpose.

There is a special rule for a nonworking spouse or one who made no more than $2,000. Under these circumstances, your total contribution as a couple can be increased to the lesser of what the two of you made or $4,000 though no more than $2,000 can be put in either spouse's name.

Although the general rule permits deductible IRA contributions of up to $2,000, not all individuals are eligible for the tax deduction. If either you or your spouse is an active participant in an employer sponsored retirement plan, your ability to make a deductible contribution to your IRA may be reduced or eliminated.

However, if you and your spouse file a joint return and your modified adjusted gross income (essentially AGI before the IRA deduction) is no more than $50,000, then both of you are entitled to continue to make full deductible contributions to your own IRAs, even if one or both of you is an active participant in an employer sponsored retirement plan.

If you and your spouse's modified adjusted gross income on the joint return is between $50,000 and $60,000, then each of you will be looked at separately and either or both of you will phase-out your ability to make deductible IRA contributions depending on your individual status as an *active participant* in an *employer sponsored retirement plan*. For example, if you and your spouse have modified adjusted income of $55,000 and you are an active plan participant but your spouse is not, you may make a $1,000 deductible IRA contribution while your spouse makes a $2,000 deductible contribution.

If you and your spouse's modified adjusted gross income is between $60,000 and $150,000, then the ability of each of you to make a deductible IRA contribution depends on your own individual lack of active plan participation. If you and your spouse's modified AGI is between $150,000 and $160,000, the ability of a spouse who is not an active plan participant to make a deductible IRA contribution phases out if the other spouse is an active plan participant. At $160,000 of modified AGI, neither of you can make a deductible IRA contribution if either of you is an active plan participant.

If you file a separate return while married, you can make a deductible IRA contribution so long as neither you nor your spouse is an active participant in an employer sponsored retirement plan. For the individual who files a separate return but who is or whose spouse is an active participant in an employer sponsored retirement plan, no deductible contribution to an IRA can be made if his or her modified adjusted gross income is $10,000 or more. If the separate modified adjusted gross income is less than $10,000, then a pro rata deductible contribution can be made not to exceed earned income plus alimony.

If you are married and file a separate return but you and your spouse have lived apart for the entire year, you will not be considered as married for purpose of the IRA contribution. Thus, your spouse's status as an active participant in an employer sponsored retirement plan will have no impact on your ability to make a deductible IRA contribution for yourself. If you are not an active participant in an employer sponsored retirement plan, you are eligible to make a deductible IRA contribution. If you participate in an employer sponsored retirement plan, you are eligible to make a deductible IRA contribution subject to the modified adjusted gross income limitation as if you were single.

If you were single and an active participant in your employer's retirement plan, you could still make a deductible contribution to your own IRA so long as your modified adjusted gross income did not exceed $30,000. If your modified AGI was $40,000 or more and you were an active participant in an employer sponsored plan, then no deductible IRA contribution could be made. If your modified adjusted gross income was between $30,000 and $40,000, the deduction to the IRA would be phased out.

FILING POINTER   Where a phase-out formula may have reduced your deductible IRA contribution to less than $200 (but more than $0), the law permits a minimum deductible contribution of $200.

CAUTION!   For 1997 the ability to make a deductible IRA contribution was phased out between $40,000 and $50,000 of adjusted gross income for married couples filing jointly when *either* spouse was an active participant in an employer sponsored retirement plan. The phase-out was between $25,000 and $35,000 for single individuals actively participating in a plan. The phase-out levels for married couples filing jointly and single individuals will rise beginning in 1999. By 2007 the level of phase-out for married couples will be $80,000–$100,000, by 2005 the level of phase-out for single individuals will be $50,000–$60,000. Other phase-out limits are not scheduled to change.

QUESTION: I contributed $2,000 to my IRA believing that I was not an active participant in my employer's retirement plan. I now find that I will be considered an active participant in the plan. Since my adjusted gross income will exceed the amounts that would allow me even a partial IRA deduction, what are my options?

ANSWER: Unless you treat the $2,000 contribution that you made to the IRA as a nondeductible contribution or as a Roth IRA (see the discussion later in this chapter), you will be liable for a six percent penalty tax for each year that the excess contribution remains in the IRA. To avoid the six percent penalty tax you should withdraw the $2,000 and the earnings that it has generated before the due date of your tax return, including extensions. The withdrawn contribution is not taxable to you but the earnings on the $2,000 are taxable in the year that you made the excess contribution, not in the year that the earnings were withdrawn. In addition, there will be a ten percent penalty tax on the amount of the earnings that are withdrawn. The six percent penalty tax will continue to apply each year that you do not correct the excess contribution.

QUESTION: Who is an active participant in an employer sponsored retirement plan for purposes of the IRA rules?

I retired from the Federal Government two years ago following the death of my husband and I receive my monthly government pension. I've decided to take a part-time job for a small company which has no retirement plan. Will I be able to make a deductible IRA contribution this year? I expect to have adjusted gross income of about $50,000.

ANSWER: Anyone who participates in a profit sharing plan, money purchase pension plan, defined benefit plan, government or church retirement plan, tax-sheltered annuity (see Chapter 11 for a discussion of these plans sponsored by schools and certain other tax-exempt organizations), simplified employee pension plan (SEP), or Simple plan where contributions or forfeitures are added to an account maintained in his or her name or benefits accrue on his or her behalf is an active participant in an employer sponsored plan. Form W-2 indicates whether or not an employee is an active participant for any part of the year.

Even though you receive a government pension, you will be eligible for a deductible IRA contribution. Receipt of retirement benefits is not considered active participation in an employer sponsored plan.

 CAUTION!   The participant in a profit sharing plan might find that no contributions are made on his or her behalf in a lean year for the employer. If the employee receives a few dollars of forfeitures from the accounts of departing participants, he or she would be considered an active participant in an employer sponsored retirement plan, and the result could be disqualification of the employee and possibly the employee's spouse from deductible IRA contributions depending upon income levels. An employee repeatedly faced with this situation and wishing to deduct an IRA contribution may wish to consider opting out of the employer's plan, if permitted.

FILING POINTER   If you or your spouse cannot make a deductible contribution to an IRA because of your modified adjusted gross income level, you can still make a nondeductible contribution to an IRA up to $2,000 and have the earnings on the account accumulate tax-free. As a result, even though you receive no current tax benefit for your retirement savings, the earnings on the account are accumulating on a tax deferred basis, thus allowing for a greater accumulation of capital. By filing IRS Form 8606 with your return, you designate the amount of your nondeductible IRA contribution. However, a nondeductible Roth IRA contribution would be preferable to a nondeductible traditional IRA for individuals who are eligible.

ROTH IRAs

The Taxpayer Relief Act of 1997 created a new nondeductible IRA effective in 1998 under which qualified withdrawals of contributions *and* earnings are free of tax and free of penalty (see the discussion later in this chapter) after the fourth calendar year following the initial contribution. Qualified withdrawals are those on account of death or disability, after age 59½, or (to a limited extent as discussed later in this chapter) to purchase a "first home."

Unlike a traditional IRA, a contribution to a Roth IRA can be made after age 70½ and withdrawals need not commence at that age. Irrespective of participation in an employer sponsored retirement plan, the ability to make Roth IRA contributions is phased out at modified adjusted gross income levels between $150,000 and $160,000 for married couples filing jointly, between $95,000 and $110,000 for single individuals, and between $0 and $15,000 for married individuals filing separately.

TAX PLANNING IDEA   The decision as to whether to make an IRA contribution will vary with an individual's particular circumstances. In general, however, most individuals whose personal pre-retirement needs will be met should make IRA contributions. Over a period of many years, the greatest tax saving is not in the initial IRA contribution but in the tax-free compounding of earnings.

That is why a Roth IRA in most cases is more valuable than a traditional deductible IRA. (The $2,000 IRA contribution limitation is a combined one for traditional IRAs and Roth IRAs.) The value of a $2,000 deduction today ($560 to an individual in the 28 percent bracket) from a traditional IRA will pale against the value of the exclusion in the future after the $2,000 has grown tax-free for many years in a Roth IRA. See the discussion later in this chapter as to how to convert a traditional IRA into a Roth IRA.

FILING POINTER   Even nonqualified withdrawals from Roth IRAs enjoy some degree of favorable tax treatment. Unlike partial distributions from a traditional IRA, where basis (see Chapter 5) is recovered tax free on a *pro rata* basis over the period of the anticipated income stream, partial distributions from a Roth IRA are first allocated to tax-free recovery of basis in your own contributions.

CAUTION!   The up-front tax-free recovery of basis for nonqualified withdrawals may have been unintentional as Congress rushed to enact the Taxpayer Relief Act. Within days after enactment, Congress was considering modification of this provision.

TAX PLANNING IDEA   You're never too young to start an IRA. A youngster who starts early with paper route savings or with compensation paid by a parent for household work will enjoy the benefit of decades of compound growth.

MAXIMIZING ELECTIVE DEFERRALS UNDER A 401(K) OR "SIMPLE" PLAN

A 401(k) plan is an employer sponsored retirement plan that gives employees the option of deferring a portion of compensation by directing it instead to be contributed to the plan. These plans have increased in popularity as employers have sought to have employees share the cost of their retirement security. Approximately 20 percent of American workers participate in 401(k) plans.

An employee who participates in a 401(k) plan can elect a tax-free deferral far in excess of the IRA limitation. The largest *elective deferral* possible is 25 percent of compensation before taking the subtraction of the deferred amount into account up to a dollar maximum of $9,500 annually, which will be adjusted in 1998 (probably to $10,000) and succeeding years for increases in the cost of living. The elective deferral maximum is the total amount that can be deferred for all plans.

Employers can contribute additional amounts to the 401(k) plan which are not subject to the employee's election up to an amount which, when combined with the employee's elective deferral amount, does not exceed the ceilings applicable to profit sharing plans discussed below. In fact, many 401(k) plans provide for the employer to match the first $1,000 or $2,000, for example, of employee elective deferrals. This incentive is particularly important in a small or medium-size business, because the maximum elective deferrals of highly compensated workers are tied to the average elective deferrals of the rank and file.

A Simple plan is another employer sponsored retirement plan that gives employees the option of elective deferrals. Created by the 1996 tax legislation for employers with no more than 100 employees and no other retirement plan, Simple plans were first used in 1997.

An employee who participates in a Simple plan is able to make an elective deferral up to a dollar maximum of $6,000 annually, which is adjusted for cost of living. The 25 percent of compensation limit also applies. Employers are required to make certain levels of contributions to Simple plans.

As in the case of an IRA, the earnings on employer and employee 401(k) and Simple contributions accumulate tax-free until withdrawal. The employee's right to contributions which he or she chose to put into the plan and the earnings on those contributions are fully vested, as are most employer matching contributions and the related earnings except in certain 401(k) plans. Also, as in the case of an IRA, no Social Security or Medicare taxes are saved.

See Chapter 11 as to a special "catch-up" rule on elective deferrals by members of the military.

⏰ **YEAR-END REMINDER**   Employees who have the ability to contribute to a 401(k) or Simple plan should consider maximizing their contributions before year-end. An employee in a 28 percent tax bracket electing a deferral of $9,500 to a 401(k) plan will save $2,660 in taxes; an employee in a 36 percent bracket will save $3,420.

IN BUSINESS FOR YOURSELF?—FUNDING LARGER CONTRIBUTIONS

If you are in business for yourself, you have the opportunity to defer larger amounts and let the contributions and earnings grow tax-free—through one or more *qualified retirement plans* or Simplified Employee Pension Plans (SEPs). However, you must treat employees in a non-discriminatory manner which generally means making a contribution on behalf of each of them in the same percentage of compensation as you make for yourself. In general, you may exclude part-timers and those under the age of 21 from receiving a contribution. Qualified retirement plans may generally exclude workers with less than one or two years of service depending upon the type of plan and how quickly benefits become nonforfeitable and vest; SEPs may generally exclude workers with less than three years of service.

Qualified retirement plans come in two varieties—defined contribution plans and defined benefit plans. Defined contribution plans themselves come in two primary types: money purchase pension plans and profit sharing plans.

In a defined contribution plan, whether it is a money purchase pension plan or a profit sharing plan, a separate retirement account is maintained in the name of each participating employee, and employer contributions to the plan are allocated to each account. Each employee's account is then increased by a proportionate share of investment earnings, and any losses suffered by the plan will be proportionately allocated to the employee's account. If an employee is terminated, he or she may forfeit all or a portion of the account depending upon the vesting schedule selected by the employer. Any amounts which are forfeited by the employee are normally allocated among the remaining employees and their respective accounts are increased accordingly. The total amount of employer contributions, employee contributions, and forfeitures allocated to an employee's account each year cannot exceed 25 percent of his or her compensation or, if less, $30,000 (scheduled to be indexed for increases in the cost of living but not for many years).

ILLUSTRATION _____

Participant's compensation	$70,000
Employer's contributions	$10,000

Employee's contributions	$ 3,000
Forfeitures	$ 2,000

The addition to this employee's account for the year is $15,000 (the sum of the employer and employee contributions plus the forfeitures). As this is less than 25 percent of the employee's compensation (25% of $70,000 = $17,500), the addition is within the statutory limit.

Employers contribute a fixed percentage of employee compensation to a money purchase plan each year regardless of employer profitability. In contrast, contributions by the employer to a profit sharing plan may be set up to be completely discretionary. Contributions need not be made each year and the amount of the contribution may vary annually. For this reason, profit sharing plans are very attractive for companies that are first starting out and have not yet established a history of profits or for companies which incur peaks and valleys in their profits. The employer may claim a tax deduction with respect to a contribution only to the extent that total contributions to the profit sharing plan do not exceed 15 percent of the compensation paid to the participating employees as a whole. A 401(k) plan, previously discussed, is a type of profit sharing plan. A Simple plan, also previously discussed, may be similarly set up or it may be set up as a group of IRAs.

The amount of an employer's contribution to a defined benefit plan will depend upon the retirement benefit established in the plan. An actuary must determine the employer's contribution each year depending upon assumptions made with respect to the salary progression and ages of the participating employees as well as the investment return of the plan.

A defined benefit plan can provide for an annual retirement benefit at Social Security retirement age (now age 65 but age 66 if you were born in the years 1938-1954 or age 67 if you were born in 1955 or later) of no greater than $125,000 (or, if less, the amount of the employee's average compensation during his or her highest-paid three consecutive years). What this means is that a defined benefit plan must limit the annual retirement benefit of employees to this amount, and employer contributions to the plan must be based on projecting this maximum annual benefit which will be indexed in 1997 and succeeding years.

A simplified employee pension plan is a hybrid between a qualified retirement plan and an IRA. Like qualified plans, SEPs have nondiscrimination rules, although they differ from those of qualified plans. SEPs have an annual contribution limit per participant and a deduction limit in the aggregate of 15 percent of compensation (determined exclusive of the contribution itself). In no event can a contribution exceed $24,000 per employee, inasmuch as compensation in excess of $160,000 (indexed in 1998 and succeeding years for cost of living) is ignored.

QUESTION: What is a Keogh plan?

ANSWER: A Keogh plan is simply a special name applied to a qualified retirement plan (whether it is a profit sharing plan, money purchase plan, or defined benefit plan) established by a sole proprietor for the benefit of the proprietor and the employees or by a partnership for the benefit of the partners and the employees. The same rules generally govern the operation of a Keogh plan as govern the operation of a qualified retirement plan established by a corporate employer.

CAUTION!   The deduction for contributions on behalf of a sole proprietor or partner to a money purchase pension plan is effectively limited to 20 percent of self-employment income (instead of 25 percent) determined after deducting one-half of the self-employment tax. In the case of a profit sharing plan, the deduction is limited to 13.04 percent (instead of 15 percent). The reason for this difference is to avoid a windfall to owners of unincorporated businesses who apply the percentage limitations to business profit before plan contributions, as compared to the owners of incorporated businesses who apply the percentage limitations to their salaries while retaining sufficient funds in the corporation for plan contributions. The result is parity to owners of unincorporated and incorporated businesses. The computations are quite complex, however.

TAX PLANNING IDEA   If you are an employer looking into the establishment of a retirement plan or if you are the only worker in the business and are seeking to maximize the benefit for yourself, consider combining a discretionary profit sharing plan with a ten percent mandatory money purchase pension plan. This is allowable so long as the total addition to both plans does not exceed 25 percent of compensation (20 percent of your profit if you are a sole proprietor or partner) but is no more than $30,000 as indexed. If you are near retirement and want to maximize your tax deduction and future benefit, consider establishing a defined benefit plan instead. Such a plan would probably provide you with the largest current contribution (and also the largest current tax deduction) available. Actuarially determined contributions to a defined benefit plan on behalf of an individual nearing retirement age can be far in excess of 25 percent of compensation.

TAX PLANNING IDEA   If you have other workers in your business, the selection of features for your particular type of retirement plan will be important. Although "discrimination" against employees is supposedly not permitted, owners may minimize the cost of covering others through such means as delayed vesting schedules, integration with Social Security, and (in the case of profit sharing plans) age-based and comparability formulas.

YEAR-END REMINDER   Although contributions to a qualified retirement plan need not be made until after year-end to be deductible, the plan itself must be in place before the end of the employer's tax year.

The employer's retirement plan will be in existence if there is a written plan executed before the end of the year that has been formally adopted by the employer before year end. So long as the contribution is made to an established retirement plan before the due date of the employer's income tax return, including extensions, a deduction can be claimed. For example, if a calendar-year corporation has established a retirement plan before December 31, 1997, the corporation need not make its contribution for 1997 before March 15, 1998, the due date of the corporation's tax return for 1997. The contribution deadline can be extended for an additional six months if the corporation timely files a request to extend the due date of its corporate return.

A SEP may be started by an employer for its employees and funded for the prior year until the extended due date of the tax return—as late as October 15 of the succeeding year.

 CAUTION!   Contributions to defined benefit plans must generally be made in periodic installments or an interest charge is imposed.

INVEST YOUR RETIREMENT PLAN SAVINGS WISELY

Your retirement plan money can be invested in anything prudent; however, an IRA, SEP, or self-directed qualified plan cannot be invested in antiques, precious metals, art, or other collectibles (except certain coins).

TAX PLANNING IDEA   Although not prohibited as a retirement plan investment, you should never invest plan money in tax-exempt bonds. This is because the interest earned from tax-exempt bonds is tax-free. If retirement plan money is used to buy tax-exempt bonds, the interest in the plan account will be taxed when you take the money out of the account even though it was all generated by tax-exempt bonds. In other words, if you invest your plan money in tax-exempt bonds you will be converting tax-exempt income into taxable income as well as receiving the lesser yield usually associated with tax-exempt securities. Real estate syndications are not attractive investments either, inasmuch as tax deferred retirement plans do not need sheltering benefits associated with real estate.

CAUTION!   In the event of a poor retirement plan investment, no tax loss can be claimed on the investor's personal return. Consequently, you should act conservatively with plan investments and reserve any speculative investments for nonretirement plan money.

UNHAPPY WITH YOUR YIELD?—DIRECT TRANSFERS AND ROLLOVERS

If you are unhappy with the yield of your retirement plan and you are the trustee (permitted only with certain types of plans) or you have a plan where you direct the investments, you can change investments without changing plans. In other cases, you may seek to change the trustee without changing plans. However, in certain plans sponsored by financial institutions, you may need to change the plan itself.

Alternatively, you may receive notice that you are to receive a distribution from a qualified retirement plan in which you have participated.

In many cases you can avoid paying taxes by a direct trustee-to-trustee transfer of funds between plans or, in a lesser number of cases, by rollover in which you can negotiate and hold funds for up to 60 days (120 days as discussed later in this chapter for acquisition delays of "first-time" home buyers) before reinvestment.

More specifically, an individual's interest in a qualified retirement plan can be transferred directly to another qualified retirement plan. Any portion of a distribution from a qualified retirement plan not attributable to tax-free return of employee after-tax contributions can be transferred tax-free to a traditional IRA or rolled over to another qualified retirement plan unless the distribution is a periodic (one of a series of substantially equal payments either tied to life expectancies or over a specified period of at least ten years) or minimum (discussed below) distribution.

In a traditional IRA, you may direct an IRA-to-IRA transfer at any time; however, an IRA-to-IRA rollover is permitted only once every 365 days.

In general, an IRA may not be directly transferred or rolled over into a qualified retirement plan. However, a conduit traditional IRA, meaning one composed exclusively of amounts previously in a qualified retirement plan plus earnings on those amounts, may be directly transferred or rolled over to a qualified retirement plan. A SEP is generally treated as an IRA for purpose of transfers.

CAUTION!   A Simple plan has its own rules, generally permitting transfers to another Simple plan or, after two years participation, to a traditional IRA.

CAUTION!   Roth IRAs have special rollover rules. Like traditional IRAs, a direct Roth IRA to Roth IRA transfer is permitted at any time; however, a rollover between Roth IRAs is permitted only once every 365 days.

Roth IRAs may not be transferred into traditional IRAs. However, traditional IRAs may be transferred into Roth IRAs without penalty by reporting the rollover amount less the amount attributable to any nondeductible contributions as income. Such transfers are not available to married individuals filing separately and to others with modified adjusted gross income in excess of $100,000 as computed without taking the transfer into income.

 FILING POINTER   On a transfer from a traditional IRA into a Roth IRA, pay the tax liability from current income or savings in order to transfer the gross distribution into the Roth IRA for maximum future tax-free growth.

TAX PLANNING IDEA   Despite the requirement of current payment of tax, the transfer of amounts in traditional IRA accounts into Roth IRAs will make sense for many individuals. Prime candidates for moving into Roth IRAs from existing traditional IRAs are those taxpayers with small balances or those with larger balances but with many anticipated years of in-plan growth. Taxpayers with net operating losses (see Chapter 1) may even be able to absorb the income without the payment of any taxes.

 FILING POINTER   If a traditional IRA is transferred into a Roth IRA in 1998, the income may be reported ratably in the years 1998-2001. Do not miss out on this one-time opportunity if you will benefit by the conversion! Keep your income below the required threshold in 1998 to permit the transfer.

TAX PLANNING IDEA   If a Roth IRA makes sense for you and your retirement funds are in a qualified retirement plan under which you can control distributions, especially one to which no new contributions will be made, consider a transfer of funds into a traditional IRA and a second transfer to a Roth IRA.

CAUTION!   Income tax withholding is required at a rate of 20 percent on any distribution of $200 or more from a qualified plan that is eligible to be transferred tax-free and is not the subject of trustee-to-trustee direct transfer. Recipients of distributions from qualified plans not intending to use distributed funds should arrange direct transfers of their balances rather than rollovers. Distributions from IRAs and SEPs are not subject to withholding.

CAUTION!   Any amount transferred to and retained in an IRA cannot ultimately qualify for the special tax treatment discussed later in this chapter which is available for lump sum distributions from qualified retirement plans. However, if otherwise eligible for special treatment and not commingled with other IRA money, it may be transferred back into a qualified retirement plan in order to qualify for the special treatment.

TAX PLANNING IDEA   If you are waiting for a tax refund or other funds needed in order to make an IRA contribution for the current filing year, an alternative, although a bit risky, is to take a distribution from your existing IRA. Utilize the funds to make the needed current contribution. However, you must be careful to reinvest the distributed funds within 60 days. In 1990, IRS issued a letter ruling not binding on other individuals that would allow a tax-free rollover within the 60 days back to the same account from which the funds were withdrawn.

AVOIDING PENALTIES ON RETIREMENT PLAN DISTRIBUTIONS

A taxable distribution from a qualified retirement plan which is not directly transferred or rolled over to another qualified plan or IRA is subject to a ten percent penalty unless the distribution is made:

1. On or after the date the participant reaches the age of 59½;
2. After the death of the participant (in which case special distribution rules apply to the beneficiary);
3. On account of the participant's disability;

4. As part of a series of substantially equal periodic payments made over a period of time equal to the participant's life expectancy or the joint life expectancy of the participant and his or her beneficiary;

5. To cover medical expenses and payment does not exceed the amount allowable as a medical expense deduction;

6. As a transfer to the non-participant spouse or former spouse pursuant to a Qualified Domestic Relations Order (QDRO) (discussed in Chapter 8); or

7. After the participant terminates employment after reaching the age of 55.

A taxable distribution from an IRA (including a SEP) which is not directly transferred or rolled over to another IRA or, if a conduit IRA, to a qualified plan is subject to a ten percent penalty unless the distribution is made:

1. On account of any of 1-5 above;

2. As a transfer to a spouse or former spouse upon a marital termination;

3. To the extent of family health insurance premiums after 12 consecutive weeks of receiving unemployment compensation (or after 12 consecutive weeks without self-employment) and until 60 days of reemployment (or self-employment) provided the withdrawal is made in the same or succeeding year of eligibility for the withdrawal;

4. To the extent of tuition, fees, and room and board paid during the year for undergraduate, graduate, or post-secondary vocational study of the taxpayer or his or her spouse, child, or grandchild (effective in 1998 for expenses incurred and paid in 1998); or

5. To a maximum of $10,000 less similar lifetime withdrawals to purchase a principal residence within 120 days for the taxpayer, spouse, child, grandchild, or ancestor of the individual or spouse (effective in 1998). Eligibility requires that the individual or spouse not have owned a principal residence within the two years leading up to the date of contract or construction.

A taxable distribution from a Simple plan which is not directly transferred or rolled over to another Simple plan or IRA will also generally be subject to a ten percent penalty unless the distribution is made on account of one of the exemptions applicable to IRAs. However, the penalty is generally 25 percent in the first two years of plan participation.

Not only are you penalized for a *premature distribution*, but also you are penalized for a *late distribution* unless from a Roth IRA. You may be fortunate enough not to need your savings from your retirement plan, either because you are continuing to work or because you have other sources of income. You would like the retirement plan savings to accumulate tax-free as long as possible. However, you are required to receive your entire benefit maintained in the plan no later than the April 1 following the year in which you attain age 70½ or, alternatively, you must take a minimum distribution by that same April 1 date and have subsequent annual minimum distributions paid to you no later than each December 31, commencing in the same calendar year, over your life expectancy or that of you and your beneficiary. If you continue to work, minimum distributions from a qualified plan but not a traditional IRA can typically be delayed until the April 1 following when you cease work.

Failure to begin distributions by the required distribution date will subject the retirement savings to a 50 percent penalty tax computed on the difference between the minimum amount you were required to take out and the amount that was actually distributed to you.

A third penalty for receiving an excess retirement distribution in a single year or for an excess accumulation at death was repealed by the Taxpayer Relief Act of 1997 retroactive to January 1, 1997.

 FILING POINTER In the case of a delay in acquisition of a principal residence, funds may be restored to an IRA within 120 days of withdrawal.

CAUTION! A greater than five percent owner must commence minimum distributions in all cases by the April 1 of the year following when he or she reaches age 70½ irrespective of continuing to work. This requirement generally applied to everyone prior to 1997.

FILING POINTER A non-five percent owner who is over age 70½ and has commenced minimum distributions from a qualified retirement plan while continuing to work may now stop until he or she ceases work so long as the trustee approves the suspension of disbursements under the terms of the plan.

FILING POINTER It usually makes sense to take only minimum distributions when you have no need for the extra funds. By taking only the minimum distribution required by law, you are spreading the income over a number of years as well as allowing amounts remaining in the plan to grow due to the continuing tax-free nature of the earnings. For example, if your life expectancy is 11 years, take your plan distribution over the 11-year period as adjusted each year based upon your new life expectancy rather than over a shorter period of time.

CAUTION! While your initial distribution must be taken by April 1 of the applicable year, subsequent annual distributions must be taken by December 31 commencing in the same calendar year as the first April 1 disbursement.

 YEAR-END REMINDER You should not wait until the early months of the year following the year when you reach age 70½ to commence distributions if two distributions in the same calendar year would move you into a higher marginal tax bracket. Rather, take your initial distribution by December 31 of the year when you reach age 70½.

 CAUTION! You should avoid a premature retirement plan distribution if at all possible even if the purpose is a valid one. The net proceeds to you may be quite small after taxes and penalty.

ILLUSTRATION

Bob needs $15,000 to make a down payment on a vacation home. He has faithfully made contributions to an IRA, all of which were deducted by him. The IRA has a total balance of $15,000. Bob withdraws $15,000 from the account to use for his down payment. If Bob is under 59½ years old at the time of the distribution, not only must he include the $15,000 in income but he also must pay a $1,500 penalty on the premature withdrawal. So after taxes, Bob, who is in the 31 percent bracket, nets only $8,850 from the withdrawal ($15,000 less $4,650 in federal taxes and less the $1,500 penalty). Bob should consider borrowing the $15,000 down payment from family or other lenders. If Bob borrows $15,000 at seven percent for five years, his monthly payment will be less than $300 and the interest can be claimed as an itemized deduction if the loan is secured by the home.

TAX OPTIONS ON DISTRIBUTIONS FROM RETIREMENT PLANS

When you can receive money which has been accumulated for your benefit in a qualified retirement plan depends upon the terms of the plan itself. Generally the plan will provide that the benefits will be payable at normal retirement age or upon death. Some plans will provide that the benefits can be paid upon termination of employment even if that occurs before retirement. You control the payment date from an IRA.

The full amount of any distribution to you from a retirement plan which is not properly rolled over or directly transferred to another eligible plan will be taxable unless you have made nondeductible contributions to the plan in which case you will recover your contributions tax-free. If you are receiving payments over time, a portion of each payment from the retirement plan will be deemed to be a nontaxable recovery of your after-tax contribution to the retirement plan.

In general, the taxable portion of a retirement plan distribution is taxed to you as ordinary income. However, a special five-year averaging computation is available to ease the impact of certain lump sum distributions from qualified retirement plans as opposed to IRAs. Five-year averaging is available for one such distribution after you have reached age 59½ and have been an active plan participant for five years preceding the distribution. In this case you can compute the tax as if the payment were received over a five-year period of time even though the full tax is paid in the year you receive the distribution. Irrespective of marital status, use rates for single individuals to complete the tax. The effect of five-year averaging is to decrease the marginal brackets in which funds are taxed.

A SEP is considered as an IRA for purpose of distribution rules. Thus, a SEP distribution is not eligible for averaging.

CAUTION! The rules on lump sum distributions are quite complicated. There is a totally separate set of rules for individuals who reached age 50 before January 1, 1986. They may use ten-year averaging at 1986 tax rates for single individuals as an alternative to five-year averaging at current tax rates for singles. Additionally, those individuals who were participants in a plan prior to 1974 can treat a portion of the distribution as capital gain computed at the 1986 maximum rate of 20 percent.

TAX PLANNING IDEA If you have the opportunity to receive a distribution eligible for favored averaging, or for capital gain, and you do not have immediate need of the funds, you must make a determination as to whether you will be better off taxwise and economically by paying taxes in the year of the distribution at favored rates and then reinvesting remaining amounts or by transferring the distribution and taking portions as ordinary income only when needed or required by law. A determination must be made on the facts of each case; however, the latter approach is usually preferable particularly when the distributee has a number of years before distributions must commence under the law.

CAUTION! The 1996 tax legislation abolished five-year averaging after 1999. The result of this change is that only individuals who reached age 50 before January 1, 1986, will be eligible for any favorable income tax treatment on lump sum distributions after the effective date.

QUESTION: Can I borrow money from my retirement plan?

ANSWER: Subject to the terms of the retirement plan, you may borrow a limited amount against your account. Unless the borrowing is to acquire a principal residence, full repayment must be within five years. In any event, installment payments must be made on at least a quarterly basis. You can borrow up to the lesser of:

1. $50,000; or

2. The greater of $10,000 or one-half of your vested benefit.

The $50,000 amount is reduced by the excess of your highest outstanding loan balance during the one-year period prior to a subsequent loan over the loan balance on the date of the subsequent loan. For example, assume the following facts:

Vested Account Balance	$200,000
November 1, 1996, Loan Balance	$ 30,000
November 1, 1997, Loan Balance	$ 20,000
Maximum Additional Loan on November 1, 1998	$ 20,000

On November 1, 1996, the participant borrowed $30,000 from his qualified retirement plan. On November 1, 1997, when his outstanding loan balance was $20,000, he sought to borrow an additional amount from the plan. The most that he could borrow on November 1, 1997 was an additional $20,000 because the normal $50,000 cap was reduced by $10,000, representing the excess of $30,000, the highest outstanding balance, over the $20,000 outstanding balance on the date of the new loan. Any distribution over these legal limits will be considered a taxable distribution from the plan and includable in income.

CAUTION!   Interest paid on loans from retirement plans is deductible pursuant to the usual rules; however, interest paid on loans from retirement plans by key individuals, including most owners and officers, is not deductible regardless of the use to which the loan proceeds are made or whether it is secured by a qualified residence. Furthermore, no interest deduction is allowed to any employee if the loan's repayment is secured by the employee's account balance representing his or her elective deferrals in a 401(k) plan or a tax-sheltered annuity (discussed in Chapter 12).

CAUTION!   An S corporation plan cannot lend money to a more than five percent stock-holder-employee and a Keogh plan cannot lend money to a sole proprietor or a more than ten percent partner. A Simplified Employee Pension Plan (SEP) or IRA cannot lend money to the account holder except indirectly through a 60-day rollover once every 365 days.

10

BUSINESS TAX PLANNING

ORGANIZATION CHOICES FOR YOUR BUSINESS

When you decide to start a business, whether it will be your full-time occupation or a part-time venture to make extra dollars, your next decision should be the legal form in which the business will operate. In other words, should operations be conducted as a sole proprietorship, a partnership, or a corporation? There is no single right answer for everyone. Rather, various tax and nontax factors must be considered and each individual situation evaluated on its particular facts. Also, once the initial legal form of the business organization has been established, the facts and circumstances may change so as to warrant modifying the structure of the business to another legal form.

There are three basic structures under which to conduct a business—sole proprietorship, partnership, or corporation. Partnerships can be organized as either general partnerships or as limited partnerships. As discussed in Chapter 6, partnerships also include limited liability companies which generally allow all co-owners the benefit of limited liability from creditors and limited liability partnerships which are recognized in a number of states and which typically allow all co-owners the benefit of limited liability in certain circumstances only. Corporations, for federal income tax purposes, can operate as regular taxable C corporations or, if eligible, can elect to be treated as S corporations, which are generally not subject to federal income taxes at the corporate level.

Nontax considerations (such as limiting personal liability) are of equal importance to tax considerations in determining the appropriate form of business operation. But in terms of income tax considerations, the sole proprietor simply includes the net profit or loss generated by the business on his or her personal return; any profit is subject to the normal applicable personal income tax rates. Similarly, an individual partner (whether general, limited, or an LLC/LLP member) is taxed at the personal tax rates on his or her share of the partnership business operations.

A C corporation is a taxable entity and pays federal taxes on its taxable income at the following marginal rates:

If Taxable Income Is:	Marginal Tax Rate Is:
Up to $50,000	15%
$50,001-$75,000	25%
$75,001-$100,000	34%
$100,001-$335,000	39%
$335,001-$10,000,000	34%
$10,000,001-$15,000,000	35%
$15,000,001-$18,333,333	38%
Over $18,333,333	35%

This creates an effective tax rate of 34 percent for most corporations with taxable incomes over $335,000 and one of 35 percent for the most profitable corporations in America. However, *personal service corporations*, providing medical, legal, accounting, and similar services, are taxed at a flat rate of 35 percent from the first dollar of taxable income.

The corporate structure offers the owner-employee the opportunity to enjoy tax savings from participation in fringe benefit programs, which is not available when the business is operated in unincorporated form. If the business operates as a C corporation (but not as an S corporation), the shareholder-employees can, subject to nondiscrimination rules when there are other employees, have the cost of health and group term life insurance as well as unreimbursed medical expenses paid for on a tax-deductible basis by the corporation. See Chapter 2 for a discussion of fringe benefits.

An S corporation shareholder is taxed at the personal tax rates on his or her share of the S corporation business operations. Although an S corporation shareholder is taxed similarly to a partner in a partnership, restrictions on qualification and use of losses make operating as an S corporation more hazardous from a tax perspective than operating as a partnership.

The salary paid a shareholder-employee of a C or S corporation is treated like all other compensation and is subject to all payroll taxes, including unemployment and Social Security taxes. However, Social Security costs of operating in incorporated form are the same as in unincorporated form. The employee's share of the Social Security tax in 1997, including the Medicare portion, prior to indexing the base in 1998 for cost of living is 7.65 percent on the first $65,400 of salary, and the corporation pays an additional 7.65 percent for a combined total on the shareholder-employee salary of 15.3 percent (which is the self-employment tax rate on the unincorporated owner). The Medicare portion of 1.45 percent to the employee and an additional 1.45 percent to the employer (the combined rate of 2.9 percent being the same for the unincorporated owner) applies to all wages and self-employment income.

CAUTION!   While operating as a sole proprietorship or general partnership requires no formal filings, the requirements of state law must be satisfied in order to obtain legal status as a limited partnership, limited liability company, limited liability partnership, or corporation. Additionally, a corporation must file Form 2553 with the IRS within two and one-half months from the start of the year for which it seeks S corporation treatment. The IRS in its discretion may accept late-filed S elections inadvertently forgotten.

TAX PLANNING IDEA While a limited liability company is generally taxed as a partnership, about 33 states permit one person LLCs. The IRS first sanctioned these LLCs as of January 1, 1997. A sole owner of an LLC apparently files a Schedule C with his or her individual income tax return.

TAX PLANNING IDEA As a general rule, if you incorporate, S corporation status is most attractive to start-up corporations if the losses to the shareholders will be active rather than passive (see Chapter 2) and to personal service or profitable nonpersonal service corporations when income will be taxed personally in a lower or comparable bracket to corporate rates of 34 or 35 percent. In contrast, C corporation status is most attractive to nonpersonal service corporations able to take advantage of the 15 percent and 25 percent corporate marginal rate brackets, especially when there are attractive fringe benefits. C corporation status is required to obtain a 50 percent exclusion on stock gains in certain small business corporations. See Chapter 7 for a discussion of small business stock.

TAX PLANNING IDEA S corporation shareholder-employees can keep Social Security contributions low by setting modest salaries below the Social Security base. While they will pay Social Security taxes on such compensation, they will not pay any Social Security tax on remaining amounts distributed by the corporation as dividends or on earnings that are retained. This "loophole," and the fact that most states and the IRS do not yet recognize one-person LLCs, are the primary reasons why new businesses may wish to operate as S corporations as opposed to LLCs, which are otherwise generally more flexible in operation.

CAUTION! Unreasonably low compensation in relation to the value of services performed by an S corporation owner may be challenged. The IRS has commenced an audit program of the compensation paid to S corporation shareholder-employees. An audit nabbed an Idaho law firm which in 1994 lost its case in federal district court. The firm, which operated as an S corporation, never paid salary to its owner-employees and the IRS successfully reclassified amounts distributed to the shareholders from dividends to compensation.

Congress has periodically considered legislation which would restrict or eliminate the ability of S corporation owner-employees to avoid Social Security taxes through this loophole. Certain proposals have been directed at all businesses, while others have targeted only service-related businesses including health, law, engineering, architecture, accounting, actuarial services, performing arts, consulting, athletics, and most financial services as well as any other business which Treasury determines to require little capital to produce income.

SELECTION OF THE BUSINESS' FISCAL YEAR

A business operated as a sole proprietorship will use the calendar year to report its business activity. C corporations, other than personal service corporations, can select any fiscal year. These corporations should consider selecting a fiscal year based upon the business' *natural business year.* Closing the cor-poration's books and records for tax purposes in the middle of the business' busiest time may be an administrative headache and may cause the highest possible taxable income due to high inventory levels.

Partnerships, S corporations, and personal service corporations are generally required to use a calendar year to report their business activities. Alternatively, if the entity can establish that a fiscal year coincides with the entity's natural business year, the entity can request IRS permission to use that fiscal year for its business reporting. Except for certain businesses that are seasonal in nature, a natural business year will be difficult to show.

If a partnership or S corporation wishes to adopt a fiscal year which does not coincide with its natural business year, it may do so by selecting a fiscal year of September 30, October 31, or November 30. However, if an S corporation or partnership selects a September, October, or November year end, it must make a tax payment to IRS roughly equal to the value of the tax deferral available to the partners or shareholders of the partnership or S corporation.

Personal service corporations unable to show a natural business year may also elect a September, October, or November year end. A personal service corporation that opts for a September, October, or November year end will lose deductions for payments to the shareholder-employees if the corporation fails to pay proportionate shares of their salaries during the entire fiscal year.

TAX PLANNING IDEA   Selecting a year-end of January 31 for a nonpersonal service C corporation can provide some tax savings. The corporation can pay a bonus to the shareholder-employee early in the calendar year. The bonus payment is deductible by the corporation but the individual does not pay taxes (other than through withholdings) on the bonus until April 15 of the following year.

TAX PLANNING IDEA   Personal tax planning is facilitated when eligible corporations select fiscal years other than December 31. For example, if a shareholder-employee finds himself or herself in the 31 percent tax bracket but realizes that a normal December salary payment would cause "creeping" into the 36 percent bracket, the individual can enter into an agreement with the corporation in November to defer receipt of the December salary until January. This effectively avoids having his or her December salary taxed at the 36 percent rate and will have no impact on the corporation's taxable income because the January payment is in the same fiscal year as a December payment of the salary would have been.

CAUTION!   Agreements between corporations and the shareholder-employees to defer compensation will be closely scrutinized by the IRS. In order to be an effective deferral, the agreement between the employer and the employee must be entered into before the time that the compensation is earned and the corporation's obligation must be unsecured. See the further discussion of deferred compensation arrangements in Chapter 2.

ALLOCATING PRICE ON AN ASSET PURCHASE

In many instances a business will commence by purchasing assets from a seller, as opposed to purchasing an interest in the business entity itself or "starting from scratch." The allocation among assets will be extremely important to the buyer in an asset purchase.

To the extent of an allocation to inventory, the buyer will write off the cost upon the disposition of the merchandise. Capital assets such as furniture, fixtures, equipment, and vehicles will be written off over prescribed periods of time as discussed later in this chapter. When a below- market lease is acquired, an allocation to the leasehold rights is written off over the remaining period of the lease. Most intangibles, including goodwill, covenants, and lists of customers, clients, and patients, are written off over 15 years.

In many cases the seller or one or more officers of the seller will provide significant or not-so-significant consultation services. When part of the consideration for the deal is the consulting payments, these amounts, when paid, will be deductible to the business, provided they reflect the value of the services.

Purchasers generally seek allocations to those assets, such as furniture, fixtures, and equipment, as well as consulting agreements, which provide a quick write-off period. Individual or S corporation sellers seek allocations to those assets which will result in capital gain. These assets include capital items such as furniture, fixtures, and equipment but only to the extent the allocation is more than the seller's original purchase price. Allocations to goodwill, leasehold interests, and lists also offer capital gain treatment to a seller. C corporation sellers seek allocations which avoid a double layer of taxation such as to individual consulting agreements or convenants.

TAX PLANNING IDEA   The allocation among assets is important to both buyer and seller. Their interests are generally adverse except both a buyer and an individual S corporation seller may benefit from an allocation to leasehold interests or to capital assets beyond the seller's original purchase price. However, most transactions are incapable of offering any economic substance to support a significant allocation in either manner. Both a buyer and a C corporation seller may benefit from an allocation to a consulting agreement. Of course, there must be substance to the arrangement or the IRS can challenge the allocation.

CAUTION!   Sellers at or near retirement age should beware of an allocation to consultation services. Such payments constitute *earned income* and affect the right to draw Social Security benefits until age 70 when the income limitation is no longer applicable. Additionally, Social Security or self-employment tax, depending on whether the structure is under an employment or independent contractor agreement, must be paid on the income.

CAUTION!   IRS Form 8594 must be attached to the tax return of both the buyer and seller when mass assets of a business are sold and a goodwill or going concern value applies. The form will allow the IRS to overturn allocations that clearly lack substance.

CAUTION! Many states impose a sales tax to the extent that a purchase price is allocated to furniture, equipment, and similar property. Additionally, certain jurisdictions seek to apply their sales tax to seemingly intangible assets such as customer lists to the extent that they are transferred on such tangible media as paper or computer disks. Given that lists have the same tax treatment to both buyer and seller as goodwill, there is no benefit in such an allocation.

CAPITALIZE ON YOUR DEPRECIATION DEDUCTION

You can recover the cost of assets used in a trade or business over a period of time, generally five or seven years, depending upon the particular type of property and the year in which you first acquired the asset.

Tangible personal property acquired by a taxpayer for use in a trade or business (as opposed to an investment such as nontransient lodging) can be expensed to a maximum of $18,000 in 1997, $18,500 in 1998, and increasing gradually to $25,000 by 2003. This benefit, which must be elected by the due date of the tax return including extensions, eliminates the need for many small businesses to maintain depreciation schedules and accelerates the tax benefit associated with capital expenditures. The expensing of tangible personal property to these maximums is phased out in any year for a taxpayer placing in service tangible personal property costing more than $200,000, and expensing in any event cannot be used to cause or increase a business loss. Married individuals filing separately are treated as one taxpayer for purpose of expensing. See Chapter 7 for special expensing rules for businesses within empowerment zones.

Although automobiles generally qualify for write-off over five years, it takes many more years to fully depreciate expensive automobiles. The maximum write-off for an automobile used 100 percent in a taxpayer's business and placed in service during 1997 is only $11,210 in the aggregate over the first three years and is only $1,775 in each subsequent year. The actual annual write-offs are adjusted upward annually for inflation. The expensing rule for tangible personal property acquired during the year cannot be used to increase the first-year write-off.

CAUTION! The maximum annual write-offs assume 100 percent business use. If an automobile is used primarily but not exclusively for business, the actual annual write-offs must be determined by multiplying these maximums by the actual percentage of business use. Special rules apply to automobiles in which business use does not exceed 50 percent.

FILING POINTER The largest sport utility vehicles, those weighing over 6,000 pounds, are exempt from the "luxury car" rules. They can be written off over five years and qualify for the first year expensing up to the limit for the particular year.

YEAR-END REMINDER Buy needed tangible personal property by December 31 if you are eligible for the expensing of capital assets and you have not reached your limit. The dollar-for-dollar write-off will give an immediate reduction of taxable income.

FILING POINTER Although the expensing of tangible personal property may not cause or enlarge a business loss, the test is applied by considering all taxable income from the active conduct of any trade or business. Treasury Regulations indicate that compensation earned as an employee is considered as taxable income from a business. Consequently, most employees with W-2 income and small side businesses will be able to expense qualifying capital purchases up to the maximum.

CAUTION! Where more than 40 percent of the basis of newly acquired personal property, exclusive of expensed items, is acquired in the fourth quarter of the year, the depreciation deduction for personal property may be reduced under a formula which looks at the quarter in which each asset was acquired. If a taxpayer isn't careful and this rule applies, the depreciation deduction for fourth quarter purchases will be one-fourth of the deduction that otherwise would have applied.

MAKING THE IMPUTED INTEREST RULES WORK FOR YOU

When there is a sale of property and at least one payment for the property is deferred (for more than six months in some cases and for more than one year in others), an adequate rate of interest must be charged or the Internal Revenue Service will impute interest on payments due more than six months after the sale. Depending on the subject matter of the sale and the parties involved in the transaction, the required rate of interest will vary.

In general, the interest that must be charged is the lesser of nine percent, or a rate set monthly by the IRS tied to U.S. Government securities rates. The nine percent alternative is unavailable on 1997 sales in excess of $3,723,800 (indexed in 1998 and succeeding years). There are many exceptions. For example, on the sale of land between certain related parties for $500,000 or less, an interest rate of at least six percent, compounded semiannually, must be charged. Interest is not imputed in transfers related to a marital termination.

The imputed interest rules also apply to loans in excess of $10,000.

CAUTION! If the stated interest rate is less on a sale than that required by the law, then a portion of each note payment will be recharacterized as interest, deductible by the payor and taxable as interest income to the recipient. Since a portion of the amount paid by the purchaser will be recharacterized as interest, the purchaser must reduce the basis of the purchased assets by the amount that has been recharacterized as interest.

If the stated interest rate on a loan is less than that required by law, then the foregone interest is deemed to have been transferred from the lender to the borrower and then "paid" by the borrower to the lender as interest. The constructive transfer from the lender to the borrower will be characterized as a gift where the context of the transaction is other than a business setting.

If the loan is made in a business setting, such as a loan to an employee or to a shareholder, the amount of the foregone interest is taxable as additional compensation (subject to Social Security taxes) if the loan is made to an employee with no equity interest or as a dividend if the loan is made to a shareholder. The constructive payment from the borrower to the lender is taxable as interest income to the lender and perhaps deductible as an interest expense for the borrower. See Chapter 4 for the rules governing the deduction for interest expense by an individual.

TAX PLANNING IDEA   While the IRS sets a minimum interest rate, it does not set a maximum rate on sales or loans. While two parties must use a rate that is "reasonable" or face a tax restructuring if scrutinized by the IRS, purchasers in a sales transaction may particularly seek faster writeoffs through a lower sales price with a higher interest rate.

TAX PLANNING IDEA   In that the imputed interest rule is not applicable to loans up to $10,000, you can use your corporation as a bank and borrow up to $10,000 without interest. The $10,000 will be recognized as a true loan only if certain steps are taken. As with all loans, it should be documented on the books of the corporation and evidenced by a promissory note which calls for loan repayment. Of course, the loan should be paid down on some regular basis.

PAYING YOUR CHILDREN

One method of family tax planning that is often overlooked is the ability of a business owner to pay children for services that are performed for the business. So long as the children are actually performing services for the business, they can be paid a reasonable salary that will provide the business with a current tax deduction. Although the salary will be taxable to the children, this earned income will be taxed at the children's own tax rate (perhaps as low as 15 percent) and will not be subject to the "Kiddie" tax (see Chapter 1). And, as discussed in Chapter 9, the child can open an Individual Retirement Account and enjoy years of tax-free compound growth.

FILING POINTER   Children under age 18 on the payroll of their sole proprietor parent are not subject to Social Security taxes; however, the self-employment income of the parent is reduced. When the parent is below the Social Security base ($65,400 before indexing in 1998), payments justifiably made to a child of a sole proprietor as a bona fide employee result in substantial self-employment tax savings coupled with the income tax savings.

CAUTION!   Make sure you consider the impact of the child's salary on your ability to continue to claim the child as a dependent. Loss of the exemption for the child would mean the loss of a $2,650 deduction in 1997, which translates to $822 more in federal taxes for a taxpayer in the 31 percent bracket (31% × $2,650). In 1998 loss of the exemption would also mean loss of the $400 child credit if the dependent is under age 17 or loss of any available education credit if he or she is in college or vocational school. See Chapter 3 for a discussion of these credits.

 CAUTION! For wages paid to a child to be deductible, they must be both "ordinary and necessary" to your business and "reasonable" for the work that was actually done.

ILLUSTRATION

Using 1997 tax rates, here is an example of the savings that can be achieved by having your child on the payroll. Assume that you have your own sole proprietorship and your 13-year-old child works for you every day after school and on weekends, cleaning up and doing general filing. Assume further that you would have to pay $10,000 to any other person to perform the same job that your child is doing. Your business shows a profit of $40,000 before considering your child's salary and any deduction relating to self-employment tax. You are in the 31 percent federal tax bracket and the salary that you pay your child is his or her only income.

	Child Employed	Child Not Employed
Business Net Profit (before child's salary and self-employment tax deduction)	$40,000	$40,000
Child's Salary	($10,000)	0
Business Net Profit	$30,000	$40,000
Federal Income Tax on Net Profit	$ 8,643	$11,524
Self-Employment Tax	4,239	5,652
Parent's Federal Taxes on Net Profit	$12,882	$17,176
Child's Federal Income Tax	900	0
Family's Combined Federal Taxes on Net Profit	$13,782	$17,176

By choosing to pay your child for the services that he or she performs for you, the family's total federal tax liability is reduced by nearly $3,400. The self-employment tax and the federal income tax were computed after the adjustments relating to the deduction for one-half of the self-employment tax, as discussed in Chapter 1.

PAYING YOUR OTHER WORKERS— INDEPENDENT CONTRACTOR VS. EMPLOYEE

Whether to classify a worker as an independent contractor or as an employee is an important decision for any business owner. If the worker is properly classified as an independent contractor, the employer has no obligation to pay Social Security taxes or unemployment taxes on the worker's compensation or to withhold income taxes or the employee's share of Social Security taxes. The worker is solely responsible for paying his or her own tax obligation, including self-employment tax.

What allows a worker to be classified as an independent contractor, reducing the costs of business operations? An independent contractor is a worker who is free to complete a designated task by whatever means he or she feels appropriate and is only under the control of the service recipient as to the end result. An employee, on the other hand, is subject to the direction and control of the service recipient both as to the end result and as to the means used to achieve that result. Twenty questions have been developed to ascertain whether an employer-employee relationship exists. Among the most important factors indicating employee status are the following:

1. The relationship is continuing, as opposed to intermittent work.
2. The worker is performing services solely or primarily for one service recipient.
3. Training is being offered to the worker by the service recipient.

In recent years the IRS has increased its activity in the independent contractor/employee classification area despite a lack of clarity in the tax law, shifting more than 500,000 workers to employee status between 1988 and 1995 and assessing almost $1 billion in taxes, penalties, and interest. No industry is immune—a New York Federal District Court in 1996 backed up an IRS reclassification of exotic dancers as employees. During 1997 the IRS came after a posh New York country club, claiming that golf caddies were club employees.

The General Accounting Office believes that independent contractors, who comprise only 13 percent of individual taxpayers, account for 40 percent of unreported income and owe 75 percent of delinquent taxes. In a 1995 speech to the White House Conference on Small Business, then IRS Commissioner Margaret Richardson estimated that misclassification of workers as independent contractors costs the Government between $4 and $6 billion annually in tax revenues.

CAUTION!   Failure to properly classify workers as employees not only means substantial exposure to the business for the unpaid taxes but also may create personal liability for unpaid withholding tax. See discussion of this Trust Fund Recovery Penalty later in this chapter. The improper classification of workers as independent contractors also jeopardizes qualification of the retirement plans of the business.

TAX PLANNING IDEA   Because of the lack of clear guidelines governing proper classification of workers, Congress provided some relief. Under Section 530 of the Revenue Act of 1978, if the business has consistently treated a worker as an independent contractor, has filed all tax returns (including the information return to the worker reporting the amount of remuneration) consistent with independent contractor status, and has a reasonable basis for such treatment, the IRS is barred from assessing payroll taxes against the business. For purposes of this Section 530 relief, judicial precedent, IRS rulings, a prior audit of the taxpayer, or an industry standard will be sufficient to establish that the business owner had a reasonable basis for treating the worker as an independent contractor. A post-

1996 audit may only be relied upon if worker classification was an issue in the audit. Section 530 relief is not available for certain technical personnel such as engineers, computer programmers, and system analysts.

TAX PLANNING IDEA Businesses wishing to continue to treat workers as independent contractors should have written agreements with their help providing, among all else, that they may work for other businesses as well. IRS Form 1099 should be utilized to report compensation to independent contractors in excess of $600 in any year.

CONTROVERSY

Section 530 speaks of the need to show that a "significant segment" of an industry treats similar workers as independent contractors if an industry standard is to be utilized as a reasonable basis. What does the word "significant" mean? Look through several dictionaries, and you will probably interpret the term as meaning something more than minimal but something less than majority. For years, the IRS interpreted the term as requiring a majority use of independent contractors within the industry. However, the 1996 tax legislation rebuts the IRS and says that 25 percent of an industry as independent contractors is a significant segment in all cases, while a smaller percentage may suffice on a case-by-case basis.

FILING POINTER Taxpayers falling just short of qualifying under Section 530 may yet be able to resolve worker classification cases at less than 100 cents on the dollar under a two-year settlement program expiring on March 4, 1998.

CAUTION! Legislation may be on the way. Dropped from the Taxpayer Relief Act of 1997 at the last hour was a provision which would have generally broadened protection for businesses treating workers as independent contractors.

THE TRUST FUND RECOVERY PENALTY— PERSONAL LIABILITY FOR PAYROLL TAXES

While the business owner in a sole proprietorship is responsible (and all general partners in a partnership are jointly and individually responsible) for the payment of payroll taxes, responsibility in a corporation, limited liability company, or limited liability partnership requires assessment of the *Trust Fund Recovery Penalty,* formerly called *the 100 percent penalty.* This penalty, when imposed, is normally a personal assessment for income and Social Security taxes withheld in trust from the wages of employees (or not withheld due to the alleged misclassification of workers as independent contractors). When it appears that payroll taxes cannot be paid by the business entity at any time in the foreseeable future, the IRS seeks to determine the identities of the *responsible persons* and to collect the trust portions of the payroll tax liability from them.

There has been much litigation, and the courts and IRS appeals offices of this land remain crowded with Trust Fund Recovery Penalty cases. For an individual to be held responsible for the Trust Fund Recovery Penalty, he or she must have been one of the persons responsible for collection and payment of payroll taxes. In any business entity, there will be at least one person and perhaps many who have this responsibility.

The Internal Revenue Service usually interviews stockholders, directors, officers, and authorized signators of a corporation (or their LLC/LLP equivalents) in order to determine whether they are responsible persons. Many factors are considered in determining who is responsible; however, the issue usually comes down to whether the individual had or shared responsibility for financial decisions.

The most frequent cases involve:

1. A management team blaming outside investors, and outside investors pointing fingers at the management team;
2. Bookkeepers with signature authority over the bank account but who deferred to others in making the financial decisions; and
3. Family members of clearly responsible business owners (often spouses with ownership interests or who hold offices in name).

The results in each case will depend upon the particular facts. Successful defenses to the imposition of the Trust Fund Recovery Penalty usually involve the absence of willfulness as shown by one or more of the following:

1. Lack of knowledge of the delinquent payroll taxes;
2. Lack of funds to pay the taxes after learning of the delinquency; or
3. Lack of ability to make payment after learning of the delinquency, due to no signature authority or lack of an actual ability to cause others to make or order payment.

Those individuals determined to be liable are jointly and individually responsible for the payment of the Trust Fund Recovery Penalty. If the penalty is collected from one person, it is not collected from any others. As a result, many of these matters are not resolved quickly in the hope that payment will be made by someone else.

A person held liable for the Trust Fund Recovery Penalty is normally only liable to the IRS for the federal income tax withholding and Social Security withholding collected from employees (or not collected due to the alleged misclassification of workers as independent contractors). There is no personal liability for the employer matching Social Security or for unemployment taxes. Interest begins to run on the Trust Fund Recovery Penalty after there is a personal assessment, usually only after an unsuccessful appeals conference. After payment by a person found to be liable, other individuals may remain liable for other tax periods for which the prior payor was not responsible. The business, if it is still in existence, also remains liable for remaining unpaid trust portions, matching Social Security, unemployment taxes, and for penalties and interest. See Chapter 13 for a discussion of the procedures for contesting a proposed Trust Fund Recovery Penalty and of a controversy as to the time period in which that Penalty can be assessed.

CAUTION!   You should avoid being involved in any capacity with a business that does not fulfill its responsibilities concerning employee withholding. Recent court decisions have strongly backed up the IRS in most Trust Fund Recovery Penalty assessments. That you were only following orders is not in itself a defense. In one 1994 case, a federal district court found a corporate officer liable although he "essentially acted as a cabin boy on a sinking ship." That you should be met with sympathy is not in itself sufficient to cause a favorable decision. In a 1996 case, the Ninth Circuit Court of Appeals backed up a Hawaii Federal District Court decision finding a quadriplegic personally liable for the Trust Fund Recovery Penalty scant months following his crippling injury.

TAX PLANNING IDEA   Voluntary payments can be allocated to the trust portion of the employment tax liability, thereby reducing the subsequent personal liability of persons who are individually liable. Designations should be made both on the check and on accompanying correspondence that payment is to be applied against the withholdings from employee wages and not employer matching Social Security.

CAUTION!   Be careful not to let a corporate charter lapse. In such a case, the IRS may be able to hold all directors and/or officers responsible for the entire corporate debt for employment and unemployment taxes if state law renders them personally liable for corporate debt upon lapse of charter.

TAX PLANNING IDEA   For Trust Fund Recovery Penalties assessed after July 30, 1996, you have a right to bring suit under federal law for *pro rata* reimbursement by other individuals found liable for the Penalty. Upon written request, the IRS must inform you of the extent of collection activity against and the amount of payment by other responsible individuals.

COMBINING YOUR BUSINESS AND PERSONAL TRAVEL

The cost of travel away from home for business purposes is generally a deductible expense. The expense of your hotel room during the business trip is fully deductible so long as your trip requires you to be away from home overnight. However, only 50 percent of the cost of your meals is deductible on the theory that the meal contains an element of personal living expense, regardless of the meal's relationship to your business activities.

If you combine a business trip with a vacation, you may be able to write off part of the cost of the trip as a business expense. If the trip is taken primarily for business purposes, the cost of traveling to and from the destination is fully deductible (with the exception of special rules that apply to trips outside the United States). The costs of your meals and lodging while on the trip are deductible (subject to the percentage rule for the costs of the meals) to the extent that they are allocable to business activities.

All of the circumstances surrounding a combined business/pleasure trip may be examined in the event of an audit to determine if the primary purpose was business or personal. Obviously, the amount of time spent on business activities in relationship to the personal activity time will be an important factor.

Special rules cover combined business and personal trips that you take outside the United States for more than seven days. Under these circumstances , if you spend 25 percent or more of your time on personal activities, only the cost of the travel allocable to the business portion of the trip will be deductible, even though the trip's purpose was primarily business oriented.

If you do not have substantial control over arranging the itinerary for the trip abroad or if you can establish that a personal vacation was not a major consideration in deciding to take the trip, no allocation will be required and your entire travel costs will still be deductible as a business expense. If the trip abroad is primarily personal in nature, none of the travel expenses will be deductible although the expenses incurred at the destination which are allocable solely to business activities will be deductible.

FILING POINTER   Even though you are unable to deduct your spouse's travel costs unless he or she is a *bona fide* employee of the business, you will nonetheless get some break with the cost of your lodging. Only to the extent that your hotel room costs more than hotel accommodations at a single rate is a portion of the deduction denied. If there is no difference in the cost of the hotel room whether you are alone or with your spouse, then the hotel room is fully deductible even though the spouse's travel costs will not be deductible.

FILING POINTER   Even though a corporation may not fully deduct certain expenses such as spousal travel and 50 percent of meals, the disallowed amounts are not income to an employee if there is a business reason for the expense, thereby avoiding a "double-hit" (no business deduction yet income to the employee).

CAUTION!   You cannot deduct the costs of attending investment seminars or similar conventions. Similarly, the costs of traveling to a shareholders' meeting are generally not deductible.

TAX PLANNING IDEA   If you own income producing property, such as rental property, you can deduct the costs of reasonable travel to look after the property. For example, if you own a beachfront condominium in Florida, you can probably deduct the costs of travel to and from Florida in the middle of fall to get the property ready for the season and then again at the end of the rental season to close up the property.

FILING POINTER   There are other types of expenses besides airfare, meals, and lodging that are often overlooked when tallying up out-of-pocket costs away from home. Don't forget tips for the skycaps and porters, taxicabs or other transportation costs from the airport to the hotel and between the hotel and the various business sites, tips to the hotel maid, and valet service.

QUESTION: I live in Chicago and I will have to travel to San Francisco on business. I have scheduled meetings with business associates in San Francisco for each day, Monday through Friday. I hope to finish up on Friday afternoon and then spend the weekend in the wine country before my return flight to Chicago. Can I write off the cost of this trip?

ANSWER: The entire cost of the flight to and from San Francisco will be deductible as a business expense since it is clear that the primary purpose of this trip will be business orient-ed. The cost of your hotel room in San Francisco for Sunday night through Thursday night will also be fully deductible. The applicable percentage of the costs of your meals in San Francisco will also be deductible as a business expense.

In contrast, while the costs of the meals and lodging incurred during your trip into the wine country will normally not be deductible inasmuch as they are personal in nature, an exception may apply if you fly home on the Sunday following your meetings. In a 1992 letter ruling not binding on other taxpayers, the IRS indicated that the cost of lodging and the deductible cost of meals may be written off on a day without business activity if a net saving in travel cost results by staying over a Saturday night. For example, if your airfare is $200 in-stead of $600 by staying in California through Saturday night, the extra cost of meals (to the extent of the allowable percentage) and lodging are deductible if they do not exceed $400.

GETTING MEAT OUT OF YOUR BUSINESS MEALS AND ENTERTAINMENT

The deduction for business meals, including the cost of meals incurred while traveling away from home and on business, and business entertainment expenses, is limited to 50 percent of the total costs incurred.

In order to be able to deduct the applicable portion of the cost of a business meal, you must be able to establish that there is more than a general expectation of deriving a business benefit and that business discussions actually occurred directly before, during, or after the meal. No deduction for a meal expense is generally allowable unless you or one of your employees is present at the meal.

Similar rules govern the deductibility of entertainment expenses. There must be more than a general expectation of deriving a benefit related to your business. Consequently, unless the entertainment is in a business setting, significant business discussions must occur before or after the event. For example, you can deduct the applicable portion of the cost of taking your biggest customer to a play on Broadway so long as you can establish that bona fide business discussions took place either before or after the play. However, according to a 1994 Tax Court decision, you can't deduct the cost of taking your clients on Canadian and Alaskan fishing trips when business is discussed casually but the primary purpose is keeping client goodwill.

No deduction can be claimed for costs associated with an entertainment facility which you own or rent, such as a yacht or tennis court; however, taxes and allowable interest remain deductible on the entertainment facility. Where the facility is used for entertainment purposes, the costs of the actual entertainment, such as food and beverages, are deductible subject to both the percentage rule and the ability to prove the validity of the entertainment expense.

Most club dues are not deductible including dues for country, athletic, luncheon, and airline clubs. This prohibition does not apply to chambers of commerce, professional organizations, public service clubs, and similar organizations pursuant to Regulations issued by the IRS in 1995.

 TAX PLANNING IDEA   If you entertain groups of customers or clients, it's best to plan a formal agenda for meetings. In 1992 the Tax Court ruled that a repossessor couldn't deduct the appropriate percentage of the cost of sending three busloads of referral sources to Las Vegas for a weekend of entertainment and general discussions despite a significant rise in business thereafter. Four years earlier, the same court had allowed a title company to deduct the appropriate percentage of the cost of flying lawyers, realtors, and bankers to Las Vegas for entertainment combined with limited formal meetings.

No formal agenda? Here's another idea—a court-created exception to the requirement of either a business setting or bona fide business discussions. Throw a party so big that the "clear purpose is to obtain publicity as opposed to maintaining goodwill." That's what a Virginia Federal District Court determined as it permitted a deduction for the annual party of a developer whose guests included all real estate agents who sold at least two of his homes during the previous year. The party for 1989 featured cocktails, a seated dinner, and entertainment by singer Barbara Mandrell. The cost of the party—$347,000.

FILING POINTER   Don't forget that entertaining at home may very well qualify as a deductible business meal subject to the percentage limitation so long as you meet the usual standards. Of course, the added cost of feeding spouses will not be deductible unless a business purpose for the spouses' attendance can be established.

FILING POINTER   The 50 percent limitation on meals is not applicable to meals offered to the general public such as prior to a marketing presentation.

CAUTION!   The 50 percent limitation on entertainment expense is not applicable in the case of tickets given to customers and clients when you do not attend the event. In-stead, the cost is treated as a business gift which is fully deductible up to $25 per recipient per year. This will work in your favor for inexpensive tickets but to your detriment for costly tickets.

QUESTION: I am a department head employed by a major corporation and my annual bonus is based on our department's profitability. To improve morale among my staff of five, I wine and dine them a half dozen times a year. Can I deduct the cost?

ANSWER: The Tax Court says, at least in the absence of a company policy requiring the entertainment of employees under your direction, that entertainment of fellow employees is a personal and nondeductible expense.

YOUR TAX HOME—NOT WHERE THE HEART IS

Many individuals work away from home, have two homes, or have two jobs. These situations generate unique problems.

QUESTION: During the summer I am president of a company which supplies lifeguards to swimming pools in New Jersey. During the winter I manage a ski resort in Vermont. I own a home in each location, staying about six months at each place. My family lives year-round in Vermont. For which residence should I keep records and claim that I was away from home?

ANSWER: An individual's "tax home" is where that person's principal place of business is located irrespective of where his or her family resides. For example, according to a 1993 Tax Court decision, a pilot's tax home is the airport city at which the pilot is actually based as opposed to where the pilot resides. When your family resides in the locale of your principal place of business, you will be "away from home" when you travel to your secondary place of business. When your family resides in the locale of your secondary place of business, you will find it harder to deduct expenses. Your tax home remains at your principal place of business and, as such, your expenses for lodging, food, and related expenses are not deductible there. Your family's expenses at your secondary place of business are not deductible; only your individual allocable share of deductible expenses in the location of your secondary employment properly attributable to your presence there for business can be written off.

It will be necessary in your case to determine whether New Jersey or Vermont is your tax home based upon the comparative time spent, business activity, and financial return at each of your locations. The First Circuit Court of Appeals recently ruled that an individual who is not an itinerant must have a single tax home; thus you will be able to deduct appropriate costs related to the necessity of maintaining a place to live at a second location. However, you will fare better if you can show that your tax home is in Vermont.

TAX PLANNING IDEA   Most of the litigation concerning tax homes has arisen when an individual is situated in one city and is assigned to another location for a lengthy period. If the assignment is "temporary" in nature rather than "indefinite," lodging, 50 percent of food expense, and related costs at the temporary job location can be written off. Work away from home of one year or less requires examination of the facts of each case while actual work away from home of more than one year will necessarily be considered as indefinite. Consequently, an individual accepting a job or position away from his or her established home should have a contract tightly drawn in order that any obligation not extend into a second year.

CONTROVERSY

When an assignment is temporary and the tax home does not shift, transportation expenses incurred while traveling to the temporary site are deductible. What if an individual chooses to commute daily to the city where he or she is working temporarily? The Tax Court determined in 1993 that the transportation costs are still deductible. However, the IRS issued a Revenue Ruling in 1994 which would deny a deduction for daily transportation costs to temporary work sites when the individual has an office at home (see the discussion below) which is not his or her principal office.

SUBSTANTIATING YOUR TRAVEL, MEALS, AND ENTERTAINMENT EXPENSES

Unless you comply with the strict substantiation requirements of the law, no deduction is allowed for the cost of business travel, meals, and entertainment. Although the substantiation requirements are strict, they are not so onerous as to be overwhelming. All that you need to do is to be organized. Your record of travel, meals, and entertainment expenses must reflect the amount of the expense, the time and place of the expense, the business purpose of the expense, and the business relationship to you of each person who was entertained. Here's how IRS Publication 463, Travel, Entertainment, and Gift Expenses sets forth the substantiation elements for claiming these deductions:

Element to Be Proved	Travel	Entertainment
Amount	Amount of each separate expense for travel, lodging, and meals. Incidental expenses may be totaled in reasonable categories, such as taxis, daily meals for traveler, etc.	Amount of each separate expense. Incidental expenses such as taxis, telephones, etc., may be totaled on a daily basis.
Time	Date you left and returned for each trip, and number of days for business.	Date of entertainment. For meals or entertainment directly before or after a business discussion, the date and duration of the business discussion.
Place	Name of city or other designation.	Name and address or location of place of entertainment, or place of use of a facility for entertainment. Type of entertainment if not otherwise apparent. Place where business discussion was held if entertainment is directly before or after a business discussion.

Business purpose	Business reason for travel or the business benefit gained or expected to be gained.	Business reason or the business benefit gained or expected to be gained. Nature of business discussion or activity.
Business relationship	Not applicable.	Occupations or other information— such as names or other designations— about persons entertained that shows their business relationship to you. If all people entertained did not take part in business discussion, identify those who did. You must also prove that you or your employee was present if entertainment was a business meal.

You establish the elements of substantiation by maintaining a diary or log. You don't have to make entries in the diary immediately after an expenditure is made, but you must make entries at a time when you have present knowledge of expenditures. For example, once a week you could go back over the previous week and record the various elements of each of the expenses incurred during the preceding week. Receipts or other documentary evidence are not required to claim a deduction for all travel and entertainment expenses. Obviously, receipts or bills will concretely establish the amount of expenses and are therefore quite helpful. However, you need only retain the receipt or other bill in the case of lodging or in the case of any other expenditure of at least $75.

CAUTION! Failure to keep sufficient records can be costly. A manufacturing company had season tickets for football and hockey games and gave them away liberally to customers, vendors, distributors, and employees. While the company kept records of who used the tickets, the Tax Court in a 1994 decision denied a deduction because records did not indicate the business relationship of the recipients.

TAX PLANNING IDEA In lieu of maintaining a diary of actual expenses and retaining receipts for out-of-town travel, employers who reimburse their employees and self-employed individuals can claim deductions for meals and lodging based on a *per diem* allowance. Under this per diem arrangement, the business person can treat between $32 and $40 per day depending on location as the cost of his or her meals, 50 percent of which would be deductible as a business expense as discussed above. If reimbursements are made for lodging as well as for meals, the current federal *per diem* rate for localities in the continental United States is set forth in tables issued by the IRS or, under a simplified method, reimbursements can be made at a standard maximum rate of $109 per day ($166 in high cost areas) of which $32 per day ($40 per day in the high cost areas) is considered meal reimbursements.

The *per diem* method for handling meals and lodging expense should only be used where that method will provide the maximum allowable deduction.

THE OFFICE-IN-HOME DEDUCTION—EXPANDED FOR 1999

If you operate your business from your home, you may be entitled to claim certain write-offs with respect to the ownership of the property as a business deduction (known in the aggregate as the *office-in-home* deduction). IRS Form 8829 has been created to prove entitlement of business owners to the deduction. To qualify for the office-in-home deduction, the portion of your home that is used for business purposes must meet the following requirements:

1. The business use of that portion of the home must be *exclusive* and it must be used *regularly* for business purposes; and

2. The business use of that portion of the home must be the principal location of the business; a location in which you meet your patients, clients, or customers in the normal course of business; a storage place for inventory if the home is the sole location of the business (no exclusivity requirement in that case); or, in the case of a separate structure not attached to the home, must be used in connection with your business.

The write-offs that you can claim for the office-in-home deduction cannot exceed the income generated by the business at the home reduced by the normal operating expenses of the business not associated with the home (for example, office supplies, salaries, and postage) and further reduced by the portion of interest and taxes allocable to the portion of the dwelling unit used for business purposes. In other words, the office-in-home deduction can never create or increase a loss.

ILLUSTRATION

Assume the following facts:

Gross Income	$70,000
Business Expenses Unrelated to Business Use of Home	$60,000
Interest on Taxes on Home Allocable to Business Portion	$ 8,000
Expenses Related to Home Allocable to Business Portion (Insurance, Utilities, etc.)	$ 5,000
Depreciation on Home Allocable to Business Portion	$ 4,000

Because this individual's business expenses which were unrelated to the business use of the home and the interest and taxes on the home attributable to the portion used for business purposes totaled $68,000, only $2,000 ($70,000 – $68,000) of the expenses related to the home which were allocable to the office use are deductible as the office-in-home deduction. The remaining $3,000 of these expenses plus $4,000 of depreciation is carried over to the subsequent year as a possible office-in-home deduction.

Most controversies arising from the office-in-home deduction involved the definition of the "principal" location of the business. In 1993, the U.S. Supreme Court heard the case of a self-employed anesthesiologist who spent about 30–35 hours per week working at several hospitals and 10–15 hours per week doing administrative work at home in the absence of an office elsewhere. The Court determined that the doctor was not entitled to deduct home office costs in that his home was not his principal business location.

The Supreme Court decided that the principal location of a business is determined based on the "relative importance" of activities performed at each location and the "relative time" spent at each location. Because the Court failed to address situations in which conflicts might arise from the two prongs of this test, it left unanswered issues to be resolved by the IRS and the lower courts.

In a 1994 Revenue Ruling, the IRS indicated that the relative importance of the office-in-home versus other locations at which business is conducted should be determined first. Only if that test is inconclusive should the relevant time at various locations be considered.

The IRS elaborates in Publication 587, Business Use of Your Home. Under the relative importance test, the IRS would permit a deduction to a salesperson whose only office is in the home and who spends 30 of 42 hours in selling activities there and the other 12 hours calling on customers. The IRS would not permit a deduction in the converse situation, where a salesperson would spend 12 of 42 hours in the home selling activities and the other 30 hours outside of the home.

The Taxpayer Relief Act of 1997 will bring belated relief for many individuals adversely affected by the Supreme Court's 1993 decision. Effective in 1999, a home can be an individual's principal place of business if used for administrative or management activities and there is no other fixed location where such activities are conducted.

FILING POINTER The Tax Court determined several years ago that an individual need not use an entire room exclusively for business. According to the Court, it suffices that an area within a room is exclusively used for business—not even a temporary partition is required.

CAUTION! The courts have backed up the IRS position that the office-in-home deduction is unavailable to income-producing activities not constituting a business. A full-time investor consequently meeting other requirements will be denied the office-in-home deduction.

QUESTION: I live in Topeka, Kansas, where I work as a salesman for my employer. My employer's home office is in New Orleans. Although I make occasional trips to New Orleans for management meetings, I spend 95 percent of my time working in my home in the Topeka regional area. My employer does not have a branch office in Topeka, so I need my home office. I even have customers come to my home every day. Can I claim the office-in-home deduction?

ANSWER: Yes, you can claim the office-in-home deduction if the area from which you operate is used only for business and you are engaged in your sales activity on a regular basis.

Be sure you get your employer to substantiate by contract or letter the requirement that you work at home. Be as specific as possible in the job duties that are to be performed at home.

If you do qualify for the office-in-home deduction, as an employee you will be able to claim the deduction only if you itemize, and the amount of the deduction, when combined with other miscellaneous itemized deductions, exceeds two percent of your adjusted gross income. It is then subject to the overall reduction in itemized deductions by high income individuals (discussed in Chapter 1).

QUESTION: I run a day-care center out of my home and take care of three or four children each working day. My entire home is occupied ten hours a day, 250 days per year, by the kids with the exception of two bedrooms and a bathroom. On evenings and weekends all rooms are used by my family. Can I claim the office-in-home deduction?

ANSWER: A 1992 ruling by the IRS permits day-care providers to claim the office-in-home deduction through a multiple-step process for determining the percentage of interest and taxes, depreciation, and other expenses of the home which are allocable to its business use. To illustrate, if you use 1,500 square feet out of 2,000 square feet (75 percent) regularly for day care, multiply .75 times .2854. This latter fraction is based on the fact that day-care use of the home is 2,500 hours out of 8,760 hours during the year. The result is that you can deduct 21.4 percent of the expenses related to your home, subject to the requirement that the office-in-home deduction not exceed business income less other operating expenses.

In other words, the portion of the home for which you claim the office-in-home deduction is broken out not only on the basis of space but also on the basis of time.

CAUTION!   See Chapter 6 concerning the requirement of recapturing the depreciation claimed as part of the office-in-home deduction upon sale of your principal residence and use of the $250,000/$500,000 exclusion of gain. Also see Chapter 6 concerning possible partial ineligibility for the exculsion if the office-in-home deduction is claimed for a period covering more than two of the five years preceding sale.

For sales prior to the effective date of the exclusion, generally May 7, 1997, gain could not be rolled over on acquisition of a new residence or excluded by an individual over age 55 to the extent of the percentage of business use of the home. However, by ceasing business use of a principal residence prior to December 31 of the year preceding sale, an individual could apparently roll over all gain irrespective of the number of years that the office-in-home deduction was claimed.

WORKING AT YOUR HOBBY—IS THE BUSINESS FOR REAL?

Here is a situation that may sound familiar to you. Tom has a regular job as an employee, but on nights, weekends, and any free time that he can find, he works on a sideline activity such as antique sales. Or perhaps Tom isn't employed anywhere and his antique business is a full-time endeavor. Even so, Tom must be careful of the *hobby loss* rules. If these rules are applied, Tom will be able to claim a deduction beyond taxes and allowable interest only to the extent that no loss is created from the activity. In other words, a taxpayer is not permitted to claim a net loss on any activity treated as a hobby to him. This rule applies regardless of whether Tom passes the material participation tests associated with limiting deductions for losses from passive activities (see Chapter 2) and regardless of the "at risk" and basis rules (see Chapter 7).

A *rebuttable* presumption arises in the taxpayer's favor that an activity is not a hobby if the gross income derived from the endeavor exceeds the deductions in three out of five consecutive years. When the activity involves breeding, training, showing, or racing horses, the presumption will arise in favor of the taxpayer if there is a profit in two out of seven years.

Even if you cannot meet the presumption, you may still be able to claim a deduction for losses sustained in the activity if you can establish on the facts that you are engaging in the activity for the purpose of making a profit. The following factors will be analyzed to determine your motivation:

1. How you conduct the activity—is it conducted in a businesslike manner?

2. What is your expertise or the expertise of those you engage? In other words, do you know what you are doing, or do you hire somebody who is familiar with the operation that you are undertaking?

3. How much time and effort do you spend on the activity?

4. Will the assets used in the activity appreciate?

5. How successful have you been in carrying on other business endeavors?

6. What is your history of income and losses?

7. What are your financial resources from other sources?

8. What is the extent of personal pleasure obtained from your participation in the activity?

Just because a loss business is pleasurable doesn't mean that it is a hobby. It depends on the facts of each case. Noting that "suffering has never been a prerequisite to deductibility," the Tax Court ruled in 1992 that a manager of musical groups could deduct the nearly $140,000 spent in unsuccessfully promoting his wife's singing career. In the same year, the Tax Court permitted a struggling artist living off inherited money to claim large losses resulting from her unsuccessful career. Two years later the same court disallowed $60,000 worth of deductions to a father who sponsored his son's entry onto the professional golf tour. The son had won a total of $155 before dad threw in the towel. In 1996, the Tax Court allowed a tuna boat operator to claim substantial losses. In one year he caught only one fish and lost $21,000. Later that year the Tax Court allowed a trash trucker to deduct over $200,000 in losses arising from searching for gold. He found but a few coins and eventually gave up.

Lawyers themselves have been before the Tax Court. In a 1994 case, an attorney who had been raised on a farm sought to supplement his income by buying a farm. Instead, he lost $1.1 million over eight years. The Tax Court, however, permitted him to claim the losses inasmuch as he spent 500 to 700 hours per year running the farm in a "businesslike" manner by seeking advice, changing his approaches, and using "state-of-the-art" techniques.

In another 1994 case, the IRS sought to claim that an attorney was practicing law as a hobby. Over two years she reported gross income of less than $7,000 and expenses of more than $49,000. Once again citing the "businesslike manner" of the individual and the many hours that she devoted to work, the Tax Court permitted the losses.

The following are some of the other types of hobbies that can result in losses, with the presumption that they are hobbies:

Free-lance photographer

Stamp, baseball card, or coin collector

Comic book, print, or old postcard collector

Antique or rare book collector

 TAX PLANNING IDEA   To avoid or minimize scrutiny of an activity under the hobby loss rules, be sure that your books and records are kept in a businesslike manner. Take every possible step to familiarize yourself with the whole operation from beginning to end. Hire individuals to work for you to add expertise if you cannot manage it all yourself. Most important, don't stick with a pro-ject if it proves to be a bad investment—don't throw good money after bad just to claim tax losses.

YEAR-END REMINDER   If you use a cash basis of accounting to report income and expenses of an activity, you may be able to create a "profitable" year simply by delaying the payment of bills until after year end.

FILING POINTER   You may wish to elect permitted slower methods of depreciation in order to avoid a loss in early years of a business.

TAX PLANNING IDEA   If your business is subject to the five-year rule described above, a special election might save your deductions. You can elect to suspend the application of the for-profit presumption until after the five-year period has lapsed. By giving a new business five years to establish itself, you might be able to prove that the activity is conducted on a for-profit basis under the criteria listed above. You also give the business two extra years to prove that the activity is conducted on a for-profit basis. Once you make the election on IRS Form 5213, the statute of limitations for any deficiency during any year in the suspension period is extended to at least two years after the due date of the return for the last year in the five-year period.

⚠ **CAUTION!** The hobby loss rules apply beyond activities with an element of personal pleasure. The rules apply to any activity and require a profit-making intent. Consequently, in order to claim a loss related to real property not held for personal use, you must have a profit motive.

In a 1994 decision, the Tax Court struck a blow to individuals absorbing rental losses in the hope of future property appreciation. The Court determined that the renting of a property and the holding of that property for appreciation are two separate activities. The decision appears to give a "blank check" to the IRS to disallow net rental losses when there exists little likelihood of net rental gains in the foreseeable future.

WHAT IS AN "ORDINARY AND NECESSARY" BUSINESS EXPENSE?

While certain business costs must meet specific requirements under the law to be deductible, most expenses must only be "ordinary and necessary."

Harold L. Jenkins persuaded about 75 of his friends and associates to invest in a new burger chain. Three years later the company failed and was shut down. Without a legal requirement, Mr. Jenkins repaid the investors every dollar of their investment plus an interest factor.

When Mr. Jenkins deducted the payments to the investors, the IRS disallowed the deduction. The Tax Court decided in favor of Mr. Jenkins, determining that, under the facts of the case, Mr. Jenkins repaid investors to protect his business reputation.

What is an "ordinary and necessary" business expense must be determined on the facts of each case. In country music, the Court observed, an entertainer must protect his reputation or suffer financially. Harold L. Jenkins was better known as the now deceased country singer Conway Twitty, and his burger was known as the Twitty Burger.

Breaking precedent, the Court put its decision to rhyme:

> Twitty Burger went belly up
> But Conway remained true
> He repaid his investors, one and all
> It was the moral thing to do.

> His fans would not have liked it
> It could have hurt his fame
> Had any investors sued him
> Like Merle Haggard or Sonny James.

> When it was time to file taxes
> Conway thought what he would do
> Was deduct those payments as a business expense
> Under section one-sixty-two.

> In order to allow these deductions
> Goes the argument of the Commissioner

The payments must be ordinary and necessary
To a business of the petitioner.

Had Conway not repaid the investors
His career would have been under a cloud,
Under the unique facts of the case
Held: The deductions are allowed.

Cynthia Hess, known professionally as Chesty Love, had her breasts enlarged in 1988 and again in 1991. Following the first implant, Ms. Hess, an exotic dancer, quadrupled her income.

When Ms. Hess claimed a depreciation deduction for her implants, the IRS disallowed the deduction. The Tax Court decided in favor of Ms. Hess, finding that, under the facts of the case, the costs were incurred solely in furtherance of business and that Ms. Hess derived no personal benefit from what she described as a necessary "stage prop."

11

SPECIAL GROUPS OF TAXPAYERS

Certain rules and strategies apply to special groups of taxpayers. Many of these rules and strategies have applicability beyond the categories identified.

ACTORS, ACTRESSES, AND PERFORMING ARTISTS

As previously discussed, employees are able to obtain a tax benefit from employee business expenses only to the extent that the aggregate expenses exceed two percent of adjusted gross income. Very often this means that employees will lose the tax benefit of most (if not all) of their employee business expenses. A special exception to the two percent floor is carved out for certain actors, actresses, and performing artists. Individuals who qualify under this special rule are entitled to claim a deduction for their employee business expenses in full regardless of the two percent floor (see Chapter 3), irrespective of whether they itemize their deductions.

To qualify, the individual must have worked in the performing arts as an employee for at least two different employers during the year; the aggregate employee business expenses associated with this work must exceed ten percent of gross income attributable to work as a performing artist; and the artist's adjusted gross income exclusive of the employee business expenses cannot exceed $16,000. If all of these conditions are met, the actor or other performing artist is entitled to claim all employee business expenses from the profession (not just those that exceed ten percent of gross income) as a deduction in computing adjusted gross income.

For the purpose of determining whether the performing artist has worked for two different employers during the year, only those employers from whom the artist has received at least $200 in compensation are taken into account.

If the performer is married and has lived at any time during the year with his or her spouse, the couple must file a joint income tax return in order to be eligible for the special treatment. On the joint return, if both spouses qualify for the special rule, each will have to determine his or her own qualification for the special treatment by taking into account separate employment circumstances during the year and separate business expenses. However, the adjusted gross income ceiling of $16,000 remains the same regardless of whether one or both spouses is a performing artist.

For example, if Chad and Lisa are both performers, they will have to file a joint return for either one of them to be eligible for this special rule. Assuming that they file a joint return, either Chad or Lisa or both of them may be able to claim employee business expenses as an adjustment to income (rather than as an itemized deduction subject to the two percent floor) if either or both of them meet the three conditions. If Chad were a struggling actor but Lisa were a successful banker, Chad would be unable to utilize this special rule if the couple's adjusted gross income exceeded $16,000, even though his separate income from his acting jobs did not total $16,000.

If the special rule applicable to performing artists is unavailable, employee business expenses may be claimed as miscellaneous itemized deductions to the extent that they exceed two percent of adjusted gross income.

CONTROVERSY

Can valuable musical instruments be depreciated? In 1995 the Third Circuit Court of Appeals agreed with the Tax Court that a 17th-century bass viol was subject to wear and tear and was depreciable. The Court rejected the IRS argument that the viol was a treasured artwork without a useful life. IRS has indicated that it will continue to litigate similar cases outside of the Third Circuit states of Pennsylvania, New Jersey, and Delaware.

CAUTION! As discussed later in this chapter, as in the case of athletes, states are aggressively pursuing actors, actresses, and others whose multi-state performances allow states to tax *pro rata* shares of their income.

ALIEN WORKERS

An alien (a non-U.S. citizen) may be subject to U.S. income tax. The tax rules will vary depending upon whether the alien is a U.S. resident or a nonresident. *Resident aliens* are those who meet a *green card* test (they are lawful permanent residents of the United States) or those who meet a *substantial presence* test.

An individual will be considered a resident alien under the substantial presence test if he or she is in the United States for at least 31 days during the current year and 183 days during the period consisting of the current year and the two preceding years, counting all of the days of physical presence in the current calendar year but only one-third of the days of physical presence in the first preceding year and only one-sixth of the days of physical presence in the second preceding calendar year.

For example, if a citizen of Japan were present in the U.S. for all of 1995, 260 days of 1996, and 40 days of 1997, the substantial presence test for 1997 will be satisfied.

DAYS IN U.S.		
1997	40 × 1/1	= 40
1996	260 × 1/3	= 87
1995	365 × 1/6	= 61
		188

Even though an individual may meet the 31 day/183 day substantial presence test, he or she will not be considered a resident alien if temporarily present in the United States because of diplomatic status or employment with an international organization. Resident alien status will not arise in the case of a teacher present in the United States on a *J* visa, a student present on a temporary *S* or *J* visa, or a professional athlete here to compete in charitable sports events. Additionally, even though an individual may meet the substantial presence test, he or she will not be considered a resident alien for tax purposes in a particular year if present in the United States for less than 183 days and he or she has regular employment in a foreign country and demonstrates closer ties to that country than to the United States.

Resident aliens are generally subject to the same income tax rules as those that govern U.S. citizens. The resident alien is taxed on worldwide income, not just income from U.S sources. A resident alien is entitled to file a joint income tax return with a spouse only if the spouse is a U.S. citizen or resident alien. However, the resident alien may elect to treat a nonresident alien spouse as a U.S. resident. The effect of the election is to tax the couple on their worldwide sources of income. Without the election, the married resident alien must file using the higher married filing separate rates.

Resident aliens are entitled to claim a deduction for personal exemptions and are entitled to claim an exemption for a spouse even if a joint return is not filed, if the spouse has no income from U.S. sources. The resident alien may claim a deduction for personal exemptions of other individuals (for example, children and siblings) if the usual requirements for the dependency deduction are satisfied. One of the conditions is that the person to be claimed as a dependent must be a U.S. citizen, a U.S. national, or a resident of the United States, Canada, or Mexico.

Although resident aliens are generally taxed in the same manner as U.S. citizens, resident aliens who are employees of a foreign government, or of certain tax-exempt international organizations such as the World Bank, are not taxed by the U.S. on their compensation received from the foreign government or international organization.

Any individual who is not a resident alien will be taxed under the rules governing the taxation of *nonresident aliens*. These individuals are subject to U.S. income tax on their income connected with a U.S. business (including most salary income) at the same rates at which U.S. citizens are taxed. Nonresident aliens who have income from the United States not connected with a U.S. business will be subject to tax on this income on a gross basis (no deductions) at a flat 30 percent rate or, as is often applicable, at a lower rate as a result of a treaty with the other nation.

A nonresident alien is required to pay tax at the regular U.S. income tax rates on gain derived from the sale of U.S. real property, regardless of the number of days of presence in the United States. The buyer will generally be required to withhold ten percent of the amount realized on the sale to cover this liability. No withholding is required if the buyer bought the property as his or her home and it cost no more than $300,000.

See Chapter 12 for a discussion of how aliens are treated differently under the estate and gift tax laws.

An alien generally becomes a resident for tax purposes on January 1 of the year in which he or she meets either of two residency tests. However, an alien generally ceases to be a resident for tax purposes upon "permanent" return to his or her home country.

CAUTION!   The 1996 tax legislation expanded the *expatriation* provision to resident aliens. A resident alien in at least eight of the most recent 15 years losing "green card" status or being treated as a resident of another country through treaty, like a departing citizen, is subject to U.S. income tax on U.S. source income for ten years following expatriation if a principal purpose of the move was tax avoidance. An individual who had average tax liability for the most recent five years of more than $106,000 or a net worth on expatriation of at least $528,000 is presumed to have had a tax avoidance purpose. These numbers are indexed for cost of living in 1998 and succeeding years.

CAUTION!   The United States has income, estate, and gift tax treaties with many foreign countries which may also impact on the tax rules governing alien workers in the United States. The applicability of a treaty to the particular situation must be considered before any final determination is made as to liability of an alien worker for U.S. income taxes.

ATHLETES

Professional athletes require good tax planning in order to minimize tax liability for their high income years. Nonqualified deferred compensation plans (see Chapter 2) are of particular interest to the highly paid professional athlete because the amount of employer contributions to qualified retirement plans are limited by law. Under a nonqualified deferred compensation plan an athlete will typically receive payments after retirement. The obligation of the team or other payor to make these payments may not be secured or it will cause the athlete to be taxed prior to receipt of the deferred compensation.

With the reduction in the highest marginal tax bracket from 70 percent to 31 percent during the late 1980s, there was a lesser need for the athlete to seek to defer income. In most cases the athlete was better off paying taxes at yesterday's tax brackets rather than risk both higher brackets and possible default on the future obligation. With the 1993 increase in the highest marginal tax bracket to 39.6 percent, a resurgence in the use of nonqualified deferred compensation by athletes has occurred.

FILING POINTER   Fines imposed for rule breaking are deductible business expenses, distinguishable from fines assessed by federal, state, or local authorities for violations of law.

TAX PLANNING IDEA   Residency of an athlete in a state without an income tax, such as Florida or Texas, will minimize state income taxes. However, most athletes play in a number of states during the year, and states have begun aggressive efforts to tax *pro rata* shares of athletes' income based on where the services were performed.

What services are counted in the proration? Is compensation earned only for game days or is compensation earned for exhibition games and practices as well? One multi-state task force has recommended a concept of "duty days" which would cover all days in which required services were performed.

The task force did not address issues related to athletes in non-team sports such as tennis and golf who often practice in their home states between tournaments.

CLERGY

Clergy (ministers, priests, and rabbis) are not taxed on the rental value of a home or on a rental or housing allowance which is provided to them. Even though a member of the clergy is entitled to this exemption when computing regular income tax liability, there is no similar exemption in the computation of the Social Security contribution through the self-employment tax.

For purpose of this exclusion, furnishings for the home may be provided as part of the allowance. The allowance may include payments to purchase a home, including the principal and interest on a mortgage, as well as expenses directly related to maintaining a home such as utilities, property taxes, and insurance.

In connection with any such allowance paid to allow a member of the clergy to rent or provide himself or herself with a home, several limitations apply. First, the exclusion for a cash allowance or rental allowance may not exceed the fair rental value of the home, including furnishings, plus the cost of utilities. Second, the allowance must actually be used by the recipient to provide himself or herself with a residence (either by payment of rent or through payment of a mortgage), insurance, taxes, utilities, or furniture. Third, the rental allowance, when coupled with straight salary, may not exceed reasonable compensation for the services provided. Fourth, the allowance must be officially designated by the ministry as a housing or rental allowance prior to payment. The designation may be evidenced in an employment contract or in minutes of the religious organization.

For Social Security purposes, members of the clergy are considered self-employed and therefore are generally subject to the self-employment tax on their net earnings received from the religious organization. There are exceptions if the member of the clergy is a member of a religious order which has taken a vow of poverty or if he or she is affiliated with a religion conscientiously opposed to public or private insurance.

Clergy who are not exempt compute net earnings from self-employment in the same manner as a sole proprietor, meaning that he or she deducts expenses incurred in generating income.

For federal income tax withholding purposes, a minister is not considered an employee subject to income tax withholding. However, his or her income may be reported on a W-2 and he or she may voluntarily agree with the ministry to have income tax withheld in order to cover any potential income tax liability as well as self-employment tax liability. Without such withholding, a member of the clergy would normally make estimated tax payments on a quarterly basis to avoid penalty.

FILING POINTER   Even though clergy do not include the parsonage allowance in income, they are entitled to claim a deduction for interest and taxes paid on the residence.

CAUTION!   Systematic "gifts" by a congregation to clergy are attributable to services and taxable according to a 1995 decision of the Eighth Circuit Court of Appeals. Payments to clergy for performing weddings, funerals, and similar functions are also taxable. However, individual gifts to clergy may on specific facts be tax-free as arising out of disinterested generosity. (See Chapter 2 for a discussion of when is a gift really a tax-free gift.)

EXECUTIVES

Corporate executives will often be given some flexibility with respect to their compensation packages including the ability to participate in cafeteria plans, qualified retirement plans, and nonqualified plans of deferred compensation. Start-up companies and well-established companies may offer their corporate executives the ultimate fringe benefit—the opportunity to acquire an equity interest in the company through stock options. The options to acquire the employer stock can be in the form of incentive stock options or nonqualified options. Participation in either of these types of compensation plans will require individual analysis and consideration of both the tax ramifications and the economic ramifications of the opportunity. Qualified retirement plans are discussed in Chapter 9; the other named benefits are discussed in Chapter 2.

TAX PLANNING IDEA   Executives nearing retirement who are in a 36 or 39.6 percent tax bracket should give serious consideration to deferring income to post-retirement years, when they will often be in a lower tax bracket.

FARMERS

Farmers are required to capitalize, rather than deduct, the cost of raising plants and animals that have a pre-productive period of more than two years. If the crop's or animal's pre-productive period is two years or less, and a farmer uses a cash method of accounting, the costs of growing the crop or raising the animal can be expensed.

As with other taxpayers, farmers are eligible to depreciate their equipment and other depreciable assets. Under this system of cost recovery, three-year property includes breeding hogs, tractor units, racehorses that are more than two years old, and any other horse over 12 years old. Breeding and dairy cattle are included in the five-year property class. Breeding and work horses 12 years old or less, farm machinery, and equipment are among the kinds of property that fall within the seven-year class of property. Farm buildings fall into the 20-year class of property.

Rather than capitalize soil and water conservation expenditures, farmers can deduct such costs if they are made consistent with a plan approved by the Soil Conservation Service of the U.S. Department of Agriculture or similar state agency. The deduction for soil and water conservation expenditures cannot exceed 25 percent of the gross income that is derived from the farming operation.

The types of expenses that can be the subject of this election are those that would otherwise be nondepreciable capital costs such as grading, terracing, contouring, or leveling land; construction of drainage ditches, earthen dams, or ponds; removal of brush; planting of trees and other windbreaks to prevent erosion; or irrigation ditches.

If a farmer holds a full-time job but engages in farming as well, he must be particularly aware of the hobby loss rules (discussed in Chapter 10). These "gentlemen farmers" are often closely scrutinized by IRS because their farming operations consistently report losses. If the farm operation is conducted with a profit motive, the losses will offset the farmer's salary income from the other job so long as the material participation and at risk rules are met.

Such farming operations will rarely be able to show a profit in three out of five years (two out of seven years for horse breeders) so as to create a presumption under the hobby loss rules that the farming activity was engaged in for profit. Even if the presumption cannot be created, gentlemen farmers should still be able to use the farm losses to offset their other income, assuming that they meet the material participation standards (see Chapter 2), satisfy the at risk rules (see Chapter 7), conduct their farming operations in a businesslike manner, educate themselves as to the latest farming techniques, and hire personnel with the appropriate expertise.

FILING POINTER   For the years 1998–2000, farmers may average income based on the sum of the tax on non-farm income plus the tax computed by applying one-third of the farm income to the marginal tax bracket of each of the three prior years.

CAUTION!   This *income-averaging* technique may not be used for the computation of alternative minimum tax (see Chapter 1) or self-employment tax (see Chapter 10).

FILING POINTER   Individuals who derive at least two-thirds of their gross income from farming need not pay any estimated taxes if they file their return and pay the tax by March 1 (a month and a half early). If the farmer's return is not going to be filed by March 1, only one instead of the usual four estimated tax payments needs to be made and that payment is due on the January 15 following the close of the year. For example, a farmer can either file his or her 1997 tax return by March 1, 1998, or make an estimated tax payment by January 15, 1998. The amount of estimated taxes that must be paid if no return will be filed by March 1 is only two-thirds of the current year's tax (or 100 percent of the preceding year's tax, if that amount is less).

HANDICAPPED INDIVIDUALS

A handicapped individual, like all other taxpayers, must include amounts received from all sources, including salary, bonuses, and investment income, in his or her gross income. If a handicapped individual receives unemployment compensation it will be fully taxable, while payments received under a worker's compensation act will be exempt from tax (see Chapter 2).

If a handicapped individual is under the age of 65, is *permanently and totally disabled*, and receives a taxable disability pension, he or she may be entitled to a tax credit. An individual will be considered to be permanently and totally disabled if he or she cannot engage in any substantial gainful activity because of a physical or mental condition. A physician must certify that the condition has lasted or can be expected to last for a minimum of 12 months or that the condition can be expected to lead to death.

The credit amount for the disabled is 15 percent of a base amount, generally $5,000 (or, if less, 15 percent of the disability income). Before figuring the amount of the credit, the base amount is reduced by any nontaxable Social Security benefits, nontaxable railroad retirement benefits, and the amount of any nontaxable pension or disability benefits paid by the Veterans Administration. The base amount is also reduced by one-half of adjusted gross income to the extent its exceeds $7,500. Thus, a single individual with nontaxable Social Security, VA, or other pension benefits of $5,000 or more, with AGI of $17,500 or more, or with a certain combination of both, will not be able to claim the credit.

ILLUSTRATION

Ken is single and 40 years old. He is permanently disabled. He received $2,000 in Social Security benefits, $6,000 from a taxable disability pension, and $6,000 of interest and dividends.

$5,000	Base Amount (lesser of $5,000 or disability income)
– 2,000	Nontaxable Social Security benefits
– 2,250	½ excess AGI ($12,000) over $7,500
$ 750	Credit Base
$ 112	Credit (15% × $750, Credit Base)

If a permanently and totally disabled individual is married, a joint return must be filed to claim the credit unless the couple did not live together at any time during the year. When a joint return is filed, the base amount is the same $5,000 if only one of the spouses is totally and permanently disabled or $7,500 if both spouses are so disabled. On a joint return, the base amount is reduced by one-half of the amount by which the couple's AGI exceeds $10,000. If a disabled person elects to file a separate return but is eligible for the credit because he or she lived apart from his or her spouse for the entire year, the base amount is $3,750 and is reduced by one-half of the amount by which adjusted gross income exceeds $5,000. This credit is calculated in conjunction with the credit for the elderly discussed in Chapter 3.

As discussed in Chapter 1, a blind individual is entitled to a higher standard deduction than other taxpayers. As discussed in Chapter 3, if an individual incurs expenses to care for a disabled spouse or dependent in order to work, a dependent care credit is available.

FILING POINTER A handicapped employee who incurs employee business expenses such as paying for an attendant in order to perform a job is entitled to claim these kinds of expenses as miscellaneous itemized deductions irrespective of whether they exceed two percent of adjusted gross income.

FILING POINTER Small businesses, meaning those with no more than 30 full-time employees or gross receipts of no more than $1 million in the previous year, can claim a tax credit equal to 50 percent of eligible expenditures in excess of $250 incurred for the purpose of complying with the Americans With Disabilities Act of 1990 by removing architectural, transportation, and other barriers for handicapped individuals. The maximum credit is $5,000. All businesses can expense up to $15,000 of the costs incurred to remove architectural and transportation barriers in order to make the business more accessible for use by handicapped people. Costs incurred that exceed $15,000 have to be capitalized and depreciated. The amount of any tax credit must be subtracted from costs eligible for expensing or depreciation.

HOUSEHOLD EMPLOYERS—THE "NANNY" TAX

Responding to the avalanche of publicity regarding the failure of various candidates for public office and political appointees to comply with payroll tax requirements for household employers, Congress in 1994 passed the Social Security Domestic Employment Reform Act. In an effort to ease the tax reporting burden placed on employers of household workers such as nannies and housekeepers, the legislation provides that household employers are not liable for Social Security taxes on wages of less than $1,000 a year paid to their domestic workers. The figure is indexed in 1998 and succeeding years for increases in average wages.

Household employers are no longer required to file federal quarterly payroll reports. Rather, Social Security, federal unemployment, and withheld federal income taxes are now paid with the employer's individual income tax return. However, only 280,000 returns reported household employees in 1995, the first year of reporting these workers on Form 1040. The IRS believes that the compliance rate was less than 20 percent.

QUESTION: I pay my 15-year-old babysitter about $25 per week throughout the year. Am I a "household employer" covered by these new rules?

ANSWER: Even though you might pay your babysitter more than $1,000 in a year, you are not a household employer. Specifically excluded from coverage by the new rules are individuals in your situation. So long as your sitter is under the age of 18 and domestic employment is not his or her principal job, you are not required to pay Social Security taxes. However, if your sitter is at least 18 years old or if babysitting is his or her principal occupation, you will be required to comply with the new rules.

CAUTION! Even though *federal* employment taxes on household employees are now paid annually on April 15, *state* law may still require that state unemployment taxes and withheld state income taxes be paid more frequently. Also, note the January 31 deadline for providing a household worker with a W-2.

CONTROVERSY

Lost in all of the hoopla surrounding payroll taxes on household workers is the possibility that certain domestic help may properly be classified as independent contractors. While a 40-hour-per-week household worker is almost certainly an employee, the half-day-per-week cleaning person may be an independent contractor. See Chapter 10 as to the classification of workers as independent contractors or employees.

INSURANCE AGENTS

Insurance agents, like other workers, can be classified as employees whose compensation is subject to Social Security taxes, unemployment taxes, and income tax withholding or as independent contractors whose net earnings from the business are subject to self-employment tax but not unemployment tax or income tax withholding. (See Chapter 10 for a discussion of the factors which are used to ascertain whether an employment relationship exists.)

If the agent is a full-time life insurance salesperson, a third classification applies. An insurance agent whose principal business activity is selling life insurance or annuity contracts is a statutory employee. As discussed in Chapter 4, such an agent will receive a W-2, and his or her compensation is subject to Social Security and Medicare withholding. However, no unemployment tax is paid on this compensation and the compensation is not subject to any income tax withholding. For purpose of deducting business expenses, he or she is an independent contractor.

An insurance agent will often have an agreement with the insurance company which will allow the agent to receive draws against commissions which the agent may earn in the future. According to a June 18, 1997 decision by the Tax Court, these advance commissions are not taxable if the advances are recognized as loans between the company and the agent and repayable on the company's demand after the agent's termination.

TAX PLANNING IDEA If you receive advance commissions which are subject to repayment, make sure that there is a written agreement to that effect or you will be taxed on receipt of the advances instead of when the commissions are earned.

CONTROVERSY

Are payments received by a former self-employed agent from an insurance company after retirement subject to self-employment tax? The IRS insisted that they were, even though the Ninth and Federal Circuit Courts of Appeal as well as the Tax Court disagreed. With the Taxpayer Relief Act of 1997, Congress got in the picture and legislated that payments after 1997 are not subject to self-employment tax if received after the agent's employment termination, the agent performs no services thereafter until at least the end of the year of payment, the agent is bound by at least a one-year covenant not to compete, and the payment amount is tied to prior year sales and/or to policy renewals. Eligibility for payment but not the amount of payment can depend on length of service.

As to payments before 1998 and as to payments that do not meet the criteria of the new law, the controversy will probably continue.

TAX PLANNING IDEA Retiring insurance agents are well advised to comply with the "safe harbor" created by the Taxpayer Relief Act of 1997 in order to avoid being caught in the controversy.

MILITARY PERSONNEL

While military pay is generally taxable, the pay of U.S. military personnel with rank below noncommissioned officer serving in a *combat zone* or *qualified hazardous duty area* is exempt from federal income tax. A commissioned officer's military pay up to $4,255 per month is currently exempt. The President determines the existence of a combat zone or qualified hazardous duty area.

Military pay receives the same exemption from tax while an individual is hospitalized as a result of wounds, disease, or injury incurred in a combat zone, for up to two years after the termination of combat activities.

Military personnel are not taxed on the amount of housing allowances, costs of living allowances, and uniform allowances which they receive. Moving expenses paid by the military are not taxed even though the time and mileage requirements applicable to other taxpayers are not satisfied. These expenses include dislocation allowances, temporary lodging expenses, and moving-in household allowances, all of which are taxable to civilians.

TAX PLANNING IDEA A 401(k) or Simple retirement plan is permitted to offer a catch-up period on missed elective deferrals by military personnel returning to prior employers. Both types of retirement plans are discussed in Chapter 9.

TAX PLANNING IDEA Service personnel often have the ability to reduce state taxes. They are generally not considered domiciles and residents of the state in which they are stationed but are deemed domiciles and residents of the state from which they entered the military. Entry into the armed services from Florida, Texas, or one of several other states without an individual income tax will minimize state income tax liability.

OVERSEAS WORKERS

Although a U.S. citizen or resident is taxed on worldwide income and must file a tax return as any other individual, he or she can elect to exclude up to $72,000 of earned income from the computation of federal gross income and may also elect to exclude (or deduct, in the case of a self-employed individual) a portion of foreign housing costs.

To be eligible for these benefits, the U.S. citizen or resident alien must have a principal place of work in a foreign country. The worker must also establish bona fide residence in a foreign country for an entire year or must establish physical presence in a foreign country for at least 330 full days during a consecutive 12-month period.

The *bona fide residence* test involves a subjective analysis of your intention with respect to your stay abroad. If you tell the foreign authorities that you are a non-resident of that foreign country, then you cannot claim that you are a bona fide resident of that country for U.S. income tax purposes. Once you have established bona fide residence abroad for a period that includes one full calendar year, then you can continue to qualify as a bona fide resident for future years until you abandon that foreign residence. Thus, even in your last year abroad, you would be considered a bona fide resident for that part of the year in which you were outside the United States.

The *physical presence* test requires that you be physically present in a foreign country for 330 days (approximately 11 months) during any 12-month period of time. It does not require that you be outside the United States for a full calendar year.

When you can satisfy the physical presence test or the bona fide residence test for only part of the year, then the $72,000 ceiling on the foreign income exclusion is prorated based on the number of days during the year in which you meet the particular test. For example, if an individual qualifies as a bona fide resident in 1998 for only 90 days, then the ceiling on the foreign income exclusion for the year would be 90/365 multiplied by $72,000 or $17,753. In a leap year, the proper fraction to use would be 90/366.

When proration is required under the physical presence test, you are entitled to count all days within a period of 12 months once you are physically present and have your tax home in a foreign country for the 330 days. The individual will want to select the 12-month period that allows for the largest exclusion.

ILLUSTRATION

Assume you worked in France from June 1, 1997, through September 30, 1998, when you left the country. During this period, you left France only for a 15-day vacation to the U.S. during December 1997. You earned $72,000 for your work in France during 1998. Your maximum 1998 exclusion is $57,797, figured as follows:

1. Start with your last full day, September 30, 1998, and count back 330 full days during which you were abroad. Not counting the vacation days, the 330th day is October 21, 1997. This is the first day of your 12-month period.

2. From October 21, 1997, count forward 12 months, to October 20, 1998, which is the last day of your 12-month period.

3. Count the number of days in 1998 that fall within the 12-month period ending October 20, 1998. Here, the number of qualifying days is 293, from January 1 through October 20, 1996.

4. The maximum 1998 exclusion is $72,000 × 293/365 or $57,797. You may exclude $57,797, the lesser of the maximum exclusion or your actual earnings of $72,000.

In addition to excluding up to $72,000 of income earned abroad, individuals who can establish a foreign tax home and pass either the bona fide residence or the physical presence test can also exclude certain employer provided housing costs from their income or deduct their excess housing costs if the housing is not employer provided.

The maximum exclusion for foreign housing costs is the excess of the housing expenses over the amount equal to 16 percent of a U.S. Government employee paid at the rate of a GS-14, Step 1 (in 1997, this rate was $64,555). In no event can the aggregate of the foreign income exclusion and the exclusion for excess housing costs exceed the taxpayer's foreign earned income.

For purposes of the foreign housing costs exclusion, housing expenses are the reasonable costs paid for housing abroad for the overseas worker and his or her family if they reside with the worker. Utilities, insurance, and rent are examples of typical housing costs eligible for the exclusion. However, housing expenses do not include deductible interest and taxes or the purchase price of a house.

CAUTION! For 1997 the income earned abroad exclusion was $70,000. From 1998–2002, it is increased in $2,000 increments. The $80,000 exclusion from 2003–2006 will be indexed for cost of living beginning in 2007.

FILING POINTER The income earned abroad exclusion is for each individual, permitting a married couple to claim twice the exclusion of a single individual. On a joint return, the housing costs exclusion may be computed jointly in which case the exclusion may only be claimed by one spouse or separately in which case housing costs may be allocated as desired.

FILING POINTER To the extent that income earned abroad cannot be excluded, taxes on that foreign source income will normally be subject to credit on the U.S. tax return. The credit will be in an amount equal to the lesser of the foreign taxes paid or the U.S. tax liability attributable to the foreign income.

CAUTION! If an individual elects either the foreign income exclusion or the excess housing exclusion, he or she cannot claim deductions or the foreign tax credit with respect to the income that has been excluded.

PUBLIC SCHOOL AND CERTAIN TAX-EXEMPT ORGANIZATION EMPLOYEES

Employees of public schools, state colleges, and universities (both academic and nonacademic staff) and employees of certain tax-exempt organizations such as churches, hospitals, and other charitable organizations may participate in a special type of retirement plan arrangement, commonly known as a *tax deferred annuity* or a *tax sheltered annuity*. Employer contributions to the tax deferred annuity are not currently taxed to the employee so long as the contribution does not exceed the lesser of:

1. $9,500 as indexed in 1998 and succeeding years for cost of living, in the case of a salary reduction arrangement;

2. An *exclusion allowance* which is one-fifth of the employee's salary for the year multiplied by the number of years of service, subtracting prior contributions from the product; or

3. The lesser of $30,000 or 25 percent of the employee's compensation determined before elective deferrals (the same as that generally applicable to defined contribution plans such that the $30,000 limit will eventually be indexed for cost of living).

Certain tax-exempt organization employees enjoy the benefit of *catch-up* provisions raising limitations in subsequent years, generally when maximum contributions have not been made for all prior years.

Like other employer sponsored retirement plans, the earnings on amounts contributed to tax deferred annuities build tax-free. Distributions from the annuities are taxable to the recipient and are subject to the same general rules as in the case of other employer sponsored retirement plans.

ILLUSTRATION

Sam is a teacher at the public school. Sam's maximum exclusion allowance in his first year of teaching is:

$$\$20,000 \times 20\% \times 1 = \$4,000.$$

Sam's salary remains the same after two years of service. Sam's exclusion allowance is:

$$\$20,000 \times 20\% \times 2 = \$8,000 - \$4,000 = \$4,000.$$

After three years of service, if Sam's salary does not increase, his exclusion allowance will remain at $4,000.

$$\$20,000 \times 20\% \times 3 = \$12,000 - (\$4,000 + \$4,000) = \$4,000.$$

As is evident, without salary increases, Sam's exclusion allowance will remain at $4,000. However, if Sam's salary increases, the exclusion allowance will increase to an amount that is greater than 20 percent of his compensation in any particular year. For example, if Sam's salary increases from $20,000 to $23,000 in his second year and $26,000 in his third year, his exclusion allowances for each of the three years are:

Year 1	$20,000 × 20% × 1 = $4,000
Year 2	$23,000 × 20% × 2 = $9,200 – $4,000 = $5,200. $5,200/$23,000 = 22.6%
Year 3	$26,000 × 20% × 3 = $15,600 – ($4,000 + $5,200) = $6,400 $6,400/$26,000 = 24.6%

 CAUTION! Prior to 1998, an employee's compensation was determined after subtracting elective deferrals.

 YEAR-END REMINDER Employee who have the ability to contribute to a tax deferred annuity should consider maximizing their contributions before year-end.

REAL ESTATE PROFESSIONALS

If you are in a real estate-related business, whether involved in development, construction, acquisition, rental, management, or brokering, your rental activities may not automatically be passive as they are for other individuals (see Chapter 2). To qualify under this special rule, you must work more than 750 hours during the year in real estate-related businesses in which you materially participate *and* a majority of your time in all businesses in which you materially participate must be in real estate. If you work in real estate as a employee, you must be at least a five percent owner of the business. (See Chapter 2 for the definition of "material participation.")

CAUTION! Excluded from the statutory list of real estate activities qualifying for the special rule are lending, consulting, and professional service (law and accounting) businesses which concentrate on real estate. Individual real estate agents probably qualify for the special rule under a broad definition of "brokering."

CONTROVERSY

What does it mean if your rental activities are not automatically passive? Does it mean that you may use rental losses to offset all of your other income without limitation? Although this may have been the intent of Congress, Treasury Regulations indicate that individuals who qualify under the special rule must still meet the tough "material participation" test (see Chapter 2) for the aggregate *rental* activities in order for rental losses to offset other income.

The hours spent on nonrental activities in real estate are ignored for this test, according to the IRS. And, if ten percent or more of aggregate gross rental income is from limited partnership interests, Proposed Regulations do not permit use of the 100-hour test or the "substantially all of the work" test to establish material participation.

FILING POINTER A real estate professional capable of qualifying under the special rule, notwithstanding the tough standard set by the IRS, will typically need to remember to elect with an originally filed return to treat all rental real estate activities as if they were one. Without an election to aggregate, each activity is separately tested for material participation and the special rule is less likely to apply. Once made, the election is generally irrevocable.

CAUTION! If a real estate professional satisfies the material participation test under the special rule, losses from rentals will offset active, portfolio, and other passive income. However, not all individuals in real estate will benefit from the special rule for this profession.

Real estate professionals with passive losses from non-real estate activities and income from real estate rentals will want the rental income to be passive in nature to permit use of these other passive losses. The election to aggregate each rental activity should then be avoided. A real estate professional must look not only at the current year but also at the future, inasmuch as an election, once made, is binding on all future years.

WAITERS, WAITRESSES, CASINO WORKERS, AND OTHER TIP-EARNING EMPLOYEES

Employees who receive tips from their customers must include the amount of the tips in their income. These tips cannot be considered as gifts.

An employee who receives $20 or more in tips during a month is required to report the amount of tips to his or her employer. The reported tips are subject to income tax and Social Security tax withholding.

The IRS believes that about one-half of tips paid at larger restaurants and two-thirds of those paid at smaller ones go unreported ($7-$10 billion annually). Additional statistics indicate that the average tip paid at a food and beverage establishment is 11.9 percent of the bill. In response, Congress enacted legislation that requires restaurants and other food and beverage establishments normally employing more than ten workers on a typical day to *allocate* a deemed amount of tip income among the employees.

The amount that must be allocated among the employees is equal to the excess, if any, of eight percent of the establishment's gross receipts over the amount of tips that the employees reported to the employer. For example, if all of the waiters and waitresses reported receiving tips amounting to five percent of the establishment's gross sales for the year, the employer would include an allocable share of the excess three percent on each employee's W-2. If the restaurant can establish that the average tips are less than eight percent, then the eight percent figure can be reduced, but not below two percent.

TAX PLANNING IDEA   It is essential that tipped restaurant workers, particularly those who do not average eight percent of receipts in tips, accurately report tip income to their employers and keep their own records of tips in order to minimize the allocation of any deemed tipped income. Many employees of large food establishments may find themselves under audit as a result of an examination of the employer's tax records to make sure that the tipped employees are reporting all of their tip income. The IRS will look at the restaurant's gross receipts and analyze the geographic region's tip habits and expect the tipped employee to have tip income based on this average. Both the numbers of audits and the extent of enforcement appear to be on the rise.

FILING POINTER   The Tax Court in 1996 determined that the gross income from tips of waiters and waitresses sharing tips with buspersons, bartenders, and others is determined after the sharing. The IRS had wanted the workers to deduct the offsets as miscellaneous itemized deductions only.

CAUTION!   The IRS has just finished a training guide for its auditors setting forth examination techniques for barbers and beauticians. They should expect greater scrutiny of their tip income. A study is underway as to compliance on the part of taxicab drivers.

12

ESTATE PLANNING
STRATEGIES

Certain income tax decisions must be made in conjunction with estate planning decisions. For example, while it might make sense from an income tax perspective to title appreciated property in the name of the elderly husband in order to get a step-up in the tax basis of the assets upon his death, estate tax needs may require that some of this property be titled exclusively in the name of the younger wife. It is wise to consider the estate tax consequences of many significant steps motivated by income tax saving considerations if there is any chance of a federal estate tax liability. In this chapter are the best strategies for all but the largest estates.

HOW THE FEDERAL ESTATE TAX SYSTEM WORKS

Basically, the federal estate tax system works as follows: On your death, if your federal taxable estate exceeds a value of $625,000 in 1998, your estate will owe federal taxes. The *marginal estate tax rates* (the rates at which the next dollar of estate assets will be taxed) start at 37 percent and rise to a maximum rate of 60 percent (including an additional five percent tax designed to create a *maximum effective rate* of 55 percent) for those leaving a taxable estate of more than $10 million.

Federal estate tax rates are applied against your federal *taxable estate*. The taxable estate is basically the net value of all of the property that you own at the time of death (including often overlooked retirement plan benefits as well as most life insurance proceeds) reduced by various deductions, the most prominent being the *marital deduction*. The full value of property transferred to a surviving spouse either outright or in certain types of trusts qualifies for the marital deduction and will reduce the gross estate.

The federal estate tax on your taxable estate can be partially or totally offset by using a *unified gift and estate tax credit* in the amount of $202,050 for 1998. This credit offsets both gift and estate tax liabilities and, to the extent that it is used to offset the tax on lifetime transfers, it is reduced and can't offset the tax on death transfers. The unified credit amount of $202,050 translates into the ability to transfer $625,000 of property tax-free. Consequently, unless your federal taxable estate exceeds $625,000, no federal estate taxes will be paid (assuming that you have not previously used any of your $202,050 credit to offset gift tax liability).

CAUTION! For 1997 the unified credit offset the first $600,000 of an individual's taxable estate. The Taxpayer Relief Act of 1997 provided for $25,000 increases in this *exemption equivalent* from 1998-2000. The exemption equivalent then rises to $700,000 in 2002, $850,000 in 2004, $950,000 in 2005, and $1 million in 2006.

TAX PLANNING IDEA Effective in 1998, decedents with qualified family owned business interests receive an exclusion designed to create an immediate effective exemption equivalent of $1.3 million which does not increase in succeeding years. A qualified business interest may be in any form; however, the decedent's extended family must own at least 30 percent of the business and the business must be owned at least 50 percent by one family, 70 percent by two families, or 90 percent by three families.

The interest passing to qualified heirs (family members or employees with at least ten years of service) must exceed 50 percent of the modified adjusted gross estate. The decedent must have owned and materially participated in the business for at least five of the eight years preceding death.

CAUTION! If within ten years of the decedent's death the qualified heirs do not continue to satisfy the material participation requirement, or if it sells the business, the tax savings are subject to graduated recapture.

CAUTION! The marital deduction is generally not available if the surviving spouse is not a U.S. citizen. The marital deduction is available in such cases, however, if the dece-dent's property is transferred to a *qualified domestic trust*, the terms of which provide that a trustee is a citizen of the United States and the surviving spouse will be paid all of the income generated by the trust. By using a qualified domestic trust, the federal estate tax on the decedent's property is deferred until principal distributions from the trust are made to the surviving spouse or until the surviving spouse's death. Hardship distributions of principal to the surviving spouse, however, are exempt from tax.

QUESTION: My wife and I jointly own a great deal of stock. When I die my wife will become the sole owner of the stock. Will this be included in my estate? If so, will the stock qualify for the marital deduction?

ANSWER: Except possibly for interests created before 1977 (see the Controversy explained in Chapter 5), one-half of husband-wife jointly held property is includable in the estate of the first spouse to die. It doesn't matter that this property may pass automatically to the survivor under the law of your state and not be subject to local probate. It also makes no difference how the property is transferred to the surviving spouse to qualify for the unlimited marital deduction. It can be transferred to the spouse by operation of law where the decedent owns the property with the surviving spouse either as a tenant by the entirety with the right of survivorship or as community property. It can be transferred under the terms of a contract, where, for example, the spouse is the beneficiary of a life insurance contract on the deceased spouse's life. It can be transferred under the terms of a will or the laws of intestacy which govern if there is no will. Because of the unlimited marital deduction, even if the value of your stock portfolio is in the millions of dollars, there need be no federal estate taxes due at the time of your death. The problem, of course, will arise upon the death of your spouse.

Federal estate tax planning more often than not involves planning for the taxes that will be due at the time of the death of the second spouse.

ILLUSTRATION

Mr. Saveless died in 1998 owning a gross estate valued at $1.25 million, all of which was left to his wife. There were no federal estate taxes due at the time of his death. At the time of the death of Mrs. Saveless in the following year (assuming that she lives off the income, doesn't consume the principal, and there is no appreciation or depreciation in the value of the property), her gross estate will be the same $1.25 million. Barring remarriage, she will not be entitled to a marital deduction, so her taxable estate will be $1.25 million. The pre-credit federal tax liability on a $1.25 million estate is $448,300. If Mrs. Saveless has her full $211,300 unified credit available to her in 1999, the federal tax liability at her death, without considering the credit for state death taxes, will be $237,000. The children of this marriage will inherit, after the death of their parents, only $1,013,000 ($1.25 million less $237,000 in federal taxes) as shown below:

On Death of First Spouse:		On Death of Second Spouse:	
$1,250,000	Gross Estate	$1,250,000	Gross Estate
(1,250,000)	Marital Deduction	(0)	Marital Deduction
$0	Taxable Estate	$1,250,000	Taxable Estate
$0	Federal Tax	$ 448,300	Tentative Federal Tax
		(211,300)	Unified Credit
		$ 237,000	Federal Tax
		$ 237,000	Combined Federal Estate Tax

THE BYPASS TRUST—THE BEST SINGLE STEP IN ESTATE PLANNING

The $237,000 tax bite in the preceding illustration can be easily avoided with basic estate planning. The $237,000 liability is a result of the first spouse's failure to use his unified credit. Because the husband, as the first spouse to die, left his entire $1.25 million estate to his wife, there was no tentative federal tax against which to use the unified credit. The credit was therefore wasted. The key to federal estate tax planning is to make use of the unified credit on the death of the first spouse and thereby avoid overloading the estate of the second spouse. To use the unified credit, you can't leave all property to your surviving spouse. Instead, you can transfer up to the exemption equivalent ($625,000 in 1998) to a qualifying trust established for the benefit of your spouse. Alternatively, you can transfer up to the exemption equivalent to your children, to a trust for your children, or to a trust for your spouse and children.

ILLUSTRATION

When Mr. Savemore died in 1998, he left $625,000 to his wife but he provided for the remaining $625,000 to be left in trust for the benefit of his wife and children. Unlike Mr. Saveless, the husband here has a tentative federal tax of $202,050. Assuming he has available to him a full unified credit of $202,050, no federal taxes will be due at the time of Mr. Savemore's death—the same result as in the first illustration. However, on the death of Mrs. Savemore in 1999, again assuming no consumption, appreciation, or depreciation, her gross estate will be equal to $625,000. Her taxable estate will be $625,000, but she will owe no federal estate taxes because of the availability of her unified credit. The remaining $625,000 which was transferred to a trust for the benefit of Mrs. Savemore and the couple's children will not be part of her taxable estate, because Mrs. Savemore will not be treated as having the equivalent of ownership of the trust property. As a result, the family's combined federal estate tax liability is $0, a saving of $237,000. The family is able to transfer the full $1.25 million estate to the children as shown below:

On Death of First Spouse:		On Death of Second Spouse:	
$1,250,000	Gross Estate	$ 625,000	Gross Estate
(625,000)	Marital Deduction	(0)	Marital Deduction
$ 625,000	Taxable Estate	$ 625,000	Taxable Estate
$ 202,050	Tentative Federal Tax	$ 202,050	Tentative Federal Tax
(202,050)	Unified Credit	(211,300)	Unified Credit
$ 0	Federal Tax	$ 0	Federal Tax
		$ 0	Combined Federal Estate Tax

QUESTION: I want to save estate taxes because I don't want my hard-earned money going to the Government and not to my children. However, my children are grown and doing well and I'm far more concerned now about my wife having enough money on which to live. How can I minimize or eliminate estate taxes and still not cause my wife to worry about money?

ANSWER: The typical estate plan, which uses a trust to keep some assets out of the estate of the surviving spouse, can distress people whose natural inclination is "I don't care about federal estate tax savings if it means that my spouse can't get everything I own." However, a trust in the amount of the exemption equivalent for the benefit of your wife can be designed to give very close to outright ownership—but with the tax savings. The trust is often called a *bypass trust, unified credit trust, credit shelter trust,* or *family trust.* Property transferred to the trust will either not qualify for the marital deduction or, if eligible, no election should be made to have the property qualify. Consequently, a taxable estate is created at the time of your death. This is what you want because basic estate planning requires a tentative federal tax liability against which to use the unified credit.

The terms of the bypass trust can be quite broad. They can provide that your wife receive all of the income generated by the assets in the trust for her entire lifetime. They can provide that she receive up to the greater of $5,000 or five percent of principal each year without a showing of need. If there is an independent trustee, the trust can provide for unlimited disbursement of principal to your wife within the discretion of the trustee. If you and your wife would rather not have an outsider, even another family member, as trustee, your wife can be trustee provided distributions of principal to her beyond the $5,000/five percent figure are limited to disbursements for *health, education, support, and maintenance.*

The bypass trust is the best single step that a married couple anticipating possible federal estate taxes can take in planning to minimize these taxes and yet maximize the survivor's security. By using this trust, you have accomplished both of your goals—reducing the federal estate tax liability and providing security and protection for your wife.

 CAUTION!   Giving the spouse the right to receive annual distributions of $5,000/ five percent of principal will result in the greater of $5,000 or five percent of the value of the trust at the time of the spouse's death being included in the spouse's federal gross estate. If the bypass trust is worth $625,000 when the spouse dies, this would mean that the spouse's federal gross estate would include $31,250 attributable to the $5,000/five percent withdrawal right. However, this is often a small price to pay to give the surviving spouse the desired security.

 CAUTION!   If the surviving spouse is to be the trustee (or a co-trustee unless the other trustees have interest which are deemed adversarial to the spouse), it is critical that proper language be utilized in setting an *ascertainable standard* for the surviving spouse to receive principal. The words "health, education, support, and maintenance" are time proven terminology, and it is clear that such a right to receive principal in a trust will not cause inclusion of the remaining assets of the trust in the estate of the surviving spouse. However, if other words are utilized, the surviving spouse may be treated as having the equivalent of outright ownership and a successful bypass of the trust amounts from the surviving spouse's estate will not be possible.

CONTROVERSY

Use of other words such as "comfort" when an ascertainable standard is required is risky and will invite challenge from the IRS. The courts look on a case by case basis as to whether this standard is met based on how the exact wording is interpreted under the law of the decedent's domicile. In 1993 the Tenth Circuit Court of Appeals, after analyzing Florida law, found that the terminology "continued comfort, support, maintenance, or education" created an ascertainable standard and reversed the pro-IRS decision of the Tax Court.

 CAUTION!   Under current law, a bypass trust is advisable when the combined assets of a couple significantly exceed the survivor's exemption equivalent. With the rising exemption equivalent, that threshold may be as low as $700,000 or as high as perhaps $1 million depending upon age, anticipated future accumulations, and the number of descendants who might receive gifts using the annual gift tax exclusion (see the discussion later in this chapter).

THE MULTIPURPOSE QTIP TRUST

Many individuals do not want to leave all or part of their estate to their surviving spouse outright. They may be concerned about the surviving spouse's ability to manage a significant estate and may want the expertise of a professional manager. They may want to protect the estate from a new spouse. They may want to provide for the children of a prior marriage yet still offer the surviving spouse security during his or her lifetime. All of these concerns, as well as the elimination of estate taxes upon the death of the first spouse, can be alleviated through the use of a *Qualified Terminable Interest Property (QTIP) trust.*

Property passing into a QTIP trust will qualify for the marital deduction if an appropriate election is made by the personal representative (executor) of the estate. If at the death of the surviving spouse there are any assets remaining in the trust for which a QTIP election was made, their value will be includable in the estate of the surviving spouse just as if the property had been left to the surviving spouse outright.

To qualify property in the QTIP trust for the marital deduction, the surviving spouse must be the sole income beneficiary of the trust and must be paid all of the income generated by the QTIP trust at least annually. Distributions of principal follow the same rules as in the case of the bypass trust; they may be mandatory, nonexistent, discretionary without limitation where there is an independent trustee, or subject to such language as health, education, support, and maintenance if the surviving spouse will be trustee. However, no distribution of the QTIP trust principal can be made to any individual other than the surviving spouse so long as he or she is alive.

The QTIP trust is an excellent vehicle to provide security and income to the surviving spouse during his or her lifetime yet ensure that, upon the surviving spouse's death, the trust principal, to the extent that it has not been used for the benefit of the surviving spouse during his or her lifetime, will pass to the beneficiaries designated in the will of the first spouse. For example, QTIP trust language can provide that upon the death of the surviving spouse the trust assets will be distributed among the children of the first spouse from a previous marriage. If the first spouse does not use a QTIP trust and leaves the property to the surviving spouse outright, there can be no assurance that the remaining estate upon the death of the surviving spouse would be left to the children from the prior marriage of the first spouse to die.

QUESTION: I like the idea of a QTIP trust. I am scared that my husband would remarry in the event of my death and could be influenced to divert funds away from our children upon his subsequent death. In fact, I like the idea of a QTIP so much that I would like to see all of my separately owned property go into this trust or into a trust where my husband and children could both benefit. Are these any problems associated with this idea?

ANSWER: There are two significant difficulties. First, if you wish to avoid federal estate taxes upon your death, assuming your husband survives, you must limit the amount which goes into the bypass trust where your children as well as your husband can be beneficiaries to the exemption equivalent ($625,000 in 1998 rising to $1 million by 2006). This trust will not qualify for the marital deduction. The balance of your estate can go into the QTIP trust in which your husband must be the only beneficiary during his lifetime.

The second difficulty is that your husband may be able to object to the arrangement depending upon the law in your home state. Many states require that a certain fraction of an individual's probate estate (usually one-third or one-half) go to the surviving spouse. A transfer to either type of trust is not the same as a bequest to the surviving spouse. Consequently, your husband may have the ability to challenge the disposition of at least a portion of the assets. However, if he insists on receiving a portion of the estate outright, state law may require him to give up any interest in the remainder of the estate.

FUNDING THE BYPASS OR QTIP TRUST

If a bypass or a QTIP trust is to be utilized, there must normally be sufficient separately owned assets in order to fund the trust. If all assets are owned jointly with the spouse and there is a right of survivorship, usually called ownership by *tenants by the entirety* in non-community property states, the assets will all pass automatically to the surviving spouse and there will be nothing left with which to fund the trust.

Life insurance is ideal for funding the bypass trust through designation of the trust as beneficiary (or designation of the estate as beneficiary if the provisions of your will would have these assets going into either of these trusts). If insurance and other separate property are insufficient, or if life insurance will be transferred to an irrevocable trust during your lifetime, it may be advisable to separate certain tenants by the entirety property into a tenancy in common in order to have assets to fund the trust upon the death of the first spouse. (See the discussion on life insurance trusts later in this chapter.)

CAUTION! When tenants by the entirety property is converted into a tenancy in common or is transferred to one of the two spouses, it becomes attachable by the separate creditors of either spouse. The severing of a tenancy by the entirety should only be accomplished with a review of your casualty insurance situation to minimize the risk of loss of assets in the event of a suit arising from an accident in the home or on the road. Consideration should also be given to the domestic relations questions under state law.

CAUTION! Designation of the trust as beneficiary of qualified retirement plan benefits as opposed to the surviving spouse will result in the loss of the ability to roll over the retirement proceeds to an Individual Retirement Account (see Chapter 9) and thus the continued deferral of income tax on the retirement benefits.

TAX PLANNING IDEA   An alternative solution would be to name the surviving spouse as the primary beneficiary of the retirement benefits and the trust as the secondary beneficiary. Then the surviving spouse can, through the use of a *disclaimer*, direct some or all of the retirement benefits to the trust if needed to fully utilize the deceased spouse's unified credit. This technique affords the couple the flexibility of maximizing estate tax savings after taking into account the income tax consequences of the beneficiary designation.

TAX PLANNING IDEA   If one spouse has minimal assets in separate name, he or she should consider using a *disclaimer trust* in the will in order to receive disclaimed inheritances not only of property distributed under the will but also of certain jointly held and other property passing outside of the will. Pursuant to the disclaimer, the inheritance would pass to a trust for benefit of the surviving spouse. By using this post-mortem disclaimer, the surviving spouse avoids an overfunding of his or her separate estate but becomes the lifetime beneficiary of the disclaimed inheritance as in the case of a bypass trust.

CAUTION!   Tenants by the entirety property, or other husband-wife jointly held property with right of survivorship, cannot be disclaimed following death unless state law permits severance of the joint ownership by unilateral action of one spouse during the lifetime of both.

However, under Proposed Regulations issued in 1996 which would be effective only after the Regulations become final, the survivorship interest in such property could be disclaimed if the property was acquired after 1954 but before 1982. These Proposed Regulations state that a surviving joint tenant cannot in any event disclaim any portion of a jointly held bank or brokerage account which is attributable to the survivor's contribution toward its acquisition. In that not all jointly held property may be disclaimed following death, planning to fund a disclaimer trust with interests in jointly held property should only be utilized with care.

THE BENEFITS OF LIFETIME GIFTS

Each person can give $10,000 in cash or property to any person or any number of persons each year without any gift or estate tax implications. The recipient must receive a *present interest* in the property, meaning a right to enjoy the gift immediately.

Consequently, an individual with three children and five grandchildren can give a total of $80,000 in any single year to these close family members without any reduction of the unified credit. If the donor is married and funds are coming from jointly held property, or if the spouse consents when the funds are coming from separately held assets of the donor, the $80,000 figure is effectively doubled to $160,000.

Thus, in the case of larger families particularly, it is possible to reduce the estate size significantly through a program of lifetime gifts to family members.

QUESTION: My wife and I inherited eight large tracts of land from my father two years ago. The real estate agent told me that I could sell the property for about $150,000. However, my wife and I would rather give the land to our four children so that they can develop it or hold on to it, at their option. If we do give the property to our children, what are the tax ramifications?

ANSWER: Assuming that you have made no other gifts to your children during the year, you can give $20,000 worth of the real estate to each of your four children without incurring a gift tax liability. Even more important is the fact that neither of you will have used any of your unified credit. Next year, the remaining real estate can be given to the four children using most of the next year's $10,000/$20,000 annual gift tax exclusion. The benefit to you is that you remove the $150,000 from your current estate and also ensure that the potential appreciation escapes federal estate taxes. You can accomplish your goal by gifts of entire tracts, of fractional interests in all tracts, or of interests in a real estate entity formed to hold the property. You should normally choose the approach which minimizes state and local transfer taxes.

TAX PLANNING IDEA   On occasion, it is advisable to make gifts in excess of the $10,000 per donor per donee annual exclusion. When property is owned that figures to go up significantly in value, it may be wise to utilize the unified credit for a lifetime gift in order to remove this appreciating asset from the estate before it goes up significantly in value.

CAUTION!   You will normally not want to give property which has already appreciated significantly in value, however. It is usually better to let assets which have already gone up significantly in value remain with the original owner in order to pass them to the younger family members through inheritance after receiving a step-up in the income tax basis. The result is that the capital gain is forgiven (see Chapter 5).

CAUTION!   Congress has periodically considered legislation which, if enacted, would limit total annual gifts which can be made utilizing the annual gift tax exclusion per beneficiary. With less frequency, Congress has also considered ending the step-up in tax basis following death. In such case there would be no particular advantage in retaining significantly appreciated assets until death.

YEAR-END REMINDER   Older individuals facing estate tax liability upon death, particularly one whose spouse has predeceased or who is otherwise unmarried, should determine the advisability of year-end estate reduction through gifts within the $10,000 annual exclusion. When there is a quick need for estate reduction, consider the spouses of children and grandchildren as possible recipients, further increasing the number of possible beneficiaries for the purpose of maximizing the annual exclusion in the aggregate. Remember also that this $10,000 exclusion per donor per donee is computed on a calendar year basis. Consequently, when the initial round of gift giving to family members in order to reduce estate size occurs late in the year, a second round of gifts in the following January can be accomplished. Remember that such a program in a certain estate tax situation will save at least $3,700 in estate taxes for each $10,000 annual exclusion utilized.

CAUTION!   The donee must present a year-end check to his or bank by December 31 or the gift will be considered as made in the following year. The IRS has dropped its prior position that the check needed to clear by year-end.

Gifts of other assets raise similar issues as to the year in which they are completed, requiring care on the part of the taxpayer. A father who wrote a letter to his son in 1974 giving him stock in a family business but who didn't endorse the stock certificate to his son until 1988 survived IRS scrutiny only when the Fifth Circuit Court of Appeals reversed the Tax Court on April 5, 1997 and determined that the gift occurred in 1974.

CAUTION!   Gifts by a holder of a power of attorney on behalf of another individual pose another problem. Any gift made by the "attorney" must be authorized under the document or by state law.

FILING POINTER   The purchase of an Education IRA or tuition certificate (see Chapter 2 as to both) in the name of another is considered to be a gift of a present interest at the time of the purchase qualifying for the annual exclusion on gifts. The donor may elect to treat a purchase of a tuition certificate as made ratably in the current year and in the four succeeding years in order to maximize use of the annual exclusion.

CAUTION!   The $10,000 annual gift tax exclusion will be indexed for cost of living beginning in 1999. Because indexing is in $1,000 increments, a rise to $11,000 is unlikely until 2001 or 2002.

TAX PLANNING IDEA   Gifts between spouses not only allow creation of a spouse's separate estate in order to fund a bypass or QTIP trust, but also permit a couple to place the most highly appreciated property in the name of the older spouse or the spouse with health problems in order to obtain the largest possible step-up in the tax basis of the property at death. (See Chapter 5 for a discussion of the increased basis at death.) However, a spouse who receives a gift from the other spouse must survive more than one year for a bequest back to the donor spouse to enjoy the basis step-up.

These interspousal transfers can generally be freely made, inasmuch as gifts between spouses qualify for the unlimited marital deduction.

CAUTION! If the recipient spouse is not a U.S. citizen, no marital deduction is available for gifts. Rather, the first $100,000 of gifts each year to a non-U.S. citizen spouse is excluded from federal gift tax.

CAUTION! You cannot effectively reduce the size of your estate by transferring title of property to another individual but retaining the right to live in the property or to receive income from the property for the remainder of your life or by transferring title to your name and that of another individual as joint owners with rights of survivorship. Property transferred in this manner is includable in the transferor's estate at its date of death value. If your goal is to reduce your federal taxable estate, you must relinquish not only legal title to the property but also any formal or informal understanding that you will receive benefits from the property in the form of a right to live in the property or the right to the income generated by the property.

THE BENEFITS OF REVOCABLE TRUSTS

A *revocable trust* is a trust which you establish and fund during your lifetime where you retain the power to terminate the trust at any time. No federal income, gift, or estate taxes are saved by using a revocable trust. Any income generated by the assets held in a revocable trust will be included on the trust creator's income tax return. There is no gift of property placed in a revocable trust since the creator can always change his or her mind and get the property back. The Taxpayer Relief Act of 1997 clarified prospectively as of August 6, 1997 that gifts from a revocable trust are treated in the same manner as direct gifts from the trust's creator. Furthermore, any assets remaining in a revocable trust at the time of the creator's death will be included in the federal gross estate so that the creator will not have diminished the size of his or her estate.

Why then use a revocable trust? Revocable trusts are useful tools to provide professional lifetime management for an estate. For example, you may be considering a particular financial institution to manage your estate after your death and you want to test the institution's management skills and investment return.

A second use of a revocable trust is to guard against the potential disability of its creator. By having a trustee as the legal owner of investment assets there will be no gap in management of assets should you become disabled. The management of your assets will continue following your disability just as the trustee had managed your assets before your disability. Without a revocable trust, upon your incapacity it might be necessary for your family to have the courts name a formal guardian of your assets. Thus, potentially expensive guardianship proceedings are avoided by using a revocable trust.

A third use of a revocable trust is to save on probate costs. Depending upon the jurisdiction, the size of your estate, the composition of your estate, and the size of your family, the probate process may be complicated and costly. By using a revocable trust you avoid the probate concerns. The assets of the revocable trust are often not subject to public disclosure as would be the assets which pass under the terms of your will. There is no delay in having your heirs benefit from your estate as there might be if they had to wait for the probate of your estate to be completed.

CAUTION!   Whether using a revocable trust will save any state inheritance taxes for you will vary from jurisdiction to jurisdiction. Many states subject revocable trusts to inherit-ance tax although they are exempt from the probate process.

CAUTION!   Careful thought should go into use of a revocable trust. Unless all separately titled assets are transferred into the trust, the probate process is generally not avoided. The transfer of most assets will require retitling of property. The transfer of certain assets (real estate, stocks, and automobiles, for example) will require recordation of the legal change in ownership. Many individuals find both the transfer process and the subsequent handling of the trust to be a nuisance.

Consequently, many individuals prefer to delay utilization of a revocable trust for all assets until such time as they no longer wish to administer their assets. During the interim, a revocable trust may be the best suited for separately titled real property and personal effects located outside of the state of domicile. An *ancillary probate* in the second state can be avoided by transferring those assets to a living trust.

THE BENEFITS OF IRREVOCABLE TRUSTS

An *irrevocable trust* is one that is formed during the creator's lifetime and the creator retains no power to revoke the terms of the trust. Once signed, the terms of such an instrument cannot be modified or revoked. The creator of the irrevocable trust is not taxed on the income generated by the trust assets so long as he or she does not retain control over the trust assets and receives no benefit from the trust. Rather, the trust or the income beneficiaries of the trust pay tax on the income generated by the trust's investments.

What are some of the uses of irrevocable trusts? Many individuals use an irrevocable trust for the same reason that they make outright gifts of property—they want to reduce the size of their estate. However, they form trusts instead of making outright gifts because they do not want the recipients to have outright ownership of the gift property either because of age or other circumstances. Perhaps the creator of a trust may want to provide one person with the benefit of the gift property for a period of time and then transfer the enjoyment to another party. For example, a father may want to provide financial security for his daughter for her lifetime and upon her death have the assets transferred to his grandchildren.

CAUTION!   A completed gift occurs upon creation and funding of most irrevocable trusts, and therefore the federal gift tax laws (and, to the extent applicable, state gift tax laws) must be considered. The annual gift tax exclusion may not apply to gifts transferred by means of an irrevocable trust because such gifts often do not involve a present interest. This means that a gift by means of an irrevocable trust will often use some or all of the creator's unified credit. However, with careful drafting of the irrevocable trust instrument, gifts made through the irrevocable trust can qualify in many cases for the annual exclusion and therefore minimize or perhaps eliminate use of the creator's unified credit.

LIFE INSURANCE AS PART OF THE ESTATE PLAN

Individuals often overlook the amount of insurance that they are carrying on their life when undertaking an estate analysis. For federal estate tax purposes, if you are the owner of a life insurance policy, its value is includable in your federal estate and can very well throw you over the threshold at which there is estate tax liability. Life insurance, together with retirement plan benefits and appreciating real estate, will often create a taxable estate in excess of this figure in the case of many middle-class Americans.

Life insurance is an excellent candidate for lifetime gifts. It will usually have only a nominal value, or its cash surrender value will be much smaller than its face value so that the cost of making a lifetime gift of an insurance policy is minimal in comparison to the cost of having to include the death benefit proceeds in one's gross estate. So long as the transfer of complete ownership of a policy occurs more than three years prior to death, the insurance proceeds payable to the beneficiary are not includable in the estate of the deceased individual.

TAX PLANNING IDEA A gift of the life insurance policy can be made either outright or, more often, to an irrevocable trust under which the surviving spouse can receive a lifetime income interest with the principal passing to the children without inclusion of the proceeds in either spouse's estate. Life insurance trusts should be especially considered by a couple facing a certain estate tax liability upon the second death even with use of bypass trusts.

CAUTION! Future estate tax legislation may restrict or eliminate the ability to remove life insurance from an estate by transferring the incidents of ownership. Individuals contemplating steps to remove life insurance from their estate should consider acting in the near future to benefit from likely "grandfather" rules exempting previously acquired or transferred policies from harsher treatment.

GENERATION SKIPPING TO AVOID TAX PIGGYBACKS

If you start with $1 and lose 40 percent in taxes and then subsequently lose 40 percent of the remainder in taxes, you have kept 36 cents. The estate and gift tax structure is generally designed to do just that, generation after generation.

Many wealthy families were able to avoid the cumulative effect of estate and gift taxes by retaining assets in trust for generations. They were not included in the estate of descendants for a number of generations because those heirs were not outright owners of the property. The only restriction on these trusts was one from the English *common law*—that outright title had to vest within 21 years following the death of the last descendant of the creator who was alive when the trust came into existence. This *Rule Against Perpetuities* still allowed a trust to hold assets for as long as 100 years or more without added taxes at each generation level.

In 1976, Congress first passed a *generation skipping tax.* Essentially, this tax is designed to ensure that even transfers in trust are taxed at each generation level. However, each individual has a $1 million exemption for generation skipping transfers, allowing a couple with a large estate to leave $2 million in trust for grandchildren, with their children enjoying rights to income and certain rights to principal during their lives. The generation skipping tax exemption will be indexed for cost of living in 1999 and succeeding years.

TAX PLANNING IDEA   Bypass trusts, QTIP trusts, lifetime gifts, and irrevocable trusts are techniques to be considered for estate tax savings by individuals whose federal gross estates exceed the threshold for tax liability, $625,000 in 1998 and climbing only gradually before more rapid increases carry that threshold to $1 million in 2006. The generation-skipping trust is one of many techniques best suited as a tax planning mechanism for much larger estates. Other tax-saving strategies for much larger estates include charitable lead and remainder trusts as well as trusts (GRATs, GRUTs, and QPRTs) in which the creator retains an interest for a period of years. Each of these techniques saves taxes by reducing the gift tax value of the transferred property.

13

DEALING WITH THE
INTERNAL REVENUE SERVICE

Your experiences with America's largest and most powerful collection agency can be made less burdensome by understanding the most important considerations in dealing with the Internal Revenue Service. That these are set forth in the 13th chapter is purely coincidental.

ALWAYS FILE YOUR TAX RETURN ON TIME

Tax filing time is stressful for many Americans. In fact, one in five individuals declared in a recent survey that the period around April 15 is the most stressful time of year. Many of these individuals owe money to the IRS and don't have it. Unfortunately, a large percentage believe that the proper method of dealing with a tax liability that cannot be paid by the due date is to send in the return late. This is generally the wrong decision.

In the case of an individual return, you will be facing a five percent per month combined late filing/late payment penalty for the first five months of tardiness (15 percent per month if willful). This penalty will usually be difficult to abate, because lack of funds is not reasonable cause for late filing. Penalties taper off after five months to one-half of one percent per month. In addition, you will be paying interest at prescribed rates which are adjusted every quarter.

But, if you file the tax return and fail to enclose a check, you will be billed for any liability plus interest plus one-half of one percent per month late payment penalty. Consequently, if you owe the IRS $5,000 and pay five months late, your penalty will be $125. However, if you do not file the return on time, your penalty will be $1,250—ten times as much.

FILING POINTER   If you request an extension of the April 15 filing deadline (about five percent of individual filers get an automatic four-month extension to August 15 by filing IRS Form 4868), you will not be subject to the late filing penalty. However, the filing extension does not extend the time for payment of your tax bill beyond April 15; thus the lesser late payment penalty will apply.

CONTROVERSY

In order for a further extension request to as late as October 15 to be valid and the late filing penalty to be inapplicable, it is unclear as to whether you must make a bona fide and reasonable estimate of your tax liability and pay the unpaid portion of the estimated liability with the second extension request. Temporary Regulations issued on January 3, 1996 are silent on the issue, and the IRS is handling the issue inconsistently.

NONFILERS—TAKE ADVANTAGE OF INFORMAL AMNESTY

The Internal Revenue Service has an informal amnesty program under which individuals and other nonfilers of income, payroll, and other tax returns may file back tax returns, even those delinquent for many years, without fear of criminal prosecution. The IRS will normally not require back filings beyond six to eight years if the most recent tax returns are filed. However, unless abated, penalties and interest are computed on any taxes owed on the back returns that are filed.

The program commenced for individual income tax in 1992 and was extended in the following year to corporate and other taxpayers as well as to payroll and other types of taxes. In order to take advantage of informal amnesty, the IRS must not have commenced any inquiry, audit, or investigation of the taxpayer and, in the case of income tax returns, income must be from legal sources. The taxpayer must cooperate in determining tax liability as accurately as possible and must pay any delinquency to the extent of the ability to pay. If future returns are not filed, the IRS may reopen the case within five years.

The informal amnesty program is designed to bring an estimated 7½ to 10 million nonfilers (including accountants and lawyers), mostly self-employed and owing a collective estimated $14 billion, back into the tax system.

CONTROVERSY

The current amnesty program has been considered informal inasmuch as the Justice Department is the agency responsible for prosecution. However, a New York Federal District Court ruled in 1996 that both IRS and the Justice Department are bound by the policy, allowing a chronically late tax attorney to avoid prosecution. The government may yet try to get a different result with different facts and a different taxpayer.

CAUTION!   In any event, the IRS is continuing to seek prosecution of nonfilers who have not come forward and are caught. If you are contacted by a representative of the Criminal Investigation Division (CID) of the Internal Revenue Service (they will identify themselves as such), or if an examiner indicates that he or she may turn the case over to the CID, run—don't walk—to an attorney versed in criminal tax affairs. Pending the advice of counsel, make no statements and turn over no more records to the IRS. Almost always, there is no benefit in making further statements to the IRS or in turning over privileged materials.

A criminal investigation should be taken seriously from the beginning. Statistics show that 50 to 60 percent of criminal inquiries lead to prosecutions, the vast majority of which are successful and result in jail time. Almost 3,000 individuals are convicted each year. Baseball greats Pete Rose, Darryl Strawberry, Duke Snider, and Willie McCovey have been among these recent numbers.

Referrals by CID to the Justice Department for prosecution on a per capita basis are much higher in some areas of the country than in others according to a study of 1995 referrals. Highest referral levels were from offices in Pensacola (Florida), Manhattan, and Las Vegas. Lowest referral levels were from offices in Sioux Falls (South Dakota) and Spokane (Washington).

CUT YOUR CHANCES OF BEING AUDITED

The tax law has become more complicated over the years. In the last two decades, there have been major revisions to the law in 1976, 1978, 1981, 1982, 1984, 1986, 1993, 1996, and 1997, numerous other changes of lesser importance, and new regulations, rulings, and cases issued almost daily in many important areas.

Despite these intimidating changes, most Americans can still prepare their own return (and save preparer fees that can be $100, $500, or even more). Even relatively involved returns can be prepared by people who can read and use a calculator, because tax guides such as *J.K. Lasser's Your Income Tax* have been answering tax questions Americans have had, in plain English, for over 50 years.

If your return is so complex that you require a professional tax preparer (or you simply choose to pay someone else for the trouble of preparing your return), the best single step you can take to minimize your chances of an audit is to obtain the services of a *competent* preparer. A paid preparer must place his or her Social Security number on your tax return as well as an employer identification number, if any, and this can be used to screen all returns prepared by less than scrupulous preparers.

Apart from avoiding irresponsible tax preparers, the second best step which you can take to minimize your chances of audit is to avoid outlandish and unreasonable positions, particularly those which are conspicuous on a tax return. For example, a couple in a reported case several years ago was purportedly engaged in in-home sales for profit. However, the couple reported only $526 in gross income and $18,538 in expenses including a business meeting in Hawaii. The return was understandably pulled for examination and the taxpayer was unable to prove a profit-making intent.

This is not to recommend that you abstain from taking positions which might be at odds with the Internal Revenue Service. There are many unclear or unanswered questions within the tax law, and you have the right to take a legally justifiable position even if it may counter the IRS view on the matter. The IRS position on issues may have been (or may be) declared incorrect by the Tax Court or other judicial forum. However, positions without significant basis in law or fact often stand out and increase your chances of audit.

Next, be certain that you include all required forms and supplemental documents with your tax return. For example, if you claim depreciation on an automobile or other asset used in a business or investment, you must attach IRS Form 4562 to the tax return. Failure to include this necessary form could alone trigger an audit.

A return that says too much (or too little) can generate an audit. If you own a roofing business in Boston and attend the trade convention in St. Thomas, don't state "Virgin Islands trip" under "Other Expenses" on Schedule C. Determine the proper portion allocable to travel, seminars, and business meals. Classify the component parts accordingly. On the other hand, don't group most of your business expenses into a mass category called "Miscellaneous." Group the costs under properly deductible headings.

Some individuals face likely audit in any event. One study of individual returns selected for audit showed that the common link among a high percentage of these returns was itemized deductions in excess of 35 percent of adjusted gross income. Among the many other entries or situations which can be audit-triggering by themselves or in conjunction with others are the following:

1. Claiming persons other than children, grandchildren, or parents as dependents and/or not providing the Social Security numbers of dependents;

2. Schedule C losses from a business or profession on modest gross income (intended to avoid the employee business expense limitation);

3. Travel, meals, and entertainment expenses on Schedule C disproportionate to the income;

4. The office-in-home deduction;

5. Substantial employee business expenses;

6. High medical expenses well over the 7½ percent of adjusted gross income floor;

7. Substantial points deducted as interest expense when there has been no change in a taxpayer's address;

8. Significant charitable contributions of property;

9. High interest deductions;

10. High rental losses;

11. Bad debts;

12. A high percentage of business use of a vehicle in an occupation not historically associated with extensive automobile usage;

13. Casualty losses;

14. Earned income credit (which due to its refundable nature has become a major source of fraud);

15. Obvious inaccurate depreciation;

16. Claiming material participation in activities with losses (especially with high W-2 income); and

17. Little or no tip income in a business which receives gratuities.

Are you the sole owner of a business? Do you deal in cash? Do you engage in barter transactions? The IRS study has found individuals in these groups as the biggest "tax cheats." Expect stepped-up activity here including IRS scrutiny of mortgage loan applications to see if they are consistent with tax returns. To assist auditors, the IRS is designing guidelines in at least 75 industries under its new *Market Segment Specialization Program (MSSP)*.

Even though your tax return may lack any audit-triggering entries, your return may yet be audited. The IRS has historically selected a small number of returns for audit under the *Taxpayer Compliance Measurement Program (TCMP)*. The TCMP ensures that every individual feels a degree of risk in that he or she might be audited despite an ordinary-looking return, as well as enables the IRS to learn of areas of noncompliance.

A TCMP audit is far more comprehensive and time-consuming than other audits; the examiner will want verification of most line items instead of concentrating on a handful of predetermined matters. However, individuals randomly selected for audit are four times more likely not to owe additional taxes than those whose returns stand out. TCMP audits have been at least temporarily halted due to budget constraints.

Additional audits are generated by information provided by tipsters such as neighbors and ex-spouses who received collective rewards of $5.3 million in fiscal 1993, $3.4 million in fiscal 1994, and $1.8 million in fiscal 1995. A tipster can even be an IRS agent as a New Hampshire couple found out several years ago after they parked their Rolls Royce outside a restaurant in a small town. The IRS employee made note of the license number, and the ensuing audit led to a referral to the Criminal Investigation Division and a conviction.

A correspondence audit can result if the income and deductions that you report on your tax return don't match the information returns sent to the IRS. If you mail your home mortgage payment on December 31, as a cash basis taxpayer you are entitled to a deduction in that year of payment for allowable mortgage interest. However, your lender has no way of knowing when you actually made the payment. Chances are that the lender will report to the IRS based on when it received your check.

In recent years the IRS has audited about one percent of individual income tax returns; however, it increased its audit rate to about 1.67 percent in fiscal 1995 through large numbers of correspondence audits as it commenced its efforts to raise tax compliance levels from the current 86 percent to at least 90 percent of reportable liability. Each one percent rise in the compliance level for any year raises about $9 billion. Nonetheless, budget constraints have reduced the audit rate to the current 1.18 percent.

Upper-income individuals have historically been more likely to be audited—they offer greater potential for collecting revenues. However, lower-income individuals now fall right behind, especially Schedule C filers with smaller profits —the IRS believes noncompliance is higher among businesses reporting lower income. Middle income individuals have the lowest audit rate.

The audit rate on a per capita basis is much higher in some areas of the country than in others. Highest audit rates in 1995 (the latest year for which complete statistics have been published) were in the Las Vegas, San Francisco, and Los Angeles districts. Lowest audit rates in 1995 were in the Cleveland, Cincinnati, and Albany districts. Cities with high or low audit rates do not vary substantially from year to year.

TAX PLANNING IDEA When you know that an incorrect information return has been filed with the IRS, submit an explanatory statement with the tax return if the provider of the information return will not make a correction. This may (but will not always) keep you from being among the millions of taxpayers contacted by the IRS each year for discrepancies as determined by computer reporting.

CAUTION!   Although you can take any legally justifiable position, your tax return preparer can be penalized for taking a position that does not have a "realistic possibility" of being sustained. Under Treasury Regulations, a position has a realistic possibility of success if it has at least approximately a one-in-three chance or better of prevailing on the merits. If a position is not "frivolous" but has longer odds of winning, the preparer may take that position if adequately disclosed on the return.

AUDITS, APPEALS, AND LITIGATION

The time and effort required in preparing for a meeting with an IRS examiner and ease in which the audit will be conducted is dependent upon a number of factors, including:

1. The nature of the audit;
2. The shape of your records;
3. The knowledge and experience of your Taxpayer Representative (or your knowledge if you are going to the meeting alone);
4. The knowledge and experience of the IRS examiner (training has been reduced and turnover has increased); and
5. Whether the IRS conducts an *economic reality check*, used with increasing frequency to examine whether the income reported on your return is commensurate with your lifestyle.

One of the first decisions you must make if you receive an audit notice is whether to go to the examination alone, bring your tax preparer or other professional along, or stay at home and let your attorney, CPA, or agent enrolled to practice before the IRS go to the meeting in your place. The last approach is usually the best one, unless your presence is needed to establish credibility or is required by the IRS.

Most individuals have a tendency to say too much rather than just answer the examiner's questions. This can open up new points for examination or can complicate ones being scrutinized. Additionally, most individuals will act emotionally and defensively when meeting with an examiner.

When a matter cannot be resolved with the examiner, an examination report will be prepared. If not accepted by the taxpayer, a *30-day letter* (so-called because you have 30 days to respond; 60 days if sent to you outside the United States) will be issued and the next step is an Appeals Office Conference. The conference is obtained by making a request to the local District Director pursuant to instructions in the 30-day letter. A written *protest* is required in order to obtain the conference when the total amount of proposed additional tax exceeds $10,000 for any taxable period. Instructions concerning the content of the protest are contained in the 30-day letter.

At the Appeals Conference, a taxpayer will have a greater opportunity to resolve a controversy than existed with the examiner. Appeals Officers will consider court decisions which have been contrary to the IRS as well as the hazards of litigation. A particular issue may also be settled at a certain number of cents on the dollar based on the risks of litigation.

Most tax matters are resolved at the Appeals Conference along the lines that they would be resolved by a court. If a case cannot be resolved with Appeals (as they are about 90 percent of the time), the IRS will issue a *statutory notice of deficiency*, also known as a *90-day letter* because the taxpayer has 90 days from the mailing date of the letter (150 days if sent to an address outside the United States) to forestall assessment of the tax and subsequent collection by filing a petition with the Tax Court.

Instead of filing a petition with the Tax Court, you can pay the *full* liability, file a claim for refund with the IRS (which will, in all likelihood, be denied), and then sue the IRS for a refund in U.S. District Court or in the Court of Federal Claims.

CONTROVERSY

The Second Circuit Court of Appeals and several federal district courts interpret this "full payment rule" to require a taxpayer to pay the entire amount of assessed tax, assessed penalties, and assessed interest before jurisdiction is conferred on the court. In contrast, the United States Court of Appeals for the Federal Circuit (the court which hears appeals from the Court of Federal Claims) has ruled that the full payment rule requires the taxpayer to pay only the assessed tax liability and not the assessed penalties and interest where the taxpayer is not making a substantive claim regarding the penalties and interest. The Federal Circuit would require full payment of assessed penalties and/or interest, as the case may be, if the taxpayer raises substantive arguments beyond the automatic reduction or elimination of penalties and interest when the tax liability is reduced or eliminated as a result of the court's decision.

CAUTION! Special rules apply to employment tax matters such as the Trust Fund Recovery Penalty discussed in Chapter 10. If the payroll matter cannot be resolved administratively, the IRS will make an assessment and provide notice and demand for payment. The taxpayer has 30 days from the date of notice and demand in which to post a bond equal to 150 percent of the amount in issue in order to forestall collection activity pending litigation of the matter. In the absence of a bond, the IRS has the right to begin collection activity although collection is usually held in abeyance during litigation. You commence the process generally by paying a certain *portion* of the liability, filing a claim for refund with the IRS (which in such cases will normally also be denied), and suing the IRS for a refund in U.S. District Court or in the Court of Federal Claims. The Tax Court does not hear employment tax matters.

CAUTION! Proposed Regulations would require a written protest only where the proposed additional tax liability exceeds $25,000. This change will be effective 60 days after the Regulations become final. In the meantime, follow the instructions in the 30-day letter.

CAUTION!   The time period for filing a Tax Court petition is statutory and cannot be extended, even if an individual is improperly advised by the Internal Revenue Service. Note that 90 days is generally less than three months. For example, if a notice of deficiency is issued on June 23, your Tax Court petition is due on September 21 (which is the 90th day).

TAX PLANNING IDEA   The hard facts are that taxpayers rarely win their cases in court. Recent statistics indicate that taxpayers win outright only four percent of the time in Tax Court, faring a bit better in District Court and the Court of Federal Claims. Absent clear error on the part of the IRS, a taxpayer with an attractive settlement offer must realistically look at his or her chance of success upon proceeding to court, particularly in light of legal fees and other costs of litigation.

MOVING—LET THE IRS KNOW

Failure to actually receive correspondence from the IRS will generally be no excuse for missing a deadline where the notice was sent to your "last known address." Because the IRS generally uses the address shown on your most recently filed tax return as the address of record for purposes of sending audit, deficiency, and levy notices, it is important to keep the IRS informed of any change in address by "clear and concise notice." Once a tax return has been filed, the IRS will be considered to have received a notice of the address reported on that return 45 days after receipt. However, as a result of the high volume of returns filed between February 14 and June 1, addresses shown on tax returns filed during that period will not be considered as received for this purpose until July 16.

If you move subsequent to filing your tax return, the "clear and concise" notice requirement can be met by filing Form 8822 with the Service Center where you filed your last tax return. In any event, make sure the Post Office forwards your mail. The IRS was unable to deliver $62 million in 1995 refunds to almost 100,000 taxpayers because of erroneous addresses. About 12 percent of taxpayers are unable to contest proposed tax assessments because they do not receive the 90-day letters sent to their last known addresses.

CONTROVERSY

Before the IRS adopted the "45-day rule" in 1990, the courts on numerous occasions scrutinized the issue of what constitutes a taxpayer's last known address. While most decisions favored the IRS, the courts did not universally accept the time period that the IRS claimed was needed for processing address changes. It is unclear whether the current rule will survive the scrutiny of the courts or Congress.

ABATING PENALTIES AND INTEREST

All but a few of the more than 150 types of civil penalties in the tax law will either not be assessed or are abatable in the event that reasonable cause can be shown. However, the IRS has drastically slashed its penalty abatements. For fiscal 1990, the IRS abated almost one-half

Form 8822, Change of address, page1.

Form **8822**	**Change of Address**	
(Rev. May 1995) Department of the Treasury Internal Revenue Service	▶ **Please type or print.** ▶ **See instructions on back.** ▶ **Do not attach this form to your return.**	OMB No. 1545-1163

Part I   **Complete This Part To Change Your Home Mailing Address**

Check **ALL** boxes this change affects:

1 ☐ Individual income tax returns (Forms 1040, 1040A, 1040EZ, 1040NR, etc.)
> ▶ If your last return was a joint return and you are now establishing a residence separate from the spouse with whom you filed that return, check here . . . . ▶ ☐

2 ☐ Employment tax returns for household employers (Forms 942, 940, 940-EZ, etc.)
> ▶ Enter your employer identification number here . . . . ▶ _____

3 ☐ Gift, estate, or generation-skipping transfer tax returns (Forms 706, 709, etc.)
> ▶ For Forms 706 and 706-NA, enter the decedent's name and social security number below.

▶ Decedent's name	▶ Social security number	
4a Your name (first name, initial, and last name)		**4b Your social security number**
5a Spouse's name (first name, initial, and last name)		**5b Spouse's social security number**

6 Prior name(s). See instructions.

7a Old address (no., street, city or town, state, and ZIP code). If a P.O. box or foreign address, see instructions.   Apt. no.

7b Spouse's old address, if different from line 7a (no., street, city or town, state, and ZIP code). If a P.O. box or foreign address, see instructions.   Apt. no.

8 New address (no., street, city or town, state, and ZIP code). If a P.O. box or foreign address, see instructions.   Apt. no.

Part II   **Complete This Part To Change Your Business Mailing Address or Business Location**

Check **ALL** boxes this change affects:

9 ☐ Employment, excise, and other business returns (Forms 720, 941, 990, 1041, 1065, 1120, etc.)
10 ☐ Employee plan returns (Forms 5500, 5500-C/R, and 5500-EZ). See instructions.
11 ☐ Business location

12a Business name		**12b Employer identification number**

13 Old address (no., street, city or town, state, and ZIP code). If a P.O. box or foreign address, see instructions.   Room or suite no.

14 New address (no., street, city or town, state, and ZIP code). If a P.O. box or foreign address, see instructions.   Room or suite no.

15 New business location (no., street, city or town, state, and ZIP code). If a foreign address, see instructions.   Room or suite no.

Part III   **Signature**

Daytime telephone number of person to contact (optional) ▶ ( ) _____

Please Sign Here

▶ _____   _____   ▶ _____
Your signature   Date   If Part II completed, signature of owner, officer, or representative   Date

▶ _____   _____   ▶ _____
If joint return, spouse's signature   Date   Title

For Privacy Act and Paperwork Reduction Act Notice, see back of form.   Cat. No. 12081V   Form **8822** (Rev. 5-95) of the billions of dollars in assessed penalties. During the following year, less than ten percent of penalties were abated. Today, the abatement rate remains low and the penalty structure remains so complicated that outgoing IRS Commissioner Margaret Richardson in 1997 called for an "urgent overhaul."

As previously discussed, it is often difficult to show reasonable cause in connection with the late filing of an income tax return. Among examples of reasonable cause are death or serious illness of the taxpayer or a member of his or her immediate family, unavoidable absence of the taxpayer, or destruction of business records. Illness may be either physical or psychological. In the latter case, a good affidavit from the taxpayer's psychiatrist or psychologist is essential but no guarantee of success.

Fortunately, the courts are more sympathetic than the IRS to penalty abatement. A Kentucky man several years ago filed a return three years late during a period in which he became totally paralyzed from a degenerative disease. The IRS refused to abate the late filing penalty but a federal district court was more sympathetic. To its credit, the IRS did not appeal the decision. However, see Chapter 1 concerning how the courts would not abate penalties on actress Skye Bassett for her parents' failure to file returns on her behalf when she was a youngster.

One of the most popular defenses to the late filing penalty is to blame the tardiness on a tax professional. The U.S. Supreme Court in 1985 resolved this formerly controversial area, determining that reliance on a professional to file a tax return does not take the taxpayer off the hook. However, if the professional gives improper tax advice, good faith reliance on the substantive guidance should suffice to make the penalty inapplicable.

Other penalties are much easier to abate. More than 20 years after ERISA (technically the *Employee Retirement Income Security Act of 1974* but popularly known in the tax profession as Every Rotten Idea Since Adam) overhauled the retirement plan laws, they remain such a source of confusion to taxpayers, practitioners, and the Internal Revenue Service itself that virtually every request to abate penalties for late filing of the 5500 series information return is granted.

The most severe penalties (excluding the Trust Fund Recovery Penalty discussed in Chapter 10, which is really a transfer of portions of corporate payroll tax liability to responsible individuals) are the civil fraud penalty and the negligence penalty. In the case of civil fraud, a taxpayer will pay, in addition to principal and interest, an amount equal to 75 percent of the portion of the liability which is attributable to fraud. Short of civil fraud is negligence, with a 20 percent penalty on the portion of the liability which is attributable to negligence. Interest will be imposed on the fraud or negligence penalty amount as well as on the tax deficiency.

Interest, which is imposed on tax and penalties, can be dropped to the extent attributable to *ministerial* error. Effective for 1997 returns, interest can be dropped to the extent attributable to *managerial* error as well. See the discussion of The Taxpayer Bill of Rights—Part 2 later in this chapter.

TAX PLANNING IDEA   Keep records of all telephone contact with IRS staffers. Record their names and telephone numbers along with the dates of contact. These records may be useful in abating penalties and interest.

FILING POINTER When a tax matter is pending for a long period of time, interest can approach or exceed the principal amount of tax liability, particularly during periods of high rates.

The interest rate which taxpayers pay to the IRS is adjusted quarterly, with the new rate three points above the short-term rate on federal obligations during the first month of the preceding quarter, rounded to the nearest full percent. (However, if the tides are turned and the IRS owes you money subject to the payment of interest, it pays you at one percent less.) Between July 1, 1983 and December 31, 1997, interest rates on obligations to the IRS ranged between seven percent and 13 percent though they have been much higher in the past. A special interest rate of 120 percent of the regular rate applies to certain *tax motivated transactions*. In either event, interest is compounded daily on the unpaid balance.

When it is clear that you may owe some liability but settlement of other issues will be drawn out or difficult, it often makes sense to cut the interest on that amount by paying undisputed principal and the interest on that principal. If you prevail on the remaining issues, you should owe nothing more. Under certain circumstances it is possible to designate payments as interest only.

STATUTES OF LIMITATION—SOMETIMES THEY BENEFIT YOU, SOMETIMES THEY DON'T

Suppose you had more gains on commodities trading in 1980 than you reported to the IRS. Suppose your inadvertent error is discovered many years later.

In this case, the statute of limitations would have expired long ago and is a bar to imposition of a tax deficiency. Nonetheless, on these facts, President and Mrs. Clinton made a voluntary payment of $14,615 tax and interest (no penalty) in 1994.

Not only may a statute of limitations bar imposition of a tax deficiency, but it also may bar collection on an outstanding deficiency. Absent a voluntary extension of the time period on your part, the IRS has ten years from the date of assessment of a deficiency to either collect the money or sue for a judgment (in which case the time period for collection is determined under state law).

The normal statute of limitations during which the IRS can assess a deficiency is three years from the later of the due date or the filing date of the tax return. However, the statute is six years rather than three if over 25 percent of gross income is omitted. There is an unlimited statute of limitations in the case of nonfilers or in the event of civil fraud.

A statute of limitations can work to your disadvantage as well. A claim for refund (usually on Form 1040-X in the case of an individual income tax refund or on Form 843 for employment taxes, penalties, and certain other matters) must generally be filed by the later of three years from the due date of the tax return, or two years from the date of payment. Consequently, if you filed your 1994 tax return on time and made full payment, a refund claim must be filed by April 15, 1998. The U.S. Supreme Court decided on February 18, 1997 that an individual's disability does not extend the time period for climing a refund.

CAUTION! Pursuant to a 1993 decision of the U.S. Supreme Court, even though the IRS missed a statute of limitations against an S corporation, it may still come after the shareholder for his or her share of taxes on the entity income until the expiration of the individual assessment period. Later that year the Ninth Circuit Court of Appeals determined that the same reasoning applied in the case of a partner as to taxes on his or her share of partnership income.

CONTROVERSY

Is a payment made with a filing extension really a deposit such that a refund is not subject to a statute of limitations? The Fifth Circuit Court of Appeals and the Tax Court have ruled that payments sent with extensions can be recovered at any time; the Third, Sixth, and Ninth Circuit Courts of Appeal agree with the Government that a payment made with a tax extension is subject to the usual time constraints.

ALWAYS PAY THE IRS IF YOU CAN—

Although the IRS interest rate may appear lower than some other creditors, it will often be higher when coupled with the one-half of one percent per month failure to pay penalty, when applicable. In any event, given any choice, owe on your credit cards, owe the bank, or owe your in-laws. Their collection remedies pale compared to those available to the Internal Revenue Service. And their collection departments are usually more responsive and more sympathetic to your telephone calls and letters.

When you owe money to the Internal Revenue Service, you are negotiating with a powerful counterpart. The IRS can force you as a debtor to provide a financial statement to learn of the whereabouts of your assets (existing bank accounts seem to have very little money and new bank accounts seem to be opened in many cases within a day or two of the financial statement).

While a federal tax lien exists on all property of a taxpayer as of the date of assessment, there is no public knowledge of the lien unless and until the Revenue Officer files a *Notice of Federal Tax Lien*. This Notice is filed in locations as provided by state law. A Notice of Federal Tax Lien affects an individual's credit standing (including his or her ability to borrow to pay off the IRS) as well as restricts disposition of certain property.

Without going to court, and even without filing a Notice of Federal Tax Lien, the IRS can levy and seize the property of a taxpayer. Under federal law, only the following property is exempt from levy:

1. Wearing apparel and school books necessary to the taxpayer or family members;

2. If the taxpayer is the head of a family, fuel, provisions, furniture, personal effects, firearms, livestock, and poultry to a collective maximum of $2,500 in value prior to indexing for cost of living in 1998;

3. Books and tools necessary in a trade, business, or profession to a maximum in the aggregate of $1,250 in value prior to indexing for cost of living in 1998;

4. Undelivered mail;

5. Certain payements to Congressional Medal of Honor winners;
6. So much of salary, wages, or other income necessary to comply with court ordered child support (not applicable to support provided in a voluntary separation agreement not incorporated in a court decree);
7. Military service connected disability payments; and
8. Payments under the Job Training Partnership Act.

Under a continuing levy, wages and other compensation are reachable subject to an exemption computed by formula. Also, under a continuing levy, 15 percent of unemployment compensation, Social Security benefits, workers compensation, and public assistance payments are reachable. The seizure of an individual's principal residence is unusual and normally requires the personal approval of the District Director.

State laws may create other exemptions. For example, principal residences are entirely exempt from seizure in a few states, and wages cannot be garnished in several others. In states permitting married couples to hold property as tenants by the entirety such that neither can change the nature of the ownership, assets held in this manner cannot be seized by the IRS for the debts of one spouse unless, such as in the case of a one signature bank account, the spouse could get sole access to the property.

The most frequently reached assets by the IRS are wages and bank accounts, both because of the simplicity in levying as well as the ease in obtaining information. Without resorting to obtaining a financial statement from you, the IRS can often locate your sources of wages from the W-2s attached to your most recently filed tax return and your bank accounts from the sources of interest income shown on that return. However, the IRS can seize a variety of assets. In 1994, it levied on a second-place purse awarded in a stakes race at Saratoga Race Track (the horse was reported to have nipped the Revenue Officer).

While the larger and more complex collection cases are assigned to a particular Revenue Officer, most collection matters are handled by the *Automated Telephone Collection System (ACS)*. If your delinquent account is assigned to ACS, your telephone number will be dialed periodically and automatically until you are reached. The telephones are manned by less experienced personnel, and you normally cannot arrange to deal a second time with the person initially handling your matter. ACS will not hesitate to garnish or attach if it knows where you work or have bank accounts. However, payment arrangements can most often be worked out over the telephone. Look for indication on collection correspondence that your account is being handled by ACS.

Tax delinquents owe collectively about $216 billion according to the IRS. However, the IRS is maintaining collection efforts to recover less than 20 percent of this amount. The balance represents liabilities which are either disputed, duplicated (such as multiple assessments of the Trust Fund Recovery Penalty discussed in Chapter 10), or uncollectible. Tax delinquents include hundreds of thousands of federal workers and retirees.

The General Accounting Office is critical of IRS collection efforts and, most specifically, the amount of uncollectible debt. In 1996, as an experiment, the IRS named five private collection agencies to take over some of the collection responsibility for delinquent accounts. Payment with credit cards is next as the Taxpayer Relief Act of 1997 permits taxpayers to pay their liabilities by credit card effective May 5, 1998 under regulations to be issued by the IRS. You will soon be able to pay your tax bill and get frequent flier miles too!

CAUTION! While ACS often offers a quick ability to resolve simpler collection matters, it has major problems in handling more complex matters such as unapplied payments, requests for substantiation, and requests for penalty abatement.

CAUTION! The IRS can seize a federal or state tax refund and apply it against another year's delinquent tax liability. Can the IRS seize a joint tax refund and apply it against the back tax liability owed by only one spouse? It does and shifts the burden to the couple to get part back by filing a claim for refund on IRS Form 843 and attaching Form 8379, which computes the portion of the refund not attributable to the debtor spouse.

CAUTION! In the nine community property states listed in Chapter 1, most income is treated as if it were actually earned one-half by each spouse. The result is that the IRS can normally levy against one-half of the wages and most other income of one spouse for the tax liability of the other spouse.

TAX PLANNING IDEA A couple residing in a community property state, subject to any restrictions under state law, may agree in writing that all or certain income not become part of the "marital community." In 1996 a Texas Federal District Court ruled that the IRS was constrained by a prenuptial agreement which provided that employment income earned during the marriage would remain separate property.

—BUT INSTALLMENT PAYMENTS ARE AVAILABLE IF YOU CAN'T PAY NOW

Not only are installment payments available in the event you can't pay the IRS in full, but also the procedure for obtaining a payment plan has been recently simplified, especially for debts under $10,000. About 2.7 million taxpayers receive installment agreement each year.

If you are unable to pay your tax bill now, but you can pay it off in the future, attach IRS Form 9465 to your return and indicate the monthly amount you can pay and the date each month that you want to pay. Your proposal will normally be accepted, no financial statement will be required, and no tax lien will be filed if you owe less than $10,000, plan to pay the debt within three years, and have filed all required tax returns.

A larger debt will normally require more effort to obtain a payment plan and will necessitate a detailed financial statement including a balance sheet and cash flow statement (which should support the requested monthly installments). If assigned to a Revenue Officer, a meeting may be required and an installment agreement becomes far more difficult to negotiate as the IRS scrutinizes the necessity of expenses and the ability to liquidate assets. In the process, certain actual expenses are discarded in favor of national or local standards. The result is that an installment arrangement may be difficult if you have higher than average expenses for basic needs such as housing, food, and transportation. If you have a high income, an installment arrangement may be next to impossible to achieve inasmuch as the guidelines make no distinctions above an annual income level of upper five figures.

Form 9465. Installment Agreement Request, page 1

Form **9465** (Rev. January 1996) Department of the Treasury Internal Revenue Service	**Installment Agreement Request** ▶ See instructions below and on back.	OMB No. 1545-1350

Note: *Do not file this form if you are currently making payments on an installment agreement. You must pay your other Federal tax liabilities in full or you will be in default on your agreement.*

If you can't pay the full amount you owe, you can ask to make monthly installment payments. If we approve your request, you will be charged a $43 fee. **Do not include the fee with this form.** We will deduct the fee from your first payment after we approve your request, unless you choose **Direct Debit** (see the line 13 instructions). We will usually let you know within 30 days after we receive your request whether it is approved or denied. But if this request is for tax due on a return you filed after March 31, it may take us longer than 30 days to reply.

To ask for an installment agreement, complete this form. Attach it to the front of your return when you file. If you have already filed your return or you are filing this form in response to a notice, see **How Do I File Form 9465?** on page 2. If you have any questions about this request, call 1-800-829-1040.

Caution: *A Notice of Federal Tax Lien may be filed to protect the government's interest until you pay in full.*

1 Your first name and initial / Last name / Your social security number

If a joint return, spouse's first name and initial / Last name / Spouse's social security number

Your current address (number and street). If you have a P.O. box and no home delivery, show box number. / Apt. number

City, town or post office, state, and ZIP code. If a foreign address, show city, state or province, postal code, and full name of country.

2 If this address is new since you filed your last tax return, check here . . . . ▶ ☐

3 (_____) _____ Your home phone number / Best time for us to call

4 (_____) _____ Your work phone number / Ext. / Best time for us to call

5 Name of your bank or other financial institution:

6 Your employer's name:

Address

City, state, and ZIP code

Address

City, state, and ZIP code

7 Enter the tax return for which you are making this request (for example, Form 1040). But if you are filing this form in response to a notice, don't complete lines 7 through 9. Instead, attach the bottom section of the notice to this form and go to line 10 . . . . ▶ _____

8 Enter the tax year for which you are making this request (for example, 1995) . . . . ▶ _____

9 Enter the total amount you owe as shown on your tax return . . . . ▶ $ _____

10 Enter the amount of any payment you are making with your tax return (or notice). See instructions . ▶ $ _____

11 Enter the amount you can paym each month. **Make your payments as large as possible to limit interest and penalty charges.** The charges will continue until you pay in full . . . . ▶ $ _____

12 Enter the date you want to make your payment each month. Do not enter a date later than the 28th ▶ _____

13 If you would like to make your monthly payments using **Direct Debit** (automatic withdrawals from your bank account), check here. . . . . ▶ ☐

Your signature / Date / Spouse's signature. If a joint return, BOTH must sign. / Date

Privacy Act and Paperwork Reduction Act Notice.– Our legal right to ask for the information on this form is Internal Revenue Code sections 6001, 6011, 6012(a), 6109, and 6159 and their regulations. We will use the information to process your request for an installment agreement. The reason we need your name and social security number is to secure proper identification. We require this information to gain access to the tax information in our files and properly respond to your request. If you do not enter the information, we may not be able to process your request. We may give this information to the Department of Justice as provided by law. We may also give it to cities, states, and the District of Columbia to carry out their tax laws.

In contrast to an audit situation, when it is usually better to let the Taxpayer Representative handle the matter while the taxpayer stays at home, it is usually advisable even for a taxpayer represented professionally (as he or she should be before the Collection Division) to be present at the meeting with the Revenue Officer. The face-to-face relationship allows a rapport to be created and the situation to be personalized. Sheer human nature makes it more difficult to say "no" when the affected person is sitting across the table from you. But if the Revenue Officer still says no, ask to meet with the supervisor (and perhaps, if needed, the supervisor's supervisor).

Given all of its remedies, why would the Internal Revenue Service even agree to a payment plan? First, it cuts the number of cases which must be actively worked; second, the IRS may seize a paycheck or some cash in the bank account, but most taxpayers in that situation who have options of mobility in their jobs and accounts are going to take whatever steps are necessary to be able to pay the rent or mortgage and to put food on the table; and third, if the taxpayer defaults, the same harsher remedies are available later.

The IRS charges a *user fee* of $43 for installment agreements, payable with the first installment.

CAUTION!   Even though an installment plan may be available, it should not be used when alternatives exist such as private financing. Taxpayers making timely payments often must deal with improper application of funds or installment agreements ignored by the IRS computer system.

—BUT AN OFFER IN COMPROMISE IS AVAILABLE IF YOU CAN NEVER PAY

Do you owe the IRS more money than you can ever reasonably expect to pay? Country music star Willie Nelson did. According to the press reports, the IRS in 1994 accepted $16.7 million from Mr. Nelson against a tax assessment of $32 million.

After years of routine rejection of most taxpayer settlement offers, the IRS several years ago changed its official policy and claimed to be favorably disposed toward accepting partial payment in full satisfaction of a tax debt which would otherwise probably be uncollectable. For the fiscal year ending September 30, 1996, the IRS processed 133,598 *Offers in Compromise* and accepted 27,673 Offers. Many submissions were bounced in early processing on account of unfiled returns, other tax delinquencies, incomplete forms, or insufficient amounts offered based on quick analysis.

To get your offer even processed, you must offer the IRS a *minimum* amount equal to the sum of the "quick-sale" value of your assets (in some cases net of taxes) plus 60 times your monthly cash flow after "necessary" living expenses (far less in most cases than your actual living expenses).

Joint Offers of husband and wife consider the assets and cash flow of both spouses. When only one of a married couple owes taxes, treatment appears inconsistent from district to district as to whether individual or joint cash flow is to be considered. Treatment also appears inconsistent as to the percentage of tenants by the entirety property to be taken into account where only one spouse owes the tax and the IRS can't reach the particular property.

If your Offer is processible, it will still be rejected if you are unable to convince the IRS that it would not likely ever collect the amount of your Offer. Notwithstanding Willie Nelson,

Form 656. Offer in Compromise, page 1

Department of Treasury
Internal Revenue Service

Form 656 (Rev. 1-97)

Form 656

Offer in Compromise

Item 1

Taxpayer's Name and Home or Business Address

Name

Street Address

City   State   Zip Code

Mailing Address (if different from above)

City   State   Zip Code

Item 2

Social Security Numbers

(a) Primary

(b) Secondary

Item 3

Employer Identification Number (Included in offer)

Item 4

Other Employer Identification Numbers (Not included in offer)

Item 5

To: Commissioner of Internal Revenue Service

I/we (includes all types of taxpayers) submit this offer to compromise the tax liabilities plus any interest, penalties, additions to tax, and additional amounts required by law (tax liability) for the tax type and period marked below: (Please mark an "X" for the correct description and fill-in the correct tax period(s), adding additional periods if needed.)

☐ 1040/1120 Income tax   Year(s) _____

☐ 941 Employer's Quarterly Federal Tax Return   Quarterly Period(s)

☐ 940 Employer's Annual Federal
Unemployment (FUTA) Tax Return   Year(s)_____

☐ **Trust Fund Recovery Penalty** as a
responsible person of (enter corporation name) _____

for failure to pay withholding and Federal Insurance
Contributions Act Taxes (Social Security taxes)   Period(s)_____

☐ **Other Federal taxes** (specify type and periods(s)) _____

Item 6

I/we submit this offer for the reason(s) checked below:

☐ **Doubt as to Liability**   "I do not believe I owe this amount." You *must* include a detailed explanation of the reasons you believe you do not owe the tax.

☐ **Doubt as to Collectibility**   "I have insufficient assets and income to pay the full amount." You *must* include a complete financial statement (Form 433-A and/or Form 433-B).

Item 7

I/We offer to pay $ _____

☐ Paid in full with this offer.
☐ Deposit of $_____ with this offer.
☐ No deposit.
Check one of the following boxes.
☐ Balance to be paid in ☐ 10, ☐ 30, ☐ 60, or ☐ 90 days from notice of acceptance of the offer. If more than one payment will be paid during the time frame checked, provide the amount of the payment and date to be paid on the line below.

☐ Other proposed payment terms. Enter the specific dates (mm/dd/yy format) and dollar amounts of the payment terms you propose on the lines below.

In addition to the above amount, IRS will add interest from the date IRS accepts the offer until the date you completely pay the amount offered, as required by section 6621 of the Internal Revenue Code, IRS compounds interest daily, as required by section 6622 of the Internal Revenue Code.

Form 656. Offer in Compromise, page 2

Item 8

By submitting this offer, I/we understand and agree to the following conditions:

(a) I/we voluntarily submit all payments made on this offer.

(b) IRS will apply payments made under the terms of this offer in the best interest of the government.

(c) If IRS rejects the offer or I/we withdraw the offer, IRS will return any amount paid with the offer. If I/we agree in writing, IRS will apply the amount paid with the offer to the amount owed. If I/we agree to apply the payment, the date the offer is rejected or withdrawn will be considered the date of payment. I/we understand that IRS will not pay interest on any amount I/we submit with the offer.

(d) I/we will comply with all provisions of the Internal Revenue Code relating to filing my/our returns and paying my/our required taxes for 5 years from the date IRS accepts the offer. This condition does not apply to offers based on Doubt as to Liability.

(e) I/we waive and agree to the suspension of any statutory periods of limitation (time limits provided for by law) for IRS assessment and collection of the tax liability for the tax periods identified in item (5).

(f) IRS will keep all payments and credits made, received, or applied to the amount being compromised before this offer was submitted. IRS may keep any proceeds from a levy served prior to submission of the offer, but not received at the time the offer is submitted. If I/we have an installment agreement prior to submitting the offer, I/we must continue to make the payments as agreed while this offer is pending. Installment agreement payments will not be applied against the amount offered.

(g) IRS will keep any refund, including interest, due to me/us because of overpayment of any tax or other liability, for tax periods extending through the calendar year that IRS accepts the offer. *I/we may not designate a refund, to which the IRS is entitled, to be applied to estimated tax payments for the following year.* This condition doesn't apply if the offer is based only on Doubt as to Liability.

(h) I/we will return to IRS any refund identified in (g) received after submission of this offer. This condition doesn't apply if the offer is based only on Doubt as to Liability.

(i) The total amount IRS can collect under this offer can not be more than the full amount of the tax liability.

(j) I/we understand that I/we remain responsible for the full amount of the tax liability, unless and until IRS accepts the offer in writing and I/we have met all the terms and conditions of the offer. IRS won't remove the original amount of the tax liability from its records until I/we have met all the terms of the offer.

(k) I/we understand that the tax I/we offer to compromise is and will remain a tax liability until I/we meet all the terms and conditions of this offer. If I/we file bankruptcy before the terms and conditions of this offer are completed, any claim the IRS files in the bankruptcy proceeding will be a tax claim.

(l) Once IRS accepts the offer in writing, I/we have no right to contest, in court or otherwise, the amount of the tax liability.

(m) The offer is pending starting with the date an authorized IRS official signs this form and accepts my/our waiver of the statutory periods of limitation. The offer remains pending until an authorized IRS official accepts, rejects or acknowledges withdrawal of the offer in writing. If I/we appeal the IRS decision on the offer, IRS will continue to treat the offer as pending until the Appeals Office accepts or rejects the offer in writing. If I/we don't file a protest within 30 days of the date IRS notifies me/us of the right to protest the decision, I/we waive the right to a hearing before the Appeals office about the offer in compromise.

(n) The waiver and suspension of any statutory periods of limitation for assessment and collection of the amount of the tax liability described in item (5), continues to apply: while the offer is pending (see m) above), during the time I/we have not paid all of the amount offered, during the time I/we have not completed all terms and conditions of the offer, and for one additional year beyond each of the time periods identified in this paragraph.

(o) If I/we fail to meet any of the terms and conditions of the offer, the offer is then in default, then IRS may: immediately file suit to collect the entire unpaid balance of the offer; immediately file suit to collect an amount equal to the original amount of the tax liability as liquidating damages, minus any payments already received under the terms of this offer; disregard the amount of the offer and apply all amounts already paid under the offer against the original amount of tax liability; or file suit or levy to collect the original amount of the tax liability, without further notice of any kind.

IRS will continue to add interest as required by section 6621 of the Internal Revenue Code, on the amount IRS determines is due after default. IRS will add interest from the date the offer is defaulted until I/we completely satisfy the amount owed.

Item 9

If I/we submit this offer on a substitute form, I/we affirm that this form is a verbatim duplicate of the official Form 656, and I/we agree to be bound by all the terms and conditions set forth in the official Form 656.

Under penalties of perjury, I declare that I have examined this offer, including accompanying schedules and statements, and to the best of my knowledge and belief, it is true, correct and complete.

_____

(9a) Signature of Taxpayer-proponent

_____

Date

_____

(9b) Signature of Taxpayer-proponent

_____

Date

For Official Use Only

I accept waiver of the statutory period of limitations for the Internal Revenue Service.

Signature of authorized Internal Revenue Service Official

_____

Title

most individuals who currently have or who previously had high incomes are unable to convince the IRS to settle for a portion of the liability.

If you do decide to submit an Offer, file IRS Form 656 along with a financial statement on IRS Form 433A and/or 433B. Be sure that you can come up from the amount you promise on acceptance. Even better, submit the offered amount with your compromise proposal. If the IRS rejects your Offer, it *must* return the money. The source of funds for most Offers is borrowed amounts from family and friends.

 TAX PLANNING IDEA   An Offer in Compromise should be submitted with the recognition that the IRS may counter with a larger dollar amount.

—BUT BANKRUPTCY IS GENERALLY AVAILABLE AS A LAST RESORT

If the Internal Revenue Service rejects your Offer in Compromise, if you have no means with which to make an Offer, or if you are overwhelmed by other debts, you may wish to file bankruptcy in the event that the IRS is continuing collection actions.

Most taxes are dischargeable in bankruptcy, absent willful evasion by the taxpayer and provided three years have passed from the due date of the return and two years have passed from the date the return was actually filed (or 240 days have passed from the date of an additional IRS assessment not reflected on a return). However, the trust portion of employment taxes (including the Trust Fund Recovery Penalty discussed in Chapter 10) is nondischargeable, eliminating bankruptcy as an available option when sizeable withholdings have gone unpaid.

TAX PLANNING IDEA   The bankruptcy laws affecting the discharge of taxes and the retention of assets are complex. The IRS is challenging more and more bankruptcies on grounds of willful evasion. For example, in 1996 an Indiana Federal District Court overruled the bankruptcy court and denied a debtor's discharge of income tax liability because he overstated withholding allowances on Form W-4 (see Chapter 1) to increase his take home pay. Bankruptcy counsel should be consulted as soon as the option of bankruptcy becomes a viable choice to a taxpayer even if only in the future.

CONTROVERSY

While the U.S. Supreme Court determined in 1992 that qualified retirement plans are protected under federal law from creditors in a bankruptcy proceeding, certain lower courts have subsequently determined that this decision does not extend to plans of unincorporated business owners in which the only participants are owners and their spouses as well as to Individual Retirement Accounts. These issues remain unsettled. State law may grant additional bankruptcy exemptions beyond those provided under federal law.

COMMUNICATING WITH THE IRS

The greatest frustration of taxpayers and professionals alike in dealing with the Internal Revenue Service is the failure of the IRS to quickly process correspondence or in many cases to process it at all. Nothing is more frustrating than to respond to a letter and then receive follow-up correspondence which says, "We have not heard from you." Responsive letters are sent and they too are ignored. All too often, taxpayers who owe nothing due to improperly credited checks or otherwise advise the IRS by mail upon receipt of the initial correspondence that nothing is owed. After receiving additional notices including a demand letter by certified mail, the taxpayer finds a paycheck garnished or a bank account attached. Some Service Centers generating the correspondence are worse than others.

In 1990, then IRS Commissioner Fred Goldberg told members of the Commissioner's Advisory Group that correspondence with taxpayers was the biggest problem of the IRS but that a new automatic correspondence system should result in a "dramatic improvement." Nonetheless, a 1994 General Accounting Office survey of two IRS Service Centers found that 15 percent of IRS correspondence was "incorrect, unclear, incomplete, or nonresponsive." There appears little improvement four years later.

Unless the matter has been turned over to a particular individual or office or except in the case of a collection matter handled by ACS (see the discussion earlier in this chapter), communicating by telephone usually produces comparable results. At a 1989 "town meeting" in which the IRS heard complaints by the public, taxpayers claimed to be unable to reach the Kansas City Service Center after two or three days of constant dialing. Today, the Government Accounting Office reports that four in five calls to the IRS seeking telephone assistance during tax season don't get through; the IRS disagrees and claims that 72 percent of callers get through. In any event, the error rate of the IRS on those getting past the busy signal is about ten percent. One 1996 blunder made national news when a Washington, D.C. accountant called the IRS about an estate tax issue and was asked whether *he* was the decedent.

When the urgency of the matter does not allow the IRS to be given an opportunity at responding to correspondence, the preferred approach is to visit a local district office, though this is no guarantee either of proper handling, as a Rockville, Maryland eight-year-old and his father found out in 1989, in another nationally reported blunder.

The eight-year-old first grade student had reported a tax liability of $152 on interest and dividend income but received a refund check from Philadelphia in the amount of $39,541.55. When his father visited the nearest IRS office in Wheaton, Maryland, the next day, the receptionist listened to his story and told him to take a number and wait. After an hour and 15 minutes, Dad's turn came but he ended up walking out of the office describing IRS personnel as "confused." The check did get returned the next day.

A similar error occurred in 1996 when a three-year old Pittsburgh boy received a $219,495 improper refund check from the IRS.

CAUTION! Send all important documents to the IRS by registered or certified U.S. mail. Many documents, particularly those sent to Service Centers, end up lost or misplaced. Although *certain* services of Airborne Express, DHL Worldwide, FedEx, and United Parcel Service are now treated similar to the U.S. Postal Service for purpose of determining whether a document was timely mailed, only registered or certified U.S. mail enjoys *prima facie* proof that a document was delivered.

CONTROVERSY

The Courts of Appeal are divided as to whether a taxpayer not using registered or certified mail can prove mailing of a form or document by proving that it was placed in a mailbox. The Eighth and Ninth Circuit Courts of Appeal have backed taxpayers while the Second and Sixth Circuit Courts of Appeal have backed the IRS. The U.S. Supreme Court declined to review the issue in 1996.

TAX PLANNING IDEA Each IRS district and Service Center has a *Problem Resolution Office (PRO)* to deal with procedural problems meeting select criteria which are not properly handled through regular channels. In hardship cases, use of IRS Form 911 should get immediate attention.

THE IRS AND THE DOUBLE STANDARD

Mail your tax return on the last day with insufficient postage; it will be returned and you will be considered as filing late. Address your Tax Court petition to the wrong address and miss the deadline; you will be permanently barred from Tax Court.

What if the IRS makes a mistake? In 1990, the IRS admitted that about 550,000 tax packets contained filing envelopes for the incorrect service center. In 1991, the IRS indicated that it lost in excess of $22 million as a result of its failure to sign necessary forms prior to the expiration of statutes of limitation. In 1992, at a cost of more than $175 million, the IRS sent refund checks arising from the earned income credit to 270,000 ineligible individuals. In 1993, the IRS sent huge erroneous tax bills out of its Kansas City Service Center; a Centerville, Virginia, man was dunned for back taxes in excess of $68 million. In 1994, the GAO reported that it couldn't audit the IRS in that it could not account for $2.1 billion of expenses. In 1995, the IRS sent about 43,000 improper bills to high-income individuals who had elected under a transition rule to spread their retroactive tax increase in 1993 over three years. In 1996, a former IRS historian called the agency a "black hole" of history, claming that the IRS routinely throws away documents. In 1997, the IRS sent about 90,000 notices to household employers charging them with failure to file and pay unemployment taxes, ignoring that these taxes are now paid with Schedule H of the individual income tax return.

So only taxpayers have to be perfect—and keep all of their records.

THE TAXPAYER BILL OF RIGHTS—PART 2

Concern over taxpayer problems with the Internal Revenue Service caused enactment in 1988 of a Taxpayer Bill of Rights, which provided taxpayers with many specific rights including the following:

1. The IRS must provide taxpayers with a written explanation of their rights.

2. On prior notice to the IRS, a taxpayer is permitted to make an audio recording of an interview. The IRS may also choose to record the interview, in which case a taxpayer is entitled to a copy or transcript upon request and payment of costs.

3. The IRS must abate any penalty attributable to erroneous *written* advice by an IRS employee when the advice was specifically requested and was reasonably relied upon.

4. The Problem Resolution Office of the Internal Revenue Service is given statutory authority to release levies through the use of a *Taxpayer Assistance Order.*

5. The IRS is prohibited from using tax enforcement records to evaluate the *collection* performance of Revenue Officers and their supervisors.

6. If the IRS wishes to modify or terminate an existing agreement for the payment of an outstanding tax liability in installments, it must provide the taxpayer with 30 days' notice setting forth a reason for the proposed modification.

7. The IRS must provide 30 days notice prior to a levy of assets unless tax collection is jeopardized. Banks are required to hold levied funds for 21 days to allow any correction of errors.

8. Taxpayers have the right to sue in Federal District Court if any IRS employee knowingly or negligently fails to release an IRS lien when required or if an IRS employee acts in reckless or intentional disregard of a law or regulation in connection with *collection* of a tax.

9. A taxpayer may be awarded reasonable litigation costs if he or she "substantially prevails" in the matter. In the case of an examination, expenses of the administrative appeal may also be awarded.

The belief of continuing unfairness by the IRS led to enactment of a Taxpayer Bill of Rights—Part 2, signed into law by President Clinton in 1996. Senate Finance Committee Chairman Bill Roth praised the legislation as "a victory for every taxpayer who has ever been intimidated, bullied, browbeaten, threatened, harassed, or unjustly accused or investigated by the IRS." Among the taxpayer benefits and rights included in Part 2 are the following:

1. An Office of Taxpayer Advocate is created within the IRS with broader authority to resolve matters and to alleviate hardship.

2. An appeals process in the event of modification or termination of an installment agreement.

3. Expanded interest abatement with Tax Court review possible, as in the case of penalties, of most failures to abate interest.

4. A separated or divorced individual who filed a joint return is entitled to information as to collection activity against and recovery from the spouse.

5. The IRS may withdraw a tax lien without full payment if the withdrawal is in the best interests of both the taxpayer and the IRS.

6. The IRS may return levied property if the levy was not in accordance with administrative procedures or return is in the best interests of both the taxpayer and the IRS.

The two Taxpayer Bill of Rights laws are the first steps toward establishing the principle that an agency charged each year with reviewing the personal tax strategies reflected on more than 118 million individual tax returns and more than 200 million total returns and collecting $1.5 trillion must be based upon clear and equitable procedures.

Has the legislation led to improvements in the Internal Revenue Service? Public opinion surveys show a declining approval rating for the IRS. A recent rating of 200 companies and government agencies by 46,000 people in a survey co-sponsored by the University of Michigan showed the IRS finishing dead last—just after the post office.

The natural tendency of individuals to dislike bill collectors has been inflamed by bad press. For example, when the IRS threatened to seize balls, bats, and uniforms of a California girls' preteen softball league, front page stories across the country helped cause the IRS to relent.

Despite a Senate Governmental Affairs Committee revelation in 1994 that more than 420 IRS employees had been disciplined since 1989 for misusing the IRS computer system (among other improprieties, the employees were accessing their own files as well as those of family members and celebrities), the "snooping" continues. General Accounting Office findings released on April 9, 1997 report 2,315 such incidents over the three-year period from 1994-1996 with 113 firings. Later in 1997, a Colorado Federal district judge ordered the IRS to pay $325,000 for turning over tax information on a businesswoman to the media. On September 23, 1997, the Senate Finance Committee began hearing several days of testimony from taxpayers and IRS agents as to the alleged abuses.

Meanwhile, after $4 billion of costs, the IRS is reexamining an $8 billion program to bring its computer system into the 21st century. One Assistant Commissioner has recommended that the IRS start all over again. For the first time in history, the IRS will be headed not by a tax professional; newly appointed Commissioner Charles Rossotti is a business executive with a background in technology.

There has been some good press too. IRS employees have raised money for charity in several cities by allowing the public a chance to throw pies in their faces or to dunk them underwater. Ask any two people as to whether the IRS is fair and you'll probably get two different answers.

For example, ask the man who hitchhiked last year to the Ogden, Utah, Service Center to pick up a badly needed tax refund. Ogden informed him that refund checks were issued by another IRS office; however, employees verified his refund, ordered the check to be sent to Ogden, and collected food and cash to hold him over until the refund check arrived.

Then ask the Tulsa, Oklahoma, man who drove naked to the post office a couple of years ago just before midnight on April 15 to file his tax return. He complained that the IRS had taken the shirt off his back—to say nothing about the pants off his seat.

Appendix

Investment Strategies for Your Tax Savings

The key to wealth is investment. Some people may choose to squander any money that they can keep from Uncle Sam, and that is their right. Others may need the money for their daily lives. But it's a fact that, thanks to Social Security taxes, earned income is taxed most heavily of all forms of income, and virtually no informed observer believes that this will change in the foreseeable future. So if you want your wealth to grow, you want to earn as much income as possible from sources (such as real estate and capital assets) that are taxed at relatively low rates. This way, you'll have more left to reinvest to earn even more money after the government takes its share.

We've discussed the tax benefits of owning real estate elsewhere in this book. And there's probably no better tax-favored investment than owning your own home.

But what about real estate as an investment? Here's how the various forms of real estate stack up in important categories:

Table 1. Real Estate Characteristics

Form	Income	Safety	Liquidity	Inflation Hedge	Tax Benefits	Growth
Rental real estate	Fair	Fair	Poor	Excellent	Good	Good
Raw land	None	Poor	Poor	Good	Few	Moderate
Residential real estate	None	Excellent	Poor	Excellent	Good	Good
Real estate investment trust	Good	Fair	Good	Good	Some	Moderate
Real estate limited partnerships	Good	Fair	Poor	Good	Some	Moderate

As you can see, the one problem with real estate is that you can't expect to build wealth rapidly. And, generally, its liquidity is poor. That means you might be in a bind or be forced to accept a price for your real estate below its true value if you need access to funds quickly.

Let's look at the characteristics of some forms of domestic equities:

Table 2. Domestic Equity Characteristics

Form	Income	Safety	Inflation Liquidity	Tax Hedge	Benefits	Growth
Listed common stock	Poor	Moderate	Good	Good	For corps.	Excellent
Over-the-counter common stock	Poor	Low	Moderate	Fair	For corps.	Good
Preferred stock	Good	Fair	Fair	Poor	For corps.	Moderate
Growth mutual funds	Poor	Good	Good	Good	None	Excellent
Income mutual funds	Good	Good	Good	Fair	None	Moderate
Index mutual funds	Poor	Fair	Good	Good	None	Excellent

Domestic equities (stocks and mutual funds) can offer better prospects for growth than real estate, at the cost of real estate's tax benefits. Fixed income instruments (corporate and government bonds) generally offer better income prospects than real estate or stocks. They don't, however, have the favorable growth characteristics that some forms of domestic equities offer. Let's look at the characteristics of some forms of fixed income instruments:

Table 3. Fixed Income Instrument Characteristics

Form	Income	Safety	Inflation Liquidity	Tax Hedge	Benefits	Growth
U.S. Treasury security	Good	Best	Best	Poor	State benefits	Moderate
Mortgage backed securities	Good	Fair	Fair	Poor	None	Moderate
State and local bonds	Good	Fair	Fair	Poor	Best	Moderate
Discounted state and local bonds	Fair	Fair	Fair	Poor	Good	Moderate
Corporate bonds	Good	Fair	Good	Poor	None	Moderate
Junk bonds	High	Poor	Fair	Poor	None	Moderate
Convertible bonds	Good	Fair	Fair	Fair	None	Moderate
Bond funds	Good	Fair	Good	Poor	None (except muni funds)	Moderate

There are other forms of investment as well, but the big three are real estate, stocks, and bonds. If you're a high-bracket taxpayer, you want to look at real estate and growth stocks. Both offer this tax benefit: they build up value without that growth being taxed until you sell the asset.

As an illustration of what tax-free growth can mean, let's look at a theoretical corporation, Amalgamated Widget. AW has bonds trading at $100, paying ten percent, and stock trading at $100 that (coincidentally) appreciates ten percent each year. AW pays no dividends to stockholders, partially accounting for its high growth rate.

	AW Bond		AW Stock
1997 Interest	$10.00	1997 Appreciation	
Tax on Interest		(10% of $100)	$10.00
(28% bracket)	−2.80		
Accumulated wealth after taxes	$7.20		$10.00
1998 Interest*	$10.72	1998 Appreciation	
Tax on interest		(10% of ($100 +	
(28% bracket)	−3.00	$10))	$11.00
Accumulated wealth after taxes	$14.92		$21.00
1999 Interest*	$11.49	1999 Appreciation	
Tax on interest		(10% of ($100 +	
(28% bracket)	−3.22	$21))	$12.10
Accumulated wealth after taxes	$23.19		$33.10
2000 Interest*	$12.32	2000 Appreciation	
Tax on interest		(10% of ($100 +	
(28% bracket)	−3.45	33.10))	$13.31
Accumulated wealth after taxes	$32.06		$46.41

*assuming reinvestment of interest at 10% after payment of taxes on bond interest

This principle of tax-free growth can apply in other areas (such as retirement plans), but the message here is that, if you want to build up wealth, and other factors are equal, aim for capital assets such as real estate and stock.

You probably found advice in these pages to cut your tax bill and save money. If you don't have pressing financial needs, you should look at investing that money to build wealth. Here are the asset allocation ranges we recommend for your investment portfolio, depending on whether you're aggressive (risk-tolerant) or conservative (risk-sensitive).

	Aggressive	Conservative
Real Estate	10%	20%
Domestic Equities	40%	20%
Fixed Income Instruments	20%	40%

If you're a high-income, high-bracket taxpayer, you may want to devote an additional portion of your portfolio to wealth-accumulating capital assets such as real estate, stocks, and mutual funds. If you expect to require current income, plan to devote an additional portion of your portfolio to bonds.

INDEX